RECORD MAKERS
AND
RECORD BREAKERS

Record Makers
and
Record Breakers

by

NICK IVERSEN

jD | JONATHAN DAVID PUBLISHERS
MIDDLE VILLAGE, N. Y. 11379

RECORD MAKERS

and

RECORD BREAKERS

by

NICK IVERSEN

Copyright © 1977
by
JONATHAN DAVID PUBLISHERS

Jonathan David Publishers
68-22 Eliot Avenue
Middle Village, New York 11379

Library of Congress Cataloging in Publication Data

Iversen, Nick.
  Record makers and record breakers.
  SUMMARY: Uses biographical sketches to present record per-
formances which have captivated the public in such areas as politics,
sports, science, entertainment, daily life, and aviation.
  1. Biography. [1. Biography. 2. Curiosities and wonders]
I. Title.
CT105.I9   920'.02 [920]   76-10227

ISBN 978-0-8246-0472-1

TABLE OF CONTENTS

FOR
BEVERLY
AND
SKIP

Acknowledgements

The author would like to thank the following people who, in a variety of ways, helped with the production of this book: Louis Cortelezzi, Tony Gardiner, Michael Goldstein, Ed Goodgold, Jeffrey Kindley, Cynthia Kirk, Jacob Rajs, Julius Solobkowicz, Paul Szapary, Lisa Tumbleson and Zilla.

INTRODUCTION

Among the many hundreds of individuals whose feats and contributions are mentioned in *Record Makers and Record Breakers,* some are so obscure that it has been difficult to uncover the pertinent facts about their personal lives. But every effort has been made to find such information and present it here. As to the better known personalities, my intention was to keep the biographical information sufficiently concise, since it was the *record* that was of prime importance here and since any reader interested in finding more detailed personal information would not encounter any obstacles in doing so. Biographical sketches, and often full biographies, have been written about the more famous people included in this volume.

I have attempted to keep to a minimum the number of bizarre or offbeat records that one usually finds listed in record books. The only exceptions are those in which the individual involved was famous, thus making his activities of general interest. For this reason, whereas other books may tell you about "the most automobile tires a person can eat in an hour," I would only include such information if the record holder were a celebrity. In this vein, perhaps it is not of great significance who invented snooker pool, but since it was British diplomat Neville Chamberlain, we are all entitled to share in the enjoyment of that bit of oddity.

Almost all inventors and pioneers and scientists who have extended the record of man's achievement have been included in *Record Makers.* These include Galileo and Edison, Franklin and Einstein, and others whose names have become better known than their deeds. I have taken special pains not to neglect those innovators whose names may still be unfamiliar, but whose inventions or contributions have become household words. In this category are in-

7

cluded such people as John Rand, who has long been forgotten, but whose invention of the toothpaste tube is very important to us all. The same holds true for Sylvester Graham, who gave us the graham cracker, and William Painter, who came up with the idea for a bottle cap.

The chapter on artists and the arts includes those whose creations have contributed to the enhancement of art—inventors of musical instruments, pioneers in advancing the graphic and visual arts, painters, sculptors, musicians, actors, performers of all kinds, and craftsmen in the fields of theater, film, radio and television.

Those listed in the religious, political and military leaders chapter most likely did not *intend* to set records. But they are record makers nevertheless and they were selected for inclusion chiefly because of their constant striving to better themselves or their environment. Because of this spirit, they share a place in a record book along with flyers, aerodynamic engineers, early birdmen, and astronauts who were instruments of progress on earth and in outer space.

In actuality, it is only in sports that people are first and foremost competitors. They compete against clocks, against each other, against established records. A great many of these competitors—some familiar, some unknown—in many different areas of competition are included in this volume.

Record Makers and Record Breakers is not the final word on the subject. Its purpose was not to be all-inclusive: it was meant to be enlightening, interesting, and entertaining. If you enjoy it, I will have accomplished my purpose.

NICK IVERSEN

SPORTS

Home Run King

AARON, HENRY—Hank Aaron's 20-year baseball career with the Milwaukee Braves, the Atlanta Braves, and the Milwaukee Brewers was outstanding. By the end of the 1973 season, he held the record for most runs batted in—2,133. In 1974, Hank broke Babe Ruth's existing all-time home run record of 714, and, by his retirement in 1976, he had increased that number to 755. In addition, Aaron's record of having touched 6,424 bases in Major League play remains unthreatened.

Aaron, born in Mobile, Alabama on February 5, 1934, was nicknamed "Bad Henry" because of his relentless pursuit of the batting records of the legendary Babe Ruth. A candy bar has been named after each man.

Motorcycle Champion

AGOSTINI, GIACOMO—In 1949, the Federation Internationale Motorcycliste divided world championship cycle competition into categories based on engine size. Since that time, Giacomo Agostini (1942-   ), the greatest motorcyclist ever, has won 108 of these races. In 1970 alone, he won 19 (a record) competitions.

Agostini won the 500-cubic-centimeter competition seven times (1966-1972), and the 350-cubic-centimeter competition six times (most recently in 1973). Between 1968 and 1972, Agostini won both world titles, a record not yet equalled.

Russian Super-Heavyweight

ALEXEEV, VASILI—Although an amateur athlete who regularly works as a factory supervisor in the Soviet Union, Vasili Alexeev

(1940-   ) has won every world weightlifting competition he ever entered. Greatly admired by the Russians, he has been named a Hero of the Soviet Union, an award usually reserved for military and political figures.

Alexeev, a super-heavyweight of more than 242½ pounds, holds the world records for the Snatch (413¾ pounds), Jerk (531¼ pounds) and Total Weight categories. He broke the existing records for both the Snatch and the Jerk on April 28, 1974 and, again, on June 6, 1974.

Biggest Box-Office Attraction

ALI, MUHAMMAD—Boxing heavyweight Muhammad Ali (1943-   ), whose name was originally Cassius Clay, can take credit for attracting the *smallest* crowd (2,434 fans) to a championship fight when he beat Sonny Liston in Lewiston, Maine, on May 25, 1965. But, on February 6, 1967, an indoor attendance record of 37,321 for a heavyweight bout was set at the Houston Astrodome when Ali fought Ernie Terrell and won. Four years later, on March 8, 1971, 20,455 fans paid $1,352,951—the largest sum of money ever grossed for a boxing match—to see Ali defeated by Joe Frazier in 15 rounds. Ali, personally, is alleged to have earned $10,000,000 during his career (as of April 1976), more than any fighter in history. He grosses in excess of six million dollars every time he defends his title.

Greatest Weightlifting Feat

ANDERSON, PAUL—In 1956, 23-year-old Paul Anderson became the Olympic heavyweight champion. The 364-pound Anderson held many records for lifting barbells, but he accomplished his most amazing feat when, on June 12, 1957 in Toccoa, Georgia, he raised 6,270 pounds of weight (which rested on steel trestles) *with his back!*

Paul, now retired from weightlifting competition, runs a home for wayward boys with his family in their native Georgia.

Triple Crown Jockey

ARCARO, EDDIE—Considered to be one of the greatest jockeys who ever lived, Eddie Arcaro (1916-   ) won $22.3 million in his 25-year career. The first American to win 3,000 races, Arcaro won the Kentucky Derby five times, the first being in 1938. The prestigious "Triple Crown," earned by winning the Derby, the Belmont Stakes and the Preakness in the same year, was won once by Arcaro in 1941 riding Whirlaway, and again in 1948 riding Citation.

Cincinatti-born Arcaro won his first race in 1932 at the age of 15. Having won more than 4,000 races and ridden 15,000 horses in his career, he was elected to Horse Racing's Hall of Fame in 1955, one of the first three admitted.

The Four-Minute Mile

BANNISTER, ROGER—At exactly 6:10 p.m. on May 6, 1954, on the Ifly Road Track in Oxford, England, Dr. Roger Gilbert Bannister (born in Harrow, England on March 23, 1929) completed a one-mile run in three minutes, 59.4 seconds. He thus broke the four-minute barrier and set a new world's record. Since that day, more than a dozen athletes have bettered Bannister's record. They now have a new goal: to break the three and one-half minute barrier.

Largest Golf Prize

BARBER, MILLER — The first place prize at the 144-hole World Open, held in Pinehurst, North Carolina between November 8 and November 17, 1973, was $100,000. A 42-year-old Texan, Miller Barber, won the tournament and collected the largest prize that professional golf has ever awarded. The total purse for the contest was $500,000.

Longest Jumper

BEAMON, BOB—The world record for the long jump (also called the broad jump) had hovered around 27½ feet, with jumpers knocking off an inch or so in each succeeding competition. So when Bob Beamon (1946-) jumped 29 feet, two and one-half inches on October 18, 1968 at the Mexico City Olympics, track and field enthusiasts were justifiably stunned. Since that time, no jumper has even approached 28 feet. Beamon's world record will probably stand for many years to come.

Bermuda Bowl Bridge Winner

BELLADONNA, GIORGIO—Born in 1923, Giorgio Belladonna was a member of the Italian "Blue Team" for 14 of the 15 times that the squad won the World and Olympic bridge championships in the period between 1957 and 1974. He then teamed up with Pietro Forguet and, in 1969, after winning the Bermuda Bowl—the symbol of world bridge supremacy—twelve times, retired.

Belladonna and Forguet came out of retirement to defeat an American squad and capture three more world titles, most recently in Venice in 1974. Giorgia Belladonna has accumulated more Masters Points than any living bridge player.

Participant in Most World Series

BERRA, LAWRENCE—As a member of the New York Yankees, Lawrence P. "Yogi" Berra (1925-) set the record for having played in more World Series games than any player in history. The Yankees have won 20 World Series and, of those, Berra, as catcher and left fielder, participated in 14—1947, 1949-1953, 1955-1958, 1960-1963.

After retiring as a player, Yogi became a coach and brought pennants to the Yankees in 1964 and to the New York Mets in 1969 and 1973. In 1976, he was signed as a Yankee coach.

Fastest Auto Racer

BETTENHAUSEN, GARY—The Texas 200 is held at the two-mile, banked oval (22-degree banking) track at the Texas World Speedway in College Station, Texas. The speedway is the fastest closed circuit auto racing track in the world. On October 6, 1973, Gary Bettenhausen of Monrovia, Indiana won the race at a record average speed of 181 miles per hour. Bettenhausen was driving a 2,600-cubic-centimeter turbo-charged McLaren-Offenhauser U.S. Auto Club open-wheeled racer.

Lowest 18-Hole Golf Score

BLANCAS, HOMERO—Born on March 7, 1938 in Houston, Texas, Homero Blancas holds the record for the lowest 18-hole golf score. On August 19, 1962, Blancas shot a 55 on the par 70 Premier Golf Course in Longview, Texas, recording 27 for the front nine and 28 for the back nine on the 5,002-yard course. Englishman A. E. Smith had shot a 55 way back in 1936, but the course on which he played was some 800 yards shorter than Longview.

Most Durable Football Player

BLANDA, GEORGE—In 1976, George Blanda completed his twenty-sixth season with the National Football League. He holds records for most seasons as an active player; most games played in a career (312 at the end of the 1973 season); most consecutive games (196); most points scored in a career (1,842); and most points after touchdown, leading the league seven times in that category. As a quarterback and place-kicking specialist, the 47-year-old Blanda has played for Chicago, Baltimore, Houston and his current team, the Oakland Raiders.

Teen-Age Tennis Player

BORG, BJORN—In the year 1975, Bjorn Borg of Sweden earned $220,851 in tennis prize money, the most ever won by a teenager in that sport. Borg, aged 19, won the French Open (he was defending champion), the United States Professional title, the Spanish Open and placed second in both the World Championship of Tennis playoffs and the Masters-Grand Prix. In addition, Borg was the number one player for Sweden, which won the Davis Cup for the first time in 1975. In his three-year professional career, Borg has earned more than $1 million from tennis and related ventures.

Greatest Speedsters

BREEDLOVE, CRAIG AND LEE—Norman Craig Breedlove (born March 23, 1938) set the record for the highest speed attained by a jet-engined car when he drove the 9,000-pound "Spirit of America" at 613.995 miles per hour on November 15, 1965. His wife, Lee, became the fastest woman on wheels 11 days earlier when she rode at 335.070 miles per hour in the same car. Craig's car left a six-mile-long set of skid marks when he lost control of the car during a test on the Bonneville Salt Flats.

In September, 1973, Craig set the record for the highest terminal velocity by a dragster when he drove his "English Leather Special" 377.754 miles per hour on the Salt Flats.

Greatest Football Rusher

BROWN, JIM—Drafted from Syracuse University in 1957, Jim Brown (1936-) set many football records during his years of play with the Cleveland Browns. Among them are league leader in rushing for eight seasons, most yardage in a career (12,312), highest average gain in a career (5.22 yards per carry), and most touchdowns (106) scored rushing in a career. Brown retired from football in 1965 and, among other interests, pursues a film career.

U.S. Wimbledon Winner

BUNDY, MAY SUTTON—May Bundy (1882-1975) won the Women's Singles Championship at England's Wimbledon Tennis

Classic in 1904, thus becoming the first American to win that tournament. She won Wimbledon again in 1905 and, once again, in 1907, and became the first three-time American winner of the prestigious event. Bundy, the first woman to be named to the United States Tennis Hall of Fame, died of cancer on October 4, 1975.

Tallest Basketball Player

BURLESON, TOM—The tallest active player in the National Basketball Association is Tom Burleson (1950-), center for the Western Division's Seattle Supersonics. At 7 feet 4 inches tall, Burleson is more than three inches shorter than the tallest man ever to play the game. That man is Emili Rached of Brazil, who measured 7 feet 7⅝ inches tall when he played in the 1971 Pan-American Games.

Nine Positions in One Game

CAMPANERIS, BERT—On September 8, 1965, Blanco Dagoberto Campaneris of the American League's Kansas City Athletics (now the Oakland Athletics) played pitcher, catcher, shortstop, first, second, and third bases and left, center and right fields—all *in one game*. Even Bert's flexibility didn't help the Athletics; they lost the game to the California Angels in 13 innings, by a score of five to three. Campaneris usually plays shortstop.

Fastest Men on Water

CAMPBELL, DONALD AND MALCOLM—In the 1920s and 1930s, Sir Malcolm Campbell set the world automobile speed record eight times and the world powerboat speed record twice. Upon his death in 1949, Campbell's son, Donald, continued in his father's footsteps. Like his father, he named his boats *Bluebird,* and his two and one-quarter-ton *Bluebird K7* broke the powerboat speed record in 1966. The following year, on January 4, 1967, Donald raced a turbojet-engined speedboat at 328 miles per hour. The record is considered unofficial however; it resulted in Donald's death.

Shortest Heavyweight Reign

CARNERA, PRIMO—For less than one year, from June 29, 1933 to June 14, 1934, Primo Carnera (1906-1967) was the world's heavyweight boxing champion—the shortest reign in heavyweight history. But Carnera, an Italian who was nicknamed the "Ambling Alp" because of his clumsiness, set several other records. He was the *heaviest* heavyweight, weighing 267 pounds when he knocked out Jack Sharkey in six rounds. He was also the tallest (6 feet 5.4 inches) boxer in history, possessing the largest fists (14¾-inch circumference), and the longest reach (85½ inches).

Greatest Basketball Player

CHAMBERLAIN, WILT—The Basketball record book is dominated by Wilt Chamberlain. Born on August 21, 1936, the 7 foot 2 inch, 275-pound "Stilt," as he is called, holds the record for most complete games played in one season (79, set in 1962) most consecutive complete games (47, also in 1962); most minutes played in a career (47,859); and most minutes played in one season (3,882, in 1962). The National Basketball scoring leader for seven seasons has scored the most points in a career (31,419); most points in a season (4,029, in 1962), scoring over 1,000 points for 13 seasons; and highest season scoring average (50.4 in 1962). He also holds the records for most field goals scored in a career, season and game, most free throws attempted, and most rebounds. Chamberlain's two most astounding achievements are the scoring of 100 points in one game, which he did against the New York Knickerbockers on March 2, 1962, and having never fouled out in 13 years and 1,045 games as a professional.

First Million-Dollar Race Horse

CITATION—The horse racing career of Calumet Farms' Citation extended from 1947 to 1951. When, on July 14, 1951, the six-year-old thoroughbred won the $100,000 Hollywood Gold Cup Handicap at Hollywood Park in Inglewood, California, his total earnings reached $1,085,760. Citation thus became the first race horse to win more than one million dollars.

Greatest Hitter of All Time

COBB, TY—The highest career batting average of all time (.367) belongs to baseball player Ty Cobb (1886-1961) of the Detroit Tigers. Cobb also holds the records for most base hits (4,191) and most runs scored (2,244).

A ruthless base-stealer who reportedly honed his metal spikes before each game to scare his opponents, Cobb stole 892 bases in his career—more than any other major leaguer. The record for most games played (3,033) also belongs to Cobb, whose career spanned the years 1905 to 1928.

Highest Paid Bullfighter

EL CORDOBES—Matador Manolo Benitez Perez, also known as El Cordobes, was born in Palma del Rio, Spain in 1936. He became a multimillionaire in 1966 after fighting 111 bulls at $15,000 per fight. By 1968, he commanded $25,000 for a one-half hour bullfight. In 1970, 121 bullfights earned him an estimated $1.8 million. The world's highest-paid matador has considerable landholdings in Spain, some of which he uses to train fighting bulls for the ring.

Female Tennis Money-Winner

COURT-SMITH, MARGARET—The $192,000 won in 1973 by Margaret Court-Smith (1942-) is a record for a single season's money winnings by a female tennis player. In the finals of the women's singles championship at Wimbledon in July of 1970, she defeated Billy Jean King 14-12 and 11-9 in a 46-game match that lasted two hours, 25 minutes. It was the longest contest of its kind ever played at Wimbledon. Court lost to Bobby Riggs in a Battle of the Sexes tennis match in 1973, but was avenged by King several months later.

Alpine Ski Champion

CRANZ, CHRISTEL—Since the World Alpine Ski Championships were introduced in 1931, Christel Cranz has won the most titles —12. Between 1934 and 1939, this great German all-around skier won five combined titles (Giant Slalom, Slalom, Downhill and Alpine), four Slalom titles, and three Downhill titles. In the 1936 Olympics, she won a gold medal for her performance in the Combined Championship.

Fastest Living Human

CROCKETT, IVORY—The title of "fastest human" is generally bestowed upon the man who wins the 100-yard dash. For 11 years, the record for the 100-yard dash hovered just above nine seconds, with several runners claiming the record. On May 11, 1974 in Knoxville, Tennessee, Ivory Crockett (1956-) of Southern Illinois University set a new record—an even 9.0 seconds—thus ending the dispute and winning the title.

First Prize Fight Broadcast

DEMPSEY, JACK—American prize fighter and world heavyweight champion Jack Dempsey was born William Harrison Dempsey in Manassa, Colorado in 1895. His heavyweight championship fight against France's Georges Carpentier, held on July 2, 1921, was both the first fight ever to be broadcast over radio and the first fight to gross $1 million in gate receipts. Dempsey won by a knockout in the fourth round. In each of his next four fights —including a July 4, 1923 decision over Tom Gibbons in 15 rounds (Montana) and a September 14, 1923 knockout over Luis Firpo in 2 rounds (New York)—Dempsey grossed $1 million dollars. Known as the "Manassa Mauler," Dempsey held the crown for seven years until losing to Tunney on September 23, 1926 in a decision after ten rounds in Philadelphia. This last fight grossed $2.6 million. He was beaten by Tunney in a comeback in 1927 and since that time has been a restaurateur and referee in New York City.

Longest Hitting Streak

DIMAGGIO, JOE—Known as the "Yankee Clipper" (he spent all his baseball years with the New York Yankees), Joe Dimaggio (1914-) performed the remarkable feat of hitting safely in 56 consecutive games during the 1941 baseball season. From May 15 to July 16 of that year, he made 91 hits, including 16 doubles, four triples and 15 homers, and was voted the American League's Most Valuable Player.

Dimaggio, a member of baseball's Hall of Fame, was also recipient of the Most Valuable Player Award in 1939 and 1947.

Fastest Oval Car Racer

DONOHUE, MARK—Only days before his tragic death on August 20, 1975 at Austria's Grand Prix, Mark Donohue (1937-1975) was clocked by National Association of Stock Car Automobile Racing officials at the Alabama International Speedway, Talladega, Alabama at a speed of 221.160 miles an hour for a single lap. This represents the fastest a man has ever traveled on a closed, or "oval," track. Donohue, a former Indianapolis 500 and Can-Am Championship winner, set the record in a modified Porsche 917/30 Can Am car, with a special turbo-charged, intercooled, five-liter engine. One of America's most popular racers, Donohue lost control of his Penske Formula One Grand Prix car during a practice session for the Austrian Prix and later succumbed to a freak brain injury.

Baseball Inventor

DOUBLEDAY, ABNER—United States Army Colonel Abner Doubleday, who later became a general, laid out the first baseball diamond in Cooperstown, New York, in 1839, now the site of the Baseball Hall of Fame. He drew up the first set of baseball rules, basing them loosely on the rules of the English games of cricket and rounders. Though first played in the United States as early as 1747, Doubleday is the acknowledged inventor of modern day baseball. The rules were codified in 1845 by Alexander Cartwright, based on Doubleday's ideas; the first game under these rules was played on June 19, 1846.

Most Consecutive Shutout Innings

DRYSDALE, DON—Donald S. Drysdale (1936-) of the Los Angeles Dodgers pitched 58 consecutive innings of runless baseball from May 14 to June 8, 1968, throwing six shutouts in the process. Both of these feats set new major league records. Drysdale has been a member of several pennant-winning clubs and is a recipient of the Cy Young Award. Now retired, he works as a sports announcer and lecturer.

Hockey High Scorer

ESPOSITO, PHIL—In professional ice hockey, a point is awarded to an individual for either scoring a goal or contributing an assist to the scoring of a goal. In the 1970-71 season, Phil Esposito, then center for the Boston Bruins, scored 152 points; establishing a National Hockey League record of 76 goals and 76 assists in a single season. Born February 20, 1942, Esposito, a Canadian, has scored 100 or more points in each of four different seasons and a minimum of 50 goals in each of three consecutive hockey seasons.

Olympic Gold Medal Winner

EWRY, RAYMOND C.—Since the modern Olympics were instituted in 1896, the only man to win 10 individual gold medals (that is, not as a members of a relay team or squad) is Ray Ewry. Born in 1874 in Lafayette, Indiana, this outstanding competitor won the gold medal for both the standing high jump and standing long jump in 1900, 1904, 1906, and 1908. In 1900 and 1904, he won the standing triple jump gold medals. Ewry died in 1937.

Five-Time World Drivers' Champion

FANGIO, JUAN MANUEL—Born in Balcarce, Argentina on June 24, 1911, Juan Manuel Fangio became the oldest man ever to win the World Drivers' Championship when he did so in 1957 at the age of 46. In fact, since the beginning of the event in 1950, Fangio (who drove mostly for Italy's Ferrari factory, but also for Maserati and Lancia) captured the title five times—1951, 1954, 1955, 1956 and 1957. By the time of his retirement in 1958, he had won 24 Grand Prix races.

First Grand Prix World Champion

FARINA, GIUSEPPE—An Italian medical doctor, nicknamed "Nino" Farina, captured the British, Swiss and Italian Grand Prix in 1950, thus becoming the first World Drivers' Champion as instituted by the International Automobile Federation (F.I.A.) in 1950. Farina won the September 3 race driving a Formula One-type Alfa Romeo designed by Enzo Ferrari on the Monza, Italy track.

Fastest Fastball Pitcher

FELLER, BOB—A test administered by the United States Army in the mid-1950s revealed that a fastball thrown by Cleveland Indian Bob Feller traveled at the rate of 98.6 miles per hour as it crossed home plate. Speed tests of the fastballs thrown by Nolan Ryan and others, made in the 1970s, confirmed that Feller is still the fastest living pitcher. Some pitchers dispute his title, claiming that their police-type auto speed indicators can more accurately measure a fastball.

Greatest Sulky Driver

FILION, HERVE—Harness racing, in which a horse is hitched to a sulky (a light, two-wheeled carriage seating only one person) with a driver at the reins, is a very popular form of horse racing. Canadian driver Herve Filion is the most successful driver harness racing has ever known. Born in Quebec on February 1, 1940, Filion set a record by winning 4,065 victories in his career. At Roosevelt Raceway, Long Island, New York, he recorded 605 wins in the 1972 season alone. He is still an active driver.

Youngest International Grandmaster

FISCHER, BOBBY—In 1958, at the age of 15, Chicago-born Robert J. Fischer (1943-) became an International Grandmaster, the highest class of chess player in the world. The Elo system of measuring the prowess of chess players ranks Fisher, who has an I.Q. of 187, as the greatest chess player of all time. Fischer's successful defense of his title against Boris Spassky of the Soviet

Union at Reykjavik, Iceland in 1972 was the most widely publicized chess match in history and brought the competitors more than $50,000, the most prize money since the creation of the chess federation (F.I.D.E.) Fischer has refused to defend his title and, although he has also refused to explain why, it seems apparent he believes there is no competition for him. Fischer's refusal to defend has forced the F.I.D.E. to strip him of his title.

First American Sports Writer

FORESTER, FRANK—Henry William Herbert (1807-1858), related to England's peerage, attended first-rate London schools. He came to America, and founded the *American Monthly Magazine* in 1833. In 1839, he began writing for the *American Turf Register* under the pseudonym of Frank Forester. A sports enthusiast from his youth, Frank authored many books and articles on hunting, fishing and riding and drew his own illustrations as well. His *Complete Manual for Young Sportsmen,* published in 1856, was a standard for many years. Forester, depressed over financial matters, committed suicide in New York City in 1858.

Fastest Man on Wheels

GABELICH, GARY—The fastest man on wheels was born in San Pedro, California on August 29, 1940. When driving the "Blue Flame" at the Bonneville Salt Flats, Utah on October 23, 1970, he set the record for the highest speed ever achieved by a land vehicle. The 5,000-pound, 37-foot-long landrocket was fueled by liquid natural gas/hydrogen peroxide and averaged 631.367 miles per hour over a measured kilometer. At one point during the run, Gabelich reached a speed of 650 miles per hour. "I've achieved a dream," he later said, "but I'll go faster."

Speediest Piston-Engined Dragster

GARLITS, DON—On November 23, 1973, at the National Hot Rod Association's All-Pro Supernational races, Don "Big Daddy" Garlits (1932-) drove his rear-engined AA-F dragster over the quarter-mile course in 5.8 seconds, reaching a terminal velocity of 247.25 miles per hour. His 7,948-cubic-centimeter, supercharged, Dodge V-8-engined vehicle scored the quickest elapsed time for a quarter-mile (5.78 seconds) in the same race meeting at Ontario Motor Speedway, California. Called the King of the Dragsters, Garlits equalled both his records in February of 1974.

Most Consecutive Baseball Games Played

GEHRIG, LOU—Henry Louis Gehrig (1903-1941), who began his ballplaying days while studying pre-law at Columbia University, was a member of the New York Yankees from June 1, 1925 to April 30, 1939. From the time he joined the club, until his retirement due to failing health, he never missed a game, thus setting the record for number of consecutive games played: 2,130. Gehrig, often called the "Iron Man," also set the record for most grand slam home runs in a career (23). He was the first major league player to hit four consecutive home runs in a single ball game.

LeMans Champion

GENDEBIEN, OLIVIER—Auto racing is the second most popular spectator sport (horse racing is first) in the world, particularly in Europe. The most important European auto race is the 24-hour Le Mans competition held in Sarthe, France. Excepting the war years, it has been held annually each June since 1923. The driver to have won that most prestigious of road races the greatest number of times is Frenchman Olivier Gendebien. In 1958, 1960, 1961 and 1962, Gendebien drove to victory in a car manufactured by the Italian firm of Ferrari Automobili. Interestingly, Ferrari cars have won the event most often, taking the honors a record nine times.

First Jewish Hall of Famer

GREENBERG, HANK—Signing with the Detroit Tigers at the age of 19, Hank Greenberg (1911-) went on to become one of the greatest sluggers in baseball history. He won the American League Most Valuable Player Award twice, the first time in 1935 as a rookie. In 1937, he won the title for most runs batted in, one less than Lou Gehrig's season record of 184. He previously led the American League in RBI's in 1935, and did again in 1940 and 1946. In 1938, Greenberg hit 58 homers and, in 1956, became the only Jewish player to be elected to baseball's Hall of Fame.

Youngest World Motorcycle Champion

HAILWOOD, MIKE—In 1961, 21-year-old Mike Hailwood won the world motorcycle championship in the 250-cubic-centimeter category. In 1966, he set a record of 19 wins in a season, a feat equalled only by Giacomo Agostini four years later. The great cycle champion has since moved up to Grand Prix auto racing;

he scored his first victory in 1975. Born in Oxford, England on April 2, 1940, Hailwood was made a *Member of the British Empire* for his accomplishments.

First Winner of the Indianapolis 500

HARROUN, RAY—On May 30, 1911, the first long-distance, closed track motor race was held at Indianapolis, Indiana. The 500-mile race was won by Ray Harroun. In America, as in Europe, long-distance races had previously been run on public roads closed for the day of the event. The 2½-mile oval track at Indy was initially hailed as a breakthrough for motor sport, but has since become known for its lack of safety for driver and spectator. Harroun, driving a Marmon Wasp, averaged 74.7 miles per hour for the distance.

Biggest Sports Money Winner

HENIE, SONJA—Norwegian skater Sonja Henie, born in 1912, won the Olympic figure-skating championship three times—1928, 1932, and 1936—before turning professional. As a pro, she toured in ice shows of her own creation and was featured in 11 motion pictures. Before her death in 1969, Sonja Henie had amassed a fortune worth more than $47,500,000, the largest sum ever accumulated by a sports figure.

Record Motorcycle Speed

HOBBES, DAVID—The record average speed for two motorcycle runs over a measured kilometer from a standing start is 122.77 miles per hour. The record is held by Englishman David John Hobbes (1944-), who accomplished the feat on September 30, 1972 at Elvington Airfield, Yorkshire, England, riding a supercharged Triumph Olympus II cycle. The bike was equipped with two twin-cylinder, 500-cubic-centimeter, 100-horsepower engines; methanol and nitromethane were used for fuel. Hobbes, also a professional auto race driver, has driven Formula One and Championship Endurance cars.

Longest Hockey Career

HOWE, GORDIE—Gordie Howe (1928-) skated for the Detroit Red Wings from 1946 through 1971—a total of 25 years—playing a record 1,687 games for the National Hockey League. In 1971, he joined the newly-formed World Hockey League to skate with his sons, who had just become professional ice hockey players. He retired two years later.

Howe scored more career goals, assists and points than any hockey star in history and is regarded as one of the game's all-time great players. Though his endurance was remarkable, he received more than 500 stitches during his career.

Hockey Hat Trick King

HULL, BOBBY—Besides having scored 50 or more goals in each of five seasons with the Chicago Black Hawks, Bobby Hull (1939-) has scored three or more goals in a single game (known as the "hat trick") 28 times during his 15-year National Hockey League career. Four of those times he scored four goals in a single game. Hull's skating speed has been measured at 29.7 miles per hour, faster than any hockey player ever measured. He also hits the puck at a record 118.3 miles per hour, the highest speed for a slap shot ever recorded.

Highest Basketball Scoring Average

JABBAR, KAREEM ABDUL—Jabbar, born Ferdinand "Lew" Alcindor on April 16, 1947, is often considered the heir apparent to Wilt Chamberlain's classification as the greatest basketball player of all time. The 7 foot, 2-inch, 225-pound center averaged 30.5 points per game during the first five years of his career with the Milwaukee Bucks, for whom he still plays. His lifetime field goal percentage of .553 is also unequalled. Now playing for the Los Angeles Lakers, Jabbar continues to threaten many of Wilt's records.

Greatest Nordic Skier

JERNBERG, SIXTEN—Nordic skiing—a combination of cross-country skiing of distances between 15 and 50 kilometers and ski jumping—is a World and Olympic class event. The Swedish skier, Sixten Jernberg (1929-), has won eight World Nordic titles, four in the 50-kilometer run, one in the 30-kilometer run, and three as a member of Sweden's relay team. Jernberg, in the meetings of 1956, 1960, and 1964, won a record number of Olympic skiing medals: four gold (which includes one relay), three silver, and two bronze—a total of nine.

First Black Heavyweight Champion

JOHNSON, JACK—When Jack Johnson (1878-1946) defeated Tommy Burns in a 14-round bout in Sidney, Australia on December 26, 1908, he technically became the World Heavy-

weight Boxing Champion. In no small part due to racial preju-
dice, Johnson was not officially awarded his title by the boxing
authorities until July 4, 1910. On that date, in Reno, Nevada,
he defeated James Jackson Jeffries in 15 rounds. But in a spectacular 26-round fight (a 15-round limit did not yet exist) in
Havana, Cuba on April 5, 1915, Johnson lost the crown to Jess
Willard. Recent analysis of actual fight films discount the belief
of some boxing critics that Johnson "threw" the fight.

Strikeout King

JOHNSON, WALTER—Walter Johnson (1887-1946) is the only
pitcher in baseball to have won 20 games in 10 consecutive
seasons. During his career with the Washington Senators, ex-
tending from 1907 to 1927, he pitched more shutout games (113)
and more strikeouts (3,508) than any major league pitcher in
history.

First Four-Title Golf Champion

JONES, BOBBY—Robert Tyre Jones (1902-   ) won the British
Amateur on May 31, 1930, the British Open on June 20, the
United States Open on June 12, and the United States Amateur
on September 27. He thus became the first golfer ever to hold
the four titles simultaneously. Jones was also the first American
golf champion to win the United States National Amateur two
years consecutively (1924 and 1925). He later repeated his feat
by winning the United States Amateur in 1927 and 1928.

Greatest Race Horse Winner

KELSO—This biggest money-winning thoroughbred in history was
foaled in 1957. Between 1959 and 1966, Kelso started in 63
races; he won 39, placed second 12 times, and took the third spot
twice. By the date of his retirement, March 10, 1966, Kelso had
won a record $1,977,896.

Biggest Tennis Attraction

KING, BILLY JEAN—On September 20, 1973, 30,472 tennis fans
filed into the Houston Astrodome to watch women's tennis professional Billy Jean King (1943-   ) defeat former Wimbledon
champion Bobby Riggs in straight sets. The contest, billed as
the "Tennis Match of the Century," was a test of Riggs' claim
that men were naturally superior to women.

King has won numerous titles in her tennis career. She was
the United States Open Champion in 1971, 1972 and 1974 and

the Wimbledon champion in 1966, 1967, 1968, 1972 and 1973. She currently (1976) plays for the Philadelphia Bell team of the United States professional tennis league. British pop singing star Elton John has written a song about her, entitled "B.J.K."

Cross-Country Skiing Winner

KOCH, BILL—At the age of two, Bill Koch, the "Green Mountain Kid," was already an Alpine skier. At the age of six, he was a ski jumper. This Vermont Olympian became the first American ever to win a medal in Cross-Country Skiing in the Winter Olympics. In the 1976 games at Innsbruck, Austria, in one of the big upsets of the competition, Koch took a silver medal in the 30-kilometer race. For the happy Koch, it was only the third 30-kilometer race he'd ever run.

Born in 1952, Koch has mastered a sport few Americans have seen, let alone tried. In cross-country skiing, special, thin skis are attached to a hinged binding which allows the skier to "walk" with his skis on. The skier's boots are hinged to the skis to allow forward body movement not possible in regular skiing.

No-Hitter Record Holder

KOUFAX, SANDY AND RYAN, NOLAN—Sandy Koufax (1935-) of the Los Angeles Dodgers pitched a no-hitter each season from 1962 to 1965, setting a record for the most no-hitters (four) by a major league pitcher. At the beginning of the 1975 season, Nolan Ryan (1947-) of the California Angels pitched his fourth no-hitter to tie Koufax's record. Koufax, retired from baseball, now works as an announcer; Ryan is still active and has a chance to break the record. In 1973, Ryan set a modern baseball record of his own: 383 strikeouts in a single season.

Perfect World Series Game

LARSEN, DON—On October 8, 1956, in the fifth game of the baseball World Series, held in Brooklyn, New York, Don Larsen of the New York Yankees did not allow a single Brooklyn Dodger to reach first base. He remains the only pitcher to ever hurl a perfect game in World Series history. The Yankees won the series, 4-3.

Longest Reigning Chess Champion

LASKER, EMANUEL—In 1886, an international committee was established to select dates for chess matches, and allot the winners prize money. The player who held the longest tenure as world chess champion was German-born Emanuel Lasker, who reigned from 1894 to 1921. Although several Russians held the title for many years in the 1950s and 1960s, Dr. Lasker's 27-year record as chess champion has never been threatened.

Tennis "Grand Slam" Winner

LAVER, ROD—In 1962, amateur tennis player Rodney George "Rocket Rod" Laver won the British, United States, Australian and French Tennis championships, known collectively as the "grand slam." As a professional, he accomplished the same feat in 1969, thus becoming the first man to win the "grand slam" twice. Ironically, Laver was born in Australia in 1938, the year that the tennis "grand slam" was first achieved by an American tennis player, Don Budge. Laver is still active in professional tennis, playing for the World Team Tennis Association.

Longest Reigning Heavyweight Champion

LOUIS, JOE—Joseph Louis Barrow was born in Lafayette, Alabama on May 13, 1914. This was the same Joe Louis ("The Brown Bomber") who, on June 22, 1937 in Chicago, knocked out James J. Braddock in the eighth round to win the heavyweight boxing title. From that day, until his retirement on March 1, 1949, he fought 25 title defenses, remaining undefeated and becoming the longest reigning heavyweight champ. He emerged from retirement briefly, only to be defeated by Ezzard Charles on September 27, 1950.

Most World Rodeo Titles

MAHAN, LARRY—To be considered for the All-Round title of the World Rodeo Championships, one must be able to wrestle a steer, rope a calf, ride a bull and ride an untamed horse, both with saddle and without. Larry Mahan (1943-) won the World All-Round Rodeo title (the unofficial "Best Cowboy in the World") a record six-times—1966, 1967, 1968, 1969, 1970, and 1973. Mahan, who is still active, set the record in 1973 for most prize money won in a single season at $64,447.

Longest Homer Hit

MANTLE, MICKEY—Mickey Mantle (1931-) played for the New York Yankees longer than any other player. During his career, he was voted Most Valuable Player three times, and won the home run and runs batted in crowns several times. Mantle played on 10 pennant-winning teams and held the record for striking out in a season until Yankee Bobby Bonds broke it in 1975. Perhaps the most stunning achievement of Mantle's career was when, in 1953, he hit a 565-foot home run—the longest homer ever hit.

Most Homers in 162-Game Season

MARIS, ROGER—Roger Maris (1934-) will forever go down in the baseball history books with an asterisk next to his name. In 1961, he did indeed hit 61 home runs—one more than Babe Ruth's record. But Ruth did it in 10 less games than Maris; hence, the asterisk. Maris hit his blasts for the New York Yankees in a celebrated home run duel with slugger Mickey Mantle. After the famous season, Maris was traded to the St. Louis Cardinals of the National League. With them, he faced his former teammates in the World Series of 1964, and beat them, as if in retaliation for the asterisk.

Prolific Baseball Manager

McCARTHY, JOE—With John McGraw and Connie Mack, Joe McCarthy is considered one of baseball's greatest managers. During his 14 years at the helm of the New York Yankee team, he won eight pennants and seven World Series. Four of those World Series wins were consecutive, a record unsurpassed except for that of Casey Stengel.

In his first major league managerial job, McCarthy led the previously cellar-dwelling Chicago Cubs to the National League pennant in 1929. When he won the first of his Yankee pennants in 1932, he became the first manager to win pennants in both leagues. Due to ill health, he retired from his position with the Yankees in 1946, but returned in 1948 for a several year managerial stint with the Boston Red Sox. Among the people managed by McCarthy were Lou Gehrig and Ted Williams; among those he traded were Grover Cleveland Alexander and Babe Ruth. "Marse Joe," as he was known, was elected to baseball's Hall of Fame in 1957.

Champion Bicycle Racer

MERCKX, EDDIE—Born in Belgium in 1945, Eddie Merckx is one of only two bicycle riders to have won the prestigious Tour de France five times. The Tour, begun in 1903, consists of almost a month of bicycle racing over nearly 3,000 miles of roads.

Merckx won the contest each year from 1969 to 1972, and again in 1974. Merckx also holds the record for the greatest distance covered on a bicycle in one hour's time—30 miles, 700 yards—which he set in Mexico City on October 25, 1972.

Open Road Race Winners

MERZARIO, ARTURO AND MUNARI, SANDRO—Driving a Ferrari 312P sports car, Arturo Merzari (1943-), and his co-driver, Sandro Munari, set the fastest average speed record in the 56th Targa Florio, the toughest and only remaining open road race in the world. (Such prestigious open road races as the Pan American 1000 and the Mille Miglia have been discontinued because of safety considerations.) The race, consisting of 11 laps around the island of Sicily, takes in 9,350 corners and requires thousands of gear changes. Merzari and Munari's record time of six hours, 27 minutes and 48 seconds was set on May 21, 1972.

Bobsled Champion

MONTI, EUGENIO—Bobsledding became recognized as an international sport when it was incorporated into the Olympics in 1924. Italy has won the world two-man bobsledding championship each year since 1954, with the exception of 1955, 1964, 1965 and 1970—a total of 13 times. Eugenio Monti, born on January 23, 1928, was a member of the championship Italian two-man bobsledding team for 11 of the 13 championship years.

First American-Born Chess Champion

MORPHY, PAUL C.—Twenty-year-old Paul Charles Morphy was the winner of the First Chess Congress in New York City in 1857. He followed this success with a trip to Europe where he won the Grand Tournament of the First National Chess Association in England and in France, which concluded on August 22, 1858. New Orleans-born Morphy returned to the United States on May 11, 1859 and defended his title for several years.

Greatest Car Race Winner

MOSS, STIRLING—Stirling Moss (1929-) won 167 car races between the years 1948 and 1962, eleven of which were shared with a co-driver. Among these is the classic victory he shared with Denis Jenkinson at the Mille Miglia of 1957, in which they drove a Mercedes.

Moss won 16 Grand Prix races, driving for underdog English

teams when the Italian marques of Ferrari and Maserati were dominating European racing. He retired from racing on February 11, 1962 after suffering a severe accident while racing at Good-wood in England.

Youngest Record-Breaking Swimmer

MUIR, KAREN—Karen Yvette Muir was born on September 16, 1952 in Kimberly, South Africa. On August 10, 1965, at the tender age of 12 years 328 days, she broke the world record for the 100-meter backstroke, swimming the event in one minute, 8.7 seconds in Blackpool, England. Karen thus became the youngest person to ever set or break an athletic record. She has since set other marks for women in World and Olympic swimming competition.

Powerboating Five-Time Winner

MUNCEY, BILL—Since the American Power Boating Association began awarding the Gold Cup, only Bill Muncey has won the award five times. Driving *Miss Century 21* and *Atlas Van Lines Special*, Muncey won the championship in 1956, 1957, 1961, 1962 and 1972.

The Gold Cup has been contested every year since 1903 (except for 1928, 1942-1945) and consists of a series of several races. Point totals determine the winner of the championship. Muncey, born in 1934, is still active in production and testing of unlimited hydroplane powerboats.

Basketball Inventor

NAISMITH, JAMES—Dr. James Naismith, a native of Ontario, Canada, graduated from McGill University in 1887. He taught physical education at the YMCA College in Springfield, Massachusetts, where, in 1891, he devised the game of basketball and composed its first set of rules. Naismith published these rules that same year in a book, entitled *Basket Ball Rules*. And on January 20, 1892 the first game of basketball was played—using two peach baskets and a soccer ball.

Naismith later became physical education director at the University of Kansas. In 1918, he published *The Basis of Clean Living*. The inventor of basketball died in 1939.

Football Throwing Record

NAMATH, JOE—In the year 1967, Len Dawson of the Kansas City Chiefs set an American Football League record for most consecutive passes completed (15). Five weeks later, New York Jets player Joe Willie Namath (1943-) tied the record of his quarter-backing rival in games against Miami and Boston. Namath went on to set an American Football League record for most yards gained passing (4,007). Two years later, he took his young team to the Super Bowl and the Jets became the first AFL club to win that championship.

Greatest Golf Winner

NELSON, BYRON—In 1945, Byron Nelson won 19 golf tournaments (of 31 he entered), the most ever won by an individual in a single season. Of the 19 wins, 11 were consecutive. They included the P.G.A., the United States and Canadian Opens and the Canadian P.G.A. The American golfer, born on February 4, 1912 in Worth, Texas, won prize money in 113 consecutive tournaments, also a record for professional golfers.

Longest Drive by a P.G.A. Golfer

NICKLAUS, JACK—In July, 1963, "The Golden Bear" (alias Jack Nicklaus) drove a ball 341 yards to set a United States Professional Golf Association record for the longest drive. Nicklaus has won more golf prize money—$2,009,168 by the end of 1973— than any other golfer; he won over $320,000 in 1972 alone. Moreover, Nicklaus is the only golfer to have won five major titles, 14 in all, and a record-setting four Masters Championships. He also won the World Cup a record three times.

Most Olympic Medals

NURMI, PAAVO—In the 1920, 1924 and 1928 Olympic Games, Paavo Johannes Nurmi (1897-1973) of Finland won nine gold medals and three silver medals for a total of 12, the most ever won by an Olympic athlete. Nurmi took first place in the 10,000-meter run twice, the cross-country run both as an individual and for his team twice, and the 1,500-meter, 5,000-meter and 3,000-meter runs for his team once. He twice won second place in the 5,000-meter run and once in the 3,000-meter steeplechase.

Hockey Assist Record Holder

ORR, BOBBY—In basketball, because "assisters" don't actually score the goals, the assist category is often overlooked. In ice hockey, however, individual points are awarded for assisting and, in this category, Bobby Orr (1948-) of the Boston Bruins is champ. In the 1970-71 season, he assisted on 102 goals for a single season record. His 1.31 average for assists per game is a league standard as well. Billy Taylor of the Detroit Red Wings once made seven assists in one game for a single game record.

Most World Records in a Day

OWENS, JESSE—At 3:15 p.m. on May 25, 1935, in Ann Arbor, Michigan, J.C. Owens (1914-) entered four races. They were the 100-yard dash, the long jump, the 220-yard run and the 220-yard low hurdles. By 4:00 p.m., Owens had won the four events, establishing new world records in each. The two 220-yard events were later established as 200-meter world records, for a total of six world records in track and field in 45 minutes. Owens later distinguished himself in the 1936 Olympics in Berlin by winning four events despite Hitler's prediction that no black man would beat a German athlete. The Germans did win the most medals that year, however.

Greatest Soccer Goal Total

PELE, EDSON ARANTES DO NASCIMENTO—Pele, as he is known to the soccer world, scored 1,026 goals from 1957 to 1970; this represents the highest number of goals scored in soccer during a specified period. Born in Bauru, Brazil on October 23, 1940, Pele played for a professional club, Santos, in his native land and led his country's team to victories in the prestigious World Cup in 1962 and 1970. Pele signed with the New York Cosmos of the American Soccer League in 1975 for a reported $3 million, and has since been playing exclusively in America.

First Million-Dollar Driver

PETTY, RICHARD—Richard Petty, the son of two-time Grand National Stock Car Champ Lee Petty, was the first stock car driver in the history of the National Association of Stock Car Automobile Racing to win $1 million on the race track. Petty achieved the feat on August 1, 1971. He has won the Daytona 500 mile race five times; no other driver has won it more than once. He was Grand National Champion in 1964, 1967, 1971 and 1972. Richard won 10 NASCAR races in 1974, earning over $150,000 in prize money, and perhaps five times that amount in endorsements.

Basketball Assist Champion

ROBERTSON, OSCAR—Oscar "Big O" Robertson (1938-) threw a record 7,694 free throws in his career with the Cincinnati

Royals and Milwaukee Bucks. He holds several other records as well: most free throws (19) in one half of play (against Baltimore in 1964); more than 1,000 points in a season (an accomplishment which he shares with Wilt Chamberlain, Jerry West and Bob Cousy); most free throw attempts in one half; most free throw attempts in one quarter. But the "Big O" is best known for his assists; that is, assisting another player score a basket. He has the most lifetime assists (9,887), the highest average number of assists per game in a career (9.5), and the highest average number of assists per game in a season (11.5) — all records set between 1961 and 1974.

Most Valuable Player

ROBINSON, FRANK—As outfielder for the National League's Cincinnati Reds, Frank Robinson (1935-) was voted Most Valuable Player of 1961 by the Baseball Writers' Association. In 1966, he won the award unanimously as outfielder for the American league's Baltimore Orioles. He thus became the first player to win the MVP in both major leagues. In 1975, Robinson became player-manager for the Cleveland Indians, the first black manager in the big leagues. His first time at bat for Cleveland, he hit a home run that won the game for the Indians.

First Black in Baseball

ROBINSON, JACKIE—April 11, 1947 was the day that Jackie Robinson (1919-1972) broke major league baseball's color barrier: he was signed by the National League's Brooklyn Dodgers. In his first game, an exhibition game against the New York Yankees, he played first base. Robinson's achievement led to other blacks being signed by the big leagues. Several players from the so-called Negro Leagues have since been elected to baseball's Hall of Fame, including Josh Gibson, "Cool Papa" Bell and Satchel Paige.

Five-Time Boxing Titleholder

ROBINSON, SUGAR RAY—Born Walker Smith, Jr. on May 3, 1920, the great American middleweight boxing champ, Sugar Ray Robinson, is the only boxer ever to have won the title five different times. He first held the middleweight crown after beating Jake LaMotta on February 14, 1951. He lost it, but regained it against Randy Turpin on September 12, 1951. He lost it again and regained it against Bobo Olsen on December 9, 1955. He won it again on May 1, 1957 against Gene Fullmer. His fifth win of the middleweight title was against Carmen Basilio on March 25, 1958.

Fastest Road Racer

RODRIGUEZ, PEDRO AND OLIVER, JACKIE—A road race is one in which drivers must negotiate left and right turns of varying degrees and speeds. In this respect, road races differ from races held on closed (oval) tracks, on which cars go in one direction and make only one kind of turn. The fastest road circuit is the Spa Francorchamps course in Belgium, an 8½-mile course, where the record average speed is 154.765 miles per hour. This record was set by Pedro Rodriguez of Mexico and his codriver, Jackie Oliver of England, on May 9, 1971, driving a Porsche 917K sports car. The 1,000-kilometer, 71-lap race took Rodriguez and Oliver four hours, one minute, 9.7 seconds to complete. After this race, the course was declared dangerous and was closed for track modifications.

Greatest Baseball Slugger

RUTH, GEORGE HERMAN—Although several of the records set by George Herman Ruth (1895-1948) have been broken by Henry Aaron, Babe still holds baseball's records for most long hits in a season (119), which he set in 152 games in 1921; most total bases in a season (457), also set in 1921; the highest "slugging" percentage (.690), set in his 21-year career in the big leagues; and most home runs (60) in a 154-game schedule, set in 1927.

The most feared slugger of his age, Ruth was walked more than any other man in 1923, when he set a base-on-balls record of 170.

Alpine Skiing Champion

SAILER, TONI—Anton Sailer of Austria has won a record seven Alpine Skiing Championships. Sailer won the Giant Slalom, Slalom, Downhill and Alpine Combo Competitions in 1956, a feat in itself. In 1958, he won three of those four events, losing only the Slalom. Sailer also shares the record for most gold medals at the Olympic Men's Alpine Skiing contests. In 1956, the same year that he swept the World Championships, he also won a record three gold medals at the Olympiad.

Basketball Attendance Record

SAPERSTEIN, ABRAHAM M.—On January 7, 1927, Abe Saperstein (1903-1966) founded the Harlem Globetrotters, the team that has played before more spectators than any other basketball team. In one season, 1951-1952, the Globetrotters played before more than three million spectators.

The Globetrotters are an exhibition team who bend basketball's rules slightly to achieve their unique brand of sports comedy. Some of their stars over the years have been Meadowlark Lemon and Curly Neal, known for his lack of hair and phenomenal dribbling ability.

Most Publicized Golf Hole

SARAZEN, GENE—On the last hole of the 1935 Masters Tournament, held in Augusta, Georgia, Gene Sarazen, in a moment memorable to golf fans, won first prize by scoring a double eagle two on that par five hole. "Par five" means that the unhandicapped player is expected to take five strokes to complete the hole. Sarazen finished the hole in only two strokes, one of which was a towering 300-yard drive and the other of which was a miraculous "four-wood" shot into the cup. Sarazen was a two-time United States Open champ (1922, 1932), British Open champ (1932), and three-time Professional Golfers Association champ (1922, 1923, 1933). He retired after winning the 1954 PGA senior championship cup.

Most Touchdowns in One Year

SAYERS, GALE—Jim Brown's last year in football was Gale Sayers' (1943-   ) first. In trying to prove that he was Brown's equal, Sayers established several records which are yet to be broken. In his rookie year with the Chicago Bears, Sayers scored the most points in a rookie season (132); the most touchdowns in a rookie season, or any season for that matter (22); and the most touchdowns in a game (6), a record shared with Dub Jones and Ernie Nevers.

Highest-Priced Race Horse

SECRETARIAT—Mrs. Helen Tweedy paid $6,080,000 for a thoroughbred race horse named Secretariat in February of 1973. She and 8 members of her syndicate paid $345 per ounce for the animal, eight times the price of gold. The horse proved worthy of the investment, becoming only the ninth horse in history to win the Triple Crown of racing (Kentucky Derby, Preakness and Belmont Stakes). The horse also set a world dirt track racing record of two minutes, 24.0 seconds before being put out to stud in November of 1973.

Free Throw Champion

SHARMAN, BILL—Bill Sharman (1934-), presently the coach for the Los Angeles Lakers, has made a perennial winner out of a perennial loser. As a player for the winningest basketball team, the Boston Celtics, he set the record for most consecutive free throws made in a season (55) during the 1956 season. He also led the league a record seven times in free throw percentage and holds the record for highest percentage in a season (.932).

Most Successful Jockey

SHOEMAKER, WILLIE—On September 7, 1970, Willie Shoemaker broke the long-standing "most winners" record of Johnny Longden by riding his 6,033rd winning horse. He started jockeying on March 19, 1949 and, by March 31, 1974, had ridden 6,624 first place winners. His acquired winnings during his 25-year career amounted to more than $50,000,000. On March 15, 1976, at age 44, Willie rode his 7,000th winner.

Most Football Yards

SIMPSON, O. J.—In the first game of the 1973 season, playing for the Buffalo Bills, O. J. "The Juice" Simpson (1947-) set a game record for most yards (250) rushing against the New England Patriots. That same year, he set a season's rushing record of 2,003 yards. Coming out of the University of Southern California, O. J. had broken all of his school's football records and won the Heisman Trophy for most valuable player in major college football. He also helped USC to a national championship and a Rose Bowl victory.

Most Gold Medals at One Olympics

SPITZ, MARK—Mark Spitz (1950-) of Santa Clara, California, after helping his relay teams swim to two firsts in the 1968 Olympic Games, went on to capture four individual and three relay gold medals at the 1972 competition, setting a new record for one meeting. He set world records for the 100- and 100-meter butterfly and the 100- and 200-meter freestyle. His American team set world records in the 400-meter freestyle relay, the 800-meter freestyle relay, and the 400-meter medley relay.

Inventor of the Football Tackling Dummy

STAGG, AMOS ALONZO—Amos Stagg (1862-1965) made many contributions to the game of football. He was head football coach of a major university for 57 years, longer than any other coach. In 1889, while at Yale University, using a canvas mat from the gym, Stagg made the first tackling dummy for use in football practice. While employed by the University of Chicago in 1892, physical education was made a part of the regular curriculum, a first for a private institution. The idea of the Varsity Letter was thought up by Stagg for a football awards ceremony at Chicago in 1904. Since that time, almost every institution has adopted the symbol.

First Successive World Series Victories

STENGEL, CASEY—On October 9, 1949, the New York Yankees captured baseball's World Series, having defeated the Brooklyn Dodgers, 4-1. The Yankees captured the title for the next four consecutive years, beating the Philadelphia Phillies in 1950, the New York Giants in 1951, the Brooklyn Dodgers in 1952 and, again, in 1953. No other team in baseball history has matched this feat and no small amount of credit is due the team's manager, Casey Stengel (1891-1975), whose record of victories is unsurpassed in 100 years of organized baseball.

Stengel was born in Kansas City (the initials K. C. forming the basis of his nickname) in either 1890 or 1891 and played for the Brooklyn Dodgers (1912-1917), the Pittsburgh Pirates (1918), Philadelphia Phillies (1920-21), the New York Giants (under John McGraw, 1922-1923). He finished his playing career with the Boston Braves (1924-1925).

Most Grand Prix Victories

STEWART, JACKIE—The World Drivers' Championship for Formula One has been in existence since 1950. An average of ten races per year has been held, although in 1975 there were 13 competitions. John Young Stewart (1939-), a member of the Order of the British Empire, won 27 of these races during his eight-year career. He won the World Drivers' Championship three times before his retirement at the end of the 1973 season.

Points in Grand Prix racing are awarded on a 9-6-4-3-2-1 basis for first through sixth places. Stewart accumulated 360 points, more than any other driver in the sport's history. His closest active competition is two-time world champion Emerson Fittipaldi, who had earned 234 points by the end of 1975.

Race Car Money-Winner

UNSER, AL—The older, and probably more successful, of the Unser brothers racing family, Al Unser won ten out of 18 United States Auto Club Championship races in the 1970 season. His prize money totalled $494,149, the largest single season earnings of any race car driver in history. Al captured the Indianapolis 500 and the USAC Championship Trail Cup that year and has also participated in dirt track, midget, hillclimb, Formula 5000 and stock car racing.

Back-to-Back No-Hitters

VANDER MEER, JOHNNY—As a starting pitcher for the National League Cincinnati Reds, Johnny Vander Meer (1914-) walked three men in a 3-0 hitless victory over the Boston Braves on June 11, 1938 in Cincinnati. Four days later, he no-hit the Brooklyn Dodgers in New York City, winning 6-0, for his second consecutive no-hitter, a feat unmatched in modern major league baseball. (Steve Busby of the Kansas City Royals pitched a no-hitter and a two-hitter back to back in 1975 and a similar feat was accomplished by Nolan Ryan of the California Angels in the same season.) The southpaw hurler, known as the "Dutch Master," went on to a 15-10 won-lost record in 1938, his first full season in the big leagues. Later in his career, he led the National League in strike-outs for three seasons (1941, 1943, 1944).

Most Valuable Baseball Card

WAGNER, HONUS—Baseball cards found in bubble gum packages evolved from the cigarette cards of the 1880s. The American Tobacco Company's 1912 series of baseball cards included one of John Peter "Honus" Wagner (1874-1955) but the cards bearing his photo were withdrawn after a few issues because of Wagner's strong opposition to smoking. A Honus Wagner card is now worth $250 to collectors.

Playing for Pittsburgh in the early years of organized baseball, Wagner won the National League batting crown eight times, the last in 1911. He didn't bat below .300 during his first 17 years as a player and set National League records for singles, doubles, triples and total base hits.

Most Holes-in-One

WALL, ART—Many professional golfers go through an entire career without sinking the ball into the hole on the first stroke. But

Art Wall, the Honesdale, Pennsylvania professional, has shot no less than 40 holes-in-one in his pro career . . . and he is still alive. Wall, who has won the Masters Tournament, has scored eagles (two strokes to sink the ball) from 250 yards out and further. His most recent hole-in-one was made on the 196-yard, sixteenth hole of the Inverrary Golf and Country Club, Lauderhill, Florida, in 1973.

Unassisted World Series Triple Play

WAMBSGANSS, BILL—Playing with the American League's Cleveland Indians in the fifth game of the 1920 World Series, second baseman Bill Wambsganss (1894-) caught a line drive by the Brooklyn Robins' Otto Miller. Bill tagged the player running from second to third, and then ran to tag the player running from first to second, thus making the only unassisted triple play in World Series history. Cleveland won the game 8-1.

Known as Wamby, the Ohio-born infielder was traded to Boston in 1924 and played his last year with Philadelphia in 1926. He had a lifetime batting average of .259.

Longest Pitching Career

WILHELM, HOYT—Pitchers are known to have the shortest careers in baseball. One bad year after several good ones can sometimes "finish" a pitcher. Hoyt Wilhelm (1934-) is an exception; he threw his knuckle ball for nine major league teams from 1952 to 1972 and pitched in 1,070 games, a feat unsurpassed by any pitcher. His lifetime earned run average was 2.52.

Lowest 18-Hole Women's Golf Score

WRIGHT, MARY KATHRYN—On the 6,286-yard Hogan Park Course in Midland, Texas, Mary Kathryn "Mickey" Wright (1935-) shot a 62, the lowest score ever recorded for a woman golfer. Wright shot a 30 on the front nine and a 32 on the back nine to record her 62 in November of 1964. She was a perennial contender of the Ladies' Professional Golfers' Association tour and won the competition several times. Mickey Wright retired in 1975.

Winningest Pitcher

YOUNG, CY—During his career from 1890 to 1911, Denton T. Young pitched a record 751 complete games for the Cleveland Indians, St. Louis Browns and Boston Red Sox. He won 511 of those games, also a record. He pitched a perfect game against the Philadelphia Athletics on May 5, 1904, a feat only 8 pitchers have accomplished.

Young's pitching legacy has been perpetuated by the institution of the Cy Young Award for outstanding pitcher of the year, a distinguished honor reserved for the best hurler of the year.

Women's Amateur Golf Championship

ZAHARIAS, BABE DIDRIKSON—One of the greatest all-around American athletes of the twentieth century was Babe Zaharias (1912-1956). Of the 634 track and field events she entered, she won all but 12. After being hailed as the star of the 1932 Olympics, Babe decided to teach herself golf. She won the 1946 United States Amateur title and the 1947 British Amateur, the first American to win both events. In 1948, 1950 and 1954, she won the Women's Professional Golf titles.

ARTISTS AND THE ARTS

National TV Color Broadcast

AMECHE, DON—On New Year's Day, 1954, actor Don Ameche hosted the Tournament of Roses Parade in Pasadena, California. The proceedings were aired, in color, on nationwide television, marking the first time that a coast-to-coast color television broadcast emanated from the West Coast. Presented on the National Broadcasting Company network, the spectacle of floats, marching bands and mounted horsemen was shown in 21 major cities. Ameche, born Dominic Felix Amici in 1910 at Kenosha, Wisconsin, made over 40 films, mostly for 20th Century-Fox Studios. Among his screen credits are: *Alexander's Ragtime Band, The Story of Alexander Graham Bell* and *The Three Musketeers.* His most recent film is *Picture Mommy Dead,* made in 1966.

First Black at Met

ANDERSON, MARIAN—When Giuseppe Verdi's *The Masked Ball* was performed on January 7, 1955, Marian Anderson sang the contralto part of Ulrica, the fortune teller. She thus became the first black to sing at the Metropolitan Opera. This "first" was the culmination of a great many "firsts" for Anderson, who made her debut in New York's Town Hall in 1935, after a triumphant European tour.

Born in Philadelphia in 1902, Marian Anderson began singing in the choir of the Union Baptist Church, which paid for her singing lessons. In 1938, she received the Spingarn Medal for the year's highest achievement by a Negro. She established a scholarship for promising singers in 1942, and published her autobiography in 1956. In 1958, following a State Department sponsored tour of Southeast Asia, Marian Anderson was appointed a United States delegate to the United Nations.

TV Quiz Show

BARKER, BOB—Bob Barker, the host of the television game show, *Truth or Consequences*, remained on the air, with one program, longer than any other performer. For more than 16 years—from December 31, 1956 through January 12, 1973—and 3,524 consecutive performances, Barker amused millions of television fans with the comical and embarrassing stunts he required of his contestants.

Ed Sullivan and Lucille Ball, two other frequently named candidates for the record, worked on more than one show while on television. Barker's quiz show remained essentially unchanged for 16 years.

Most Records Sold

THE BEATLES—The musical combo that has most contributed to revolutionizing the popular music industry is the Beatles. Between February, 1963 and January, 1973, they sold an estimated 545,000,000 records. The group, consisting of George Harrison and John Lennon (guitar), Paul McCartney (bass), and Ringo Starr (drums), hailed from Liverpool, England. With hits such as "I Want to Hold Your Hand," "Thank You Girl," "Help," and "Nowhere Man," the Beatles introduced a harmony vocal/guitar sound that is still popular more than a decade after their debut.

Since the group's breakup, Starr has appeared in several films, including *Candy* and *200 Motels*; Lennon has won the legal right to remain in the United States (1975); Harrison has toured America with a new band; and McCartney has toured Europe and the United States in late spring, 1976. All four have recording contracts and produce one album a year.

100,000,000 Record Sales

BERLIN, IRVING—Born in Russia on May 11, 1888, Israel Baline (or Bailin) arrived in the United States in 1893. Baline, who later changed his name to Irving Berlin, played a leading role in the evolution of the popular song from early ragtime to jazz. He wrote such classics as "God Bless America" and "Alexander's Ragtime Band." Among the numerous musical comedy scores to his credit are *Annie Get Your Gun* (1946) and *Watch Your Step* (1916).

Berlin's hit tune, "White Christmas," was first recorded in 1941. In 1970, it became the first recorded song to reach sales of 100,000,000.

First Disc Gramophone

BERLINER, EMILE—The *Berliner Gramophone,* patented in 1887 by Emile Berliner (1851-1929), was the earliest record player to use the wax disc. (Edison's and succeeding models of the record player had used cylinders.) To keep the record revolving on the turntable, the operator had to continually crank the record player. By 1896, however, a motor had been developed which kept the turntable spinning for an extended period of time. The sound produced by the Berliner gramophone was amplified by a metal horn. A hornless model, known as the *Victrola,* eventually rendered it obsolete.

First Sync-Sound Film

BERNHARDT, SARAH—In 1900, French actress Sarah Bernhardt (1844-1923) played the duel scene from *Hamlet* in the first film using sound synchronized with the movements of the characters on screen. The film, along with six other shorts, was shown at the Paris Exposition between April and November of that year. The words of Shakespeare, or of any other playwright for that matter, had never been spoken on the screen before.

In 1876, Bernhardt, wearing a jacketed trouser-suit, was photographed by Melandri in her Paris studio. No woman had ever before worn pants as an article of feminine apparel. Known as the "Divine Sarah," the French actress was born Rosine Bernard in 1844. In addition to being an accomplished Shakespearean actress, Bernhardt was a leading interpreter of Racine, Sardou and Victor Hugo, premiering plays by all of these leading contemporary French dramatists.

Most Expensive Movie

BONDARCHUK, SERGEI—The Russian government-sponsored version of Leo Tolstoy's *War and Peace* cost a reported $96 million to produce. Filmed between 1962 and 1967, and directed by and starring Sergei Bondarchuk, the complete film runs six hours and 13 minutes, with three intermissions. For the re-creation of the Battle of Borodino the same number of extras were used as were involved in the actual battle—over 120,000 troops. To ensure authenticity, the actual Russian crown jewels were used and telephone lines were removed for a 50-mile radius.

First Television Western

BOYD, WILLIAM—*Hopalong Cassidy*, which premiered on the National Broadcasting Company network on November 28, 1948, was the first of many western television shows to be produced. Actor William Boyd, who played the tall-hatted "Hoppy," won several awards for young people's programming. The series ran successfully for many years and reruns of what has almost become a classic in television programming are still being shown today.

Highest One-Film Salary

BRANDO, MARLON—For his performance as Mafia chieftain Don Corleone in *The Godfather*, Marlon Brando (born April 13, 1924) received a reported $10 million before taxes, the highest salary ever paid to a movie actor for a single picture. Brando also shared a percentage of the profits. In its first year of showing, *The Godfather* grossed over $100 million at the box office, a record at the time.

For his performance in *The Godfather*, which was based on the best-selling novel by Mario Puzo and directed by Francis Ford Coppola, Brando won an Academy Award for Best Actor, which he did not accept. In 1954, he received his first Oscar, which he *did* accept, for *On the Waterfront*. He had a successful stage career before going to Hollywood where, after his film debut in Stanley Kramer's *The Men*, he re-created his Broadway role of Stanley Kowalski in Elia Kazan's movie version of *A Streetcar Named Desire*.

First Dredger

BREUGEL, PIETER THE ELDER—Pieter Breugel the Elder (1520?-1569?) headed a family of artists who brought sixteenth century Flemish painting to its artistic peak. His work, influenced by fellow countryman Hieronymous Bosch, dealt with scenes of Flemish peasants at work and leisure, as well as depictions of the brutality of their conquerors. But Breugel is also known for another achievement. In 1561, he designed and built a dredger for the Brussels government which was used to excavate the Rupel-Scheldt Canal. Built entirely of wood, it was rolled along on logs and used to scoop the soft, swampy earth for an efficient and continuous ditch which would be filled with water, for navigation, irrigation and flood control.

First Woman Nobel Prize Winner

BUCK, PEARL—The daughter of missionary parents, American novelist Pearl Buck was born in 1898. She lived in China for the first 40 years of her life and, in 1932, won the Pulitzer Prize for *The Good Earth,* a novel based on her observations of Chinese peasant existence.

In all, Pearl Buck wrote 85 works of fiction and nonfiction. Some of her titles include: *Sons* (1932), *A House Divided* (1935), and *A Bridge for Passing* (1962). In 1938, she became the first American woman to win the Nobel Prize for literature, largely on the strength of *Fighting Angel* and *The Exile,* biographies of her father and mother, published in 1936. Ms. Buck, an active environmentalist and child welfare worker, died in 1973.

Crew Member of First Steamship

BURNS, ROBERT—The first steamship was built by Patrick Miller, an Edinburgh banker with an amateur's interest in science. The first voyage of the steamship was on the Loch of Dalswinton, near Dumfries, Scotland, where Robert Burns (1759-1796) worked for the Civil Service in the Office of Excise. Burns became a member of the steamship's crew on its first voyage.

Burns is known to most as a famous eighteenth-century Scottish poet, called "Caledonia's Bard." The poems in the Kilmarnock edition were first published in 1786 to finance his migration and that of his wife to Jamaica. Included were "The Address to a Mouse," "The Two Dogs" and "The Holy Fair."

Highest Priced Diamond

BURTON, RICHARD—Richard Burton, born on November 10, 1925 in Wales, began acting while a student at Oxford. He has starred on Broadway in *Othello* and *Hamlet* and is regarded as a leading interpreter of Shakespeare. Burton has received many international awards for his film acting, including the New York Drama Critics Circle Award (1961). He was named a C.B.E. by Queen Elizabeth in 1970.

Burton married Elizabeth Taylor in 1964 and, in 1969, presented her with a 69.24-carat, flawless diamond, purchased for $1,050,000, the highest priced diamond ever sold at auction. Separated from his wife in February, 1976, Burton returned to the stage after a decade of screen acting in the Broadway hit, *Equus.*

The Largest Mobile

CALDER, ALEXANDER—In the main terminal building of John F. Kennedy International Airport in New York City hangs a 45-foot by 17-foot movable sculpture by Alexander Calder. It is the largest mobile in the world. (The term "mobile" was coined by Marcel Duchamp when he was experimenting with new sculpture forms and was despairing of immovable statues, which he called "stabiles.")

Calder, born in Philadelphia in 1898, is the son of sculptor Alexander Stirling Calder, who made many sculptures for parks and gardens in the early part of the twentieth century. Calder fils' huge mobile weighs 600 pounds and was suspended in December of 1957.

First Woman Met Conductor

CALDWELL, SARAH—Born in 1928, Sarah Caldwell has dedicated her life to furthering the popularity of opera. She founded the Opera Company of Boston in 1957, an organization which performed new and innovative compositions as well as rarely performed European works. In November of 1975, Caldwell became the second woman in the history of the New York Philharmonic to conduct its orchestra. Although extremely proud of the accomplishment, she harbored the desire to become the first woman to conduct the Metropolitan Opera. That ambition was realized when, in January, 1976, she conducted Giuseppe Verdi's *La Traviata* to unanimous critical acclaim.

A conductor addicted to the offbeat and the eccentric, Caldwell has used slide projections, video tapes, motorcycles and circus midgets in her attempts to produce programs which will bring in more paying customers and at the same time introduce fresh interpretations of classic operatic works.

Wealthiest Classical Singer

CARUSO, ENRICO—Italian operatic tenor Enrico Caruso was born in Naples, Italy in 1873, the eighteenth child in a family of 22. His interpretation of *Vesti la giubba* (*On with the Motley*) became the first recorded aria to sell one million copies. Excerpts from Ruggiero Leoncavallo's opera, *I Pagliacci*, first made on November 12, 1902, also earned him "gold records" as single recordings.

When he died in 1921, Caruso's estate was valued at $9,000,000, the greatest fortune ever amassed by a singer.

The turning point in his career was his lead tenor performance of Giordano's *Fedora* on November 17, 1898 at the Teatro Lirico in Milan. He made his debut at New York's Metropolitan Opera House in *Rigoletto* on November 23, 1903 and toured America extensively.

Cello as Solo Instrument

CASALS, PABLO—It is unlikely that anyone has done more for the cello than Pablo Casals. His development of modern cello playing techniques has established the cello as a solo instrument. A leading interpreter of Bach and Beethoven, Casals established the Prades music festival in France (1950) and Puerto Rico (1957).

Born in Spain in 1876, Casals made his concert debut in Paris at the age of 23. He returned to his homeland and, in the 1920s, founded a symphony orchestra in Barcelona. Casals fled his native Spain after the Franco victory in 1939. He was awarded the Presidential Freedom Medal in 1963 and the United Nations Peace Medal in 1971. The renowned cellist died on October 22, 1973.

Inventor of Ball Bearings

CELLINI, BENVENUTO—Famed Italian goldsmith Benvenuto Cellini (1500-1571) studied under Michelangelo in 1519. Among his patrons during his long and interesting life were Pope Clement VII, Cosimo de Medici, and Francis I of France. Cellini's best known sculpture is a bronze group depicting *Perseus Holding the Head of Medusa.*

In 1543, after finishing a sculpture of *Jupiter,* Cellini mounted the statue on four small wooden spheres (the forerunner of ball bearings) so it could be moved backward and forward and rotated for view.

Cellini's autobiography is considered one of the classics of Renaissance literature.

Most Popular French Entertainer

CHEVALIER, MAURICE—The beloved French song and dance man, Maurice Chevalier (1888-1972), began his career at the Café des Trois Lions in Paris in 1900. He became a favorite of Hollywood in the 1930s, invariably being cast as the dashing, romantic lead in such movies as: *The Playboy of Paris, Love Me Tonight,* and *The Beloved Vagabond.* He later played character roles with distinction, including his highly acclaimed performance in *Gigi* in 1955. Chevalier toured extensively in a one-man revue featuring his songs and stories and punctuated by dance steps. His 1947-1950 tours of Europe and America were particularly successful. It was through this avenue that he became most popular and earned a reputation as the most popular French entertainer of the twentieth century. His renditions of "Louise" and "Amy" were most loved by the public.

Top-Selling Authoress

CHRISTIE, AGATHA—Born in Torquay, Devon, England on September 15, 1890, Dame Agatha Christie, later Lady Mallowan, wrote more than 80 novels of the mystery-detective variety. Her works have sold an estimated 400,000,000 copies world-wide. The paperback editions of her books sell 1.5 million copies every year in Great Britain alone. Dame Agatha's mysteries include such standard thriller titles as *Murder on the Orient Express* (1934), *Ten Little Indians* (1939), and *Hickory, Dickory Death* (1955). Her heroes and heroines are household names among mystery readers and include the characters, Hercule Poirot and Miss Marple.

Dame Agatha's play, *The Mousetrap*, has been running continuously in London since November 25, 1952, a record run for a play. It was still running strong when she died in early 1976. Another of her award-winning plays is *Witness for the Prosecution*, which opened in 1955.

Inventor of Papier Mâché

CLAY, HENRY—In 1772, Henry Clay of Birmingham, England patented a method of making paper "hard." Though the process was already known in the Orient, the idea of making "japanned" paper was new to eighteenth-century Europe. After Clay's patent expired in 1802, many of his fellow townsmen pirated the idea and, at the same time, advanced the art. But Clay was the *first* to make papier mâché in Europe.

First Classical Gold Record

CLIBURN, HARVEY LAVAN—In 1958, renowned American pianist Van Cliburn, born in Kilgore, Texas on July 12, 1934, recorded Piano Concerto No. 1 of Pyotr Ilych Tchaikovsky. By 1961, it had sold more than one million copies. By January of 1970, sales had exceeded two and one-half million, a record for a classical long-playing record. The popularity of this recording stems from Cliburn's triumph at the Moscow International Tchaikovsky

Competition on April 14, 1958. He was proclaimed the "new American Sputnik" and was hailed on both sides of the Iron Curtain for his virtuosity.

Highest Paid TV Performer

COMO, PERRY—Born in Canonsburg, Pennsylvania on May 18, 1912, Perry Como was first employed as a barber. His singing career began in Philadelphia night clubs, and led to the recording and release of several popular records.

The contract Como signed in May of 1969 with the National Broadcasting Company guaranteed him a rate of $1.25 million an hour—equivalent to $20,833 a minute—the highest hourly rate ever paid for a television performance. In return, Como was to star in four one-hour specials, for a total of $5 million. From this amount, he was required to pay those supporting artists he chose to use on the programs.

First All-Metal Sax

CONN, CHARLES GERARD—In 1888, the Conn Musical Instrument Company, of Elkhart, Indiana, produced the first all-brass saxophone for use by American military bands. A year later, Charles G. Conn (1844-1931), the company's founder and a pioneer in marching band instrument building, manufactured the first "clarionet," an instrument made entirely of metal. All clarinets had previously been made from wood.) Conn also constructed the first sousaphone from the "bell-up" designs of John Philip Sousa and, in 1908, made the first and more popular "bell-front" model. The Indiana firm still makes many of the instruments used by outdoor and military bands.

First International American Artist

COPLEY, JOHN SINGLETON—Born in Boston in 1738, John Copley was the first American painter to receive acclaim on both sides of the Atlantic. His nearly 300 oils are important for their evocative portraits of colonial life and customs. Copley lived and exhibited primarily in London, where he settled from 1774 until his death in 1815. (He disliked the fact that the colonies were cut off from the mainstream of contemporary European art.) His paintings include battle scenes of the French and Indian Wars and portraits of famous contemporary figures, including the king and queen of England. He is best known for his colonial portraits of *Mr. and Mrs. Thomas Mifflin* (1773), *Mrs. Sylvanus Bourne* (1766) *and Colonel Epis Sargent* (1760).

Inventor of the Piano

CRISTOFORI, BARTOLOMMEO—Bartolommeo di Francesco Cristofori was a harpsichord maker in Padua. When he was summoned to the court of Prince Ferdinand of Florence in 1687, the prince encouraged Cristofori to continue his work in developing a harpsichord in which the volume could be regulated, and which possessed a larger range than that of existing models. By 1711, Cristofori had produced what he called a *gravicembalo col piano e forte*, the first piano. Two years earlier, he had published a diagram describing this genuine forerunner of the modern piano. Cristofori continued to improve the instrument even after the prince had died. He extended its range (which had originally been from D to F) to more than four octaves.

Unsurpassed Record-Selling Singer

CROSBY, BING—Harry Lillis Crosby, Jr. was honored on June 9, 1960 with a platinum record commemorating the sale of his 200,000,000th record, a feat not approached by any other recording artist. From the sales of his 2,600 recorded singles and 125 recorded albums, it is estimated that Crosby has by now doubled that figure. His first record was "I've Got the Girl," made in 1926.

Born in Tacoma, Washington in 1904, "Bing" Crosby's first musical "gig" was as the drummer in the Juicy Seven jazz group in 1925. Among his many films are: *Going My Way*, for which he received the Best Actor Oscar in 1944, *The Bells of St. Mary's* (1946) and *White Christmas* (1954). The title song from the latter is his best-selling recording.

Pioneer of Music Notation

D'AREZZO, GUIDO—A Benedictine monk who lived from 995 to 1050 A.D., Guido D'Arezzo, devised the earliest system of music notation. The system consisted of lettering the notes using 15 symbols of the Roman alphabet. D'Arezzo also set down a code for indicating stops, dynamics, tempos and clef. He developed the octave, accent, and other markings still used in music today.

Designer of the Modern Violin

DA SALO, GASPARO—The grandson of Santino diBertolotti, the lutemaker, Gasparo da Salo is credited with being the first to make violins in the shape used today. The instrument had previously been shaped like a small "viol," descending from the fifteenth century troubador fiddle. De Salo introduced the "violin" shape and, by the time of Haydn (1732-1809), violins had entirely replaced viols in musical scoring and arranging.

Da Salo (1540-1609), whose shop in the northern Italian town of Brescia was noted for its fine violins, also produced violas and double basses.

The $100,000,000 Painting

DA VINCI, LEONARDO—Born the illegitimate son of Ser Piero of Vinci, Italy in 1452, Leonardo was a painter, sculptor, architect and engineer. He worked in Milan and Florence before becoming the court artist of Francis I of France, in whose service he died on May 2, 1519.

One of Da Vinci's 17 surviving paintings, his portrait of *Mona Lisa,* was assessed at $100,000,000 when it was brought to the United States in 1962, and so became, for insurance purposes, the world's most valuable painting.

Loudest Rock Band

DEEP PURPLE—Deep Purple is a British "heavy metal" group, a "hard rock" band based around an electric guitar and organ sound. In a test conducted by an association for the deaf in 1972, it was discovered that the sound emanating from Deep Purple's 10,000-watt Marshall sound system registered a record-making 117 decibels. It was reported that, at the London Rainbow Theatre engagement of Deep Purple in 1972, three people lost consciousness as a result of the loudness.

In 1976, New York's Carnegie Hall announced that it was discontinuing the performances of rock bands with a decibel level above 103 due to the "excessive noise involved."

Most Expensive Sculpture

DEGAS, EDGAR—Degas' sculpture in bronze, *Petite Danseuse de Quatorze Ans,* executed in an edition of twelve casts in 1880, brought $380,000 on May 5, 1971. It was sold by the Parke-Bernet Galleries of New York City.

Degas, born the son of a French banker in 1834, was well educated and encouraged to study law. Instead, he attended art school and developed into an artist with a singular judgment of individual form and coherent design. He died in 1917, a virtual recluse.

The Original "Radio Girl"

DE LEATH, VAUGHN—Lee de Forest (1875-1961), the American inventor of telegraphic, telephonic and radio apparatus, was passionately interested in the broadcasting of music over a newly-discovered medium—the radio wave. The developer of the audion tube in 1906, DeForest first made musical broadcasts from the Eiffel Tower in 1908, in a publicity effort to obtain funds for his inventions. And, in 1916, he introduced the first "radio girl," in the person of Vaughn de Leath.

Recording in DeForest's New York City Laboratory, Vaughn's voice became a familiar sound to all radio listeners. The original radio crooner left DeForest in 1921 to sing for station WJZ in Newark, New Jersey.

Inventor of the Clarinet

DENNER, JOHANN CHRISTOPH—Johann Denner was a prominent maker of woodwind instruments living in Leipzig, Germany in the seventeenth century. For many years, he had attempted to improve the French "chalumeau," also known as the "shawm," a popular woodwind instrument of the day. Around the year 1700, Denner invented an entirely new type of woodwind instrument. The device contained, not only keys, but, a single flat reed with which the player could control pitch. He called the instrument a "clarinet," and it soon became the rage of Nuremberg music circles. In 1913, an opera by Weigman, called *Der Klarinettemacker,* was premiered. Johann Denner was the hero.

Recipient of Most Oscars

DISNEY, WALT—The first animated talking cartoon picture was Walt Disney's *Steamboat Willie.* Produced in Hollywood and first shown in New York City on September 19, 1928, it featured Mickey Mouse, the first animal ever to "talk" on screen. From *Steamboat Willie,* Disney (1901-1966) parlayed the cartoon business into a multimillion dollar empire and, in 1971, built the world's largest amusement resort, Disney World, in Orlando, Florida. The entertainment facility, set on 27,443 acres, cost $400 million to build. Disney's film career garnered him 35 Oscars from 1931 to 1969. Brother Roy Disney took over the company's leadership after Walt's death.

First Poet Laureate

DRYDEN, JOHN—In April of 1668, John Dryden was appointed the first official Poet Laureate of England. Born in 1631, Dryden first achieved fame upon the publication of his "Heroick Stanzas" about Oliver Cromwell in 1656. But, the following year, he wrote "Astraea Redux," which celebrated the return of Charles II, demonstrating that a good poet also had to be a good politician.

Dryden also wrote plays, his tragedies being the most memorable. He translated all the major Roman poets, including Juvenal, Virgil and Ovid. He converted to Catholicism in 1687 and upon the ascension to the throne of the Protestant William III, lost his laureateship. He died in 1700.

Tallest Pre-Broadcasting Tower

EIFFEL, ALEXANDER GUSTAV—The Eiffel Tower, created for the Paris Exhibition, was completed on March 31, 1889. As designed by Alexander Gustav Eiffel, the 8,091-ton structure was originally 986 feet tall; a television aerial extended it 67 feet in 1957. The tower, which is made of iron and took over two years to complete, sways as much as five inches in high winds. The Eiffel Tower was the world's tallest structure for 40 years, until the Chrysler Building and the Empire State Building in New York were completed in 1930. More than 350 people have jumped from the top of the tower to their deaths.

Eiffel is also noted for his book, *The Resistance of the Air*, published in 1913. It greatly contributed to the science of aerodynamics.

Developer of Piano and Harp

ÉRARD, SEBASTIEN—The first *French piano*, so called because it was developed in Paris, was square and had a five octave range. Although he first produced it in 1777, Sebastien Érard only obtained a patent for the instrument in 1785 from King Louis XIV. Upon receipt of the patent, Érard, with his brother, Jean Baptiste, moved his shop to London. There he built his first grand piano in 1796. He also worked extensively with harps, developing the first double action harp in 1810, and fixing the form of the modern harp as early as 1792. Érard continued his work with pianos, inventing a combination piano and organ called the *piano organise*. Although the piano had been invented around the beginning of the eighteenth century, *Érard* made significant improvements on the hammer and key mechanisms of the instrument.

Smallest Brain on Record

FRANCE, ANATOLE—Anatole France (born Jacques Anatole Francois Thibault) received the Nobel Prize for Literature in 1921.

Born in 1844, his first novel was *Le Crime de Sylvestre Bonnard,* published in 1881, which established his reputation as an author.

France's early works were politically oriented. At one time, he worked as literary critic for the journal, *Le Temps.* Later, his writings became more satiric with a libertarian vein. They include such works as *L'Ile de Pirgouins* (*Penguin Island,* 1908), and *La Révolte des Anges* (1914).

At the time of his death in 1924, France was one of the giants of French literature. A full autopsy was performed, according to custom. France's brain was measured and was found to weigh only two pounds four ounces, the *lightest* ever recorded.

First Woman Newspaper Editor

FRANKLIN, ANN—Ann Franklin was the wife of printer James Franklin, brother of Benjamin. Her son, James Jr., founded the *Newport Mercury* in June, 1758 and, when he died in 1762, she assumed the editorship, thus becoming the first female newspaper editor. The *Mercury* was Rhode Island's oldest newspaper, and one of the oldest in the colonies. Ann served as editor of the liberal weekly publication until her death in 1763.

First Televised Movie Premiere

GABLE, CLARK—Everything about David O. Selznick's *Gone with the Wind* was spectacular: its budget, its high-powered cast, its spectacular sets and its premiere. On December 19, 1939, the New York opening of the picture was transmitted live from the Capitol Theatre. Two cameras situated in the theater lobby broadcast the excitement to anyone owning a television set. Clark Gable, the male lead in the movie, appeared briefly before the cameras when he entered the theater that evening. Gable (1901-1960), a native Ohioan, had won an Oscar for Best Actor in *It Happened One Night,* directed by Frank Capra in 1934. He was married five times; his love affair with Carole Lombard is legendary.

Largest Radio Audience

GAMBLING, JOHN—*Rambling with Gambling* was first presented on WOR radio, New York in 1925. Hosted originally by John Gambling, and currently by John Gambling, Jr., the morning news-music-talk program has two and one-half million listeners daily, more than any other show. Celebrating its fiftieth anniversary in November, 1975, *Rambling with Gambling* is the longest on-going radio program in the history of the medium.

The World's Fastest Writer

GARDNER, ERLE STANLEY—Born in Massachusetts in 1889, Earle Stanley Gardner moved to the West Coast in 1913 to study law. He initially wrote as a hobby, but, by 1932, when the first in his Perry Mason series was published, he had already authored many novels under assumed names. Between the years 1933 and 1938, Gardner wrote 1,100,000 words a year—the equivalent of a novel every six days—while still practicing law. In all, he wrote over 140 of them, dictating up to 10,000 words a day.

When he died on March 11, 1970, Gardner's novels were selling at the rate of 2,000 per hour. Total sales for his books exceed 170 million copies. When Gardner was once referred to as the world's fastest novelist, he commented: "All I ask of life is that it keep moving."

First Oscar for Best Actress

GAYNOR, JANET—Janet Gaynor received the first Academy Award for Best Performance by an Actress in 1928 and 1929 for her roles in the movies *The Last Command* (which also featured Best Actor Emil Jannings), *Seventh Heaven, Street Angel,* and *Sunrise.* The name "Oscar" was not applied to the award until 1931 when the secretary of the Academy, a Mrs. Herrick, remarked that the statue looked like her Uncle Oscar, who lived in Texas.

Gaynor received the first Best Actress Oscar for films covering a two-year period. (Thereafter, the award was generally given for work in a single film.) Born Laura Gainor in 1906, she retired from the screen in 1939, though she made one last film, *Bernardine,* in 1957.

First Jazz Piano Concerto

GERSHWIN, GEORGE—*The Piano Concerto in F* by George Gershwin (1898-1937), written in 1925, was the first symphonic music created in the jazz idiom. His *Rhapsody in Blue,* as scored by composer Ferde Grofe, was the first orchestrated jazz piece played by the Paul Whiteman Jazz Band in 1924.

Gershwin's popularity was based mostly on the success of his show tunes and pop songs, the first of which, "Swanee," made him famous. The musical comedy, *Of Thee I Sing,* which he wrote with his brother Ira, George Kaufman and Morrie Ryskind, was awarded the Pulitzer Prize in 1932, the first in that medium to receive the award. *Porgy and Bess* has been performed widely in the West and behind the Iron Curtain on State Department-sponsored tours.

First Televised Operetta

GILBERT AND SULLIVAN—Sir William S. Gilbert (1836-1911) was the librettist and Sir Arthur S. Sullivan (1842-1900) was the composer of a musical team which created 14 comic operas (also called *light operas*, or *operettas*). Their career earned them both knighthoods and gave the world lasting musical entertainment. Gilbert had been a bit of a poet and Sullivan had written "Onward Christian Soldiers" before they joined forces in 1871. Their 25-year musical collaboration produced *H.M.S. Pinafore, The Mikado* and *Iolanthe,* among others. Their *Pirates of Penzance* was the first operetta ever to be televised, appearing on June 20, 1939 on W2XBS, emanating from New York City and starring Ray Heatherton.

First Full-Length Sound Film

GRIFFITH, D. W.—The silent film, *Dream Street,* was made by director David Wark Griffith (1875-1948) for United Artists Studios early in 1921. It failed miserably when it premiered in April of that year. After the movie had closed, Griffith was persuaded by Wendell McMahill of Kellum Talking Pictures that all the film needed was *sound.* So the picture's star, Ralph Graves, returned to the studios to record a song in synchronization with the action. A crap-shooting scene was also changed to include sound. The film was then released—successfully.

Earliest Radio Music

HANDEL, GEORG FRIEDRICH—On Christmas Eve, 1906, Professor Reginald A. Fessenden presented the first advertised radio broadcast from the National Electric Signalling Company of Massachusetts. The music played was the *Largo* of German composer Georg Friedrich Handel (1685-1759). Handel, an English composer born in Germany, won wide European recognition as a composer of operas. He was commissioned by Queen Anne of England and Cosimo d'Medici of Florence.

First Jazz Composer

HANDY, W. C.—William Christopher Handy is known as the Father of the Blues. His jazz composition of 1912, called *Memphis Blues,* is considered the first jazz creation. Handy originally composed it as an election song in 1909. His *St. Louis Blues,* written in 1914, has been recorded between 900 and 1,000 times, more than any other popular song. Handy wrote several books on music and taught briefly in the music department of a small Alabama college. He died in 1958.

First Corporate Body in America

HARVARD, JOHN—John Harvard (1607-1638) was an English clergyman living in New Towne (now Cambridge), Massachusetts. When he died, he bequeathed 800 English pounds and 300 books to Cambridge College, which had been founded in 1636. The first building, constructed the following year, was paid for with Harvard's bequest. Not long after, Cambridge College—the first college in America—was renamed Harvard College in his honor.

The President and Fellows of Harvard, chartered on May 30, 1650, is recognized as the first corporate body established in America.

Highest Author's Fee

HEMINGWAY, ERNEST MILLER—Ernest Hemingway, born in Oak Park, Illinois on June 21, 1899, received his training in the reportage style of writing while working for the *Kansas City Star.* The training enabled him to interpret his experiences while an ambulance driver during World War I. In translating these experiences into the written word, the author utilized a direct and virile prose which would capture the fancy of millions of readers.

Hemingway received the Pulitzer Prize in 1953 and the Nobel Prize for Literature in 1954 for *The Old Man and the Sea.* In January of 1960, *Sports Illustrated* offered him $30,000 for a 2,000-word article on bullfighting, which had been the subject of his novel, *Death in the Afternoon.* At $15 per word, it is the highest rate ever offered a writer.

Three-Time "Best Actress" Winner

HEPBURN, KATHERINE—For her starring roles in *Morning Glory* (1933), *Guess Who's Coming to Dinner?* (1967) and *The Lion in Winter* (1968), Katherine Hepburn thrice received the Motion Picture Academy of Arts and Sciences' award for Best Performance by an Actress. She is the only woman to hold that distinction. Hepburn, whose career spans more than five decades has starred in over 75 major motion pictures and was still making movies and television plays in 1975 at the age of 66. She was born on November 9, 1909, and lives in Connecticut and California. In 1975, she filmed *Rooster Cogburn & the Lady* with John Wayne and, in 1976, she returned to the Broadway stage as the star of Edith Bagnold's comedy, *A Matter of Gravity.*

First Stereoscope

HOLMES, OLIVER WENDELL—The *stereoscope,* which simulates depth or three-dimensional images in pictures, was devised by American writer and physician Oliver Wendell Holmes (1809-1894) in 1861. The instrument consisted of two pictures which were placed side by side and examined through lenticular prisms. The images were slightly magnified and, in effect, combined into one (when a focussed distance was achieved) giving an illusion of depth. Holmes did not patent the idea.

Dr. Holmes was a teacher and, from 1847 to 1853, dean of Harvard Medical School. He was also a poet and essayist, part of the important New England school of writers which included Hawthorne, Emerson, Longfellow and Whittier. He was the father of the famed United States jurist who bore his name.

First American Woman of Letters

HOWE, JULIA WARD—The respected American Academy of Arts and Letters was established in 1904. When Julia Ward Howe was elected to the society in 1908, the first woman to be so honored, Mark Twain and Henry James were counted among its members. Howe (1819-1910), a social reformer, lecturer and poet, was the author of "The Battle Hymn of the Republic," the patriotic song widely sung during the Civil War, and first published in the *Atlantic Monthly* in 1862.

Membership to the American Academy of Arts and Letters is now (1976) selected from its parent body, the National Institute of Arts and Letters, which meets annually in May in New York City. The current president of the 50-member body is composer Aaron Copland.

Father and Son "Oscar" Recipients

HUSTON, WALTER AND JOHN—The 1948 film, *The Treasure of Sierra Madre,* brought Academy Awards to a father and son, a unique situation which has never recurred. Walter Huston won an Oscar as Best Supporting Actor and son John received one for Best Director. The picture also won the Best Screenplay award.

Walter Huston (1884-1950) had appeared unbilled in John's first directorial effort, *The Maltese Falcon*, in 1940. Among his film credits are *The Virginian, Rain,* and *Dodsworth.* He and his wife, Bayonne Whipple, started out in vaudeville together in 1914. Son John appeared in their act at the age of 3 and later boxed professionally before turning actor, cavalry officer, writer, painter, reporter and, finally, director. His most recent film, *The Man Who Would Be King* (1975), received five Oscar nominations.

First Oscar for Best Actor

JANNINGS, EMIL—The awards of the American Academy of Motion Pictures Arts and Sciences were first presented on May 16, 1929 in Hollywood, California. Eligible for competition were those movies made between August 1, 1927 and July 31, 1928. Emil Jannings received the award for Best Performance by an Actor for his work in two films: *The Way of All Flesh* and *The Last Command.* At the time of the first awards, the gold figure that was the symbol of high achievement was known as "the Statuette."

Swiss-born Jannings only worked in Hollywood from 1925 to 1929, at which time he went to Germany, where he made all of his sound motion pictures. He died in 1950.

First American Grammar Book

JOHNSON, WILLIAM SAMUEL—*The First Easy Rudiments of Grammar* . . . , published in 1765 by J. Holt of New York, was the first English grammar book written by an American for American publication. The author of the 36-page book was Dr. William Samuel Johnson (1727-1819) of Connecticut. Dr. Johnson was a postwar member of the Continental Congress and the Constitutional Convention, signing our Constitution in 1787. He was the first United States senator from Connecticut and served as the first president of Columbia University, the former King's College, from 1787 to 1800. His father was Dr. Samuel Johnson, the renowned clergyman, philosopher and societal commentator.

English Architect with Renaissance Style

JONES, INIGO—Studying in Italy in the last decade of the sixteenth century, architect and stage designer Inigo Jones (1573-1652) developed a style similar to that of the Renaissance masters. He returned to his native England as the first English architect having mastered the Renaissance style of architecture. In 1615, Jones became surveyor general of the royal buildings. The Covent Garden piazza, the first English square planned as a unit, is an outstanding example of his total use of the style, not merely for ornamental purposes. He also built the Queen's House in Greenwich and the royal banqueting hall in Whitehall in this unique style. Prior to his trip to Italy and subsequent association with the Italian Renaissance master architect Palladio, Jones had been the scenic and costume designer for the theatre troupe at the court of James I and, later, Charles I.

Person Buried Standing Up

JONSON, BEN—The royally-appointed "king's poet" of James I and Charles I of England, Ben Jonson (1573?-1637), jokingly asked his king for a square foot in Westminster Abbey, where the great and noble of England are buried. When Jonson died in 1637, Charles remembered the request and arranged for the poet/dramatist to be buried in the cathedral *in a standing position,* so as to occupy not more than a square foot of space.

Ben Jonson was a very significant playwright of his day. Performing in his second play, *Every Man in His Humour,* in 1598, was actor William Shakespeare. This work established Ben Jonson as a major playwright. His comedies—*Volpone, The Alchemist* and others—are ranked among the greatest of the Elizabethan plays.

First Abstract Expressionist Painter

KANDINSKY, WASSILY—Working mainly in Germany, Russian painter Wassily Kandinsky (1866-1944) studied and taught at the Bauhaus, an architectural school. In 1910, Kandinsky painted the first purely abstract expressionist painting, inspiring a whole new school of thought in art. His work, as he put it, was "a graphic representation of a mood and not of objects." Many critics were initially outraged at the lack of recognizable form in Kandinsky's work. His historic paper of 1912 was his first written justification of his nonobjective art. From 1921 on, he changed the thrust of his style from expressionistic abstractions to constructive abstractions. His *Composition #2* of 1910, his *Accompanied Contrast* (1935), and his *Yellow Accompaniment* (1924) are examples of his unique contributions to twentieth century art.

Japanese Nobel Prize Winner

KAWABATA, YASUNARI—The English-language translations of *Snow Country*, written in 1957, and *A Thousand Cranes*, written in 1959, are among the best examples of postwar Japanese literature. The author of those books, Yasunari Kawabata, who is respected for his gifted interpretations of Japanese character and thought, became the first Japanese to be awarded the Nobel Prize in 1968 for "expressing the essence of the Japanese mind." He committed suicide in 1972 in the style of several important postwar Japanese writers, "as if to place a punctuation mark on his work."

Movie Star on Postage Stamp

KELLY, GRACE—Philadelphia-born Grace Kelly had a five-year career as a movie actress before meeting and marrying Prince Rainier III of Monaco on April 19, 1956 in Monte Carlo. The government of Monaco issued a set of commemorative stamps in honor of the marriage. The stamps, in denominations of one to 500 francs, were made available only on the wedding day. They bore a portrait of Princess Grace and are the only postage stamps to show the face of a movie star.

Kelly made 11 films during her career, including the Alfred Hitchcock thrillers, *Dial M for Murder* and *To Catch a Thief*. Her last film was *High Society*, released just before her marriage.

Inventors of Klieg Light

KLIEGL, JOHN H. AND ANTON T.—The *Klieg light*, a very bright, hot arc light used to illuminate motion picture sets, was introduced by brothers John and Anton Kliegl in 1911. Four times more powerful than any source of artificial illumination used to date, it was considered a revolutionary advance for the motion picture industry. The instrument, which used white flame carbon for the first time, was initially used on the East Coast. Refined versions of the Klieg light are still used today for high-intensity illumination.

First Inter-City Movie Premiere

KRAMER, STANLEY—*On the Beach*, produced and directed by Stanley Kramer, was premiered on December 17, 1959 in New York and 17 other major cities throughout the world. It was the first movie to "open" in all major cities simultaneously. The story of a group of nuclear holocaust survivors, the film was based on a novel by Nevil Shute and starred Gregory Peck and Ava Gardner. Kramer also directed *Inherit the Wind, Judgment at Nuremberg* and *The Defiant Ones*.

Highest Paid Violinist

KREISLER, FRITZ—Born in Vienna on February 2, 1975, Fritz Kreisler was one of the most successful virtuosos of the twentieth century. At the time of his death in 1962, he is reputed to have been the highest paid violinist of his era—having earned in excess of $3,000,000.

Kreisler twice interrupted his highly-successful concert tours to fight for his country, first in 1889 and later in World War I, in which he was wounded. In 1943, he became an American citizen. During his distinguished career in music, Kreisler wrote some very popular violin pieces, including *Caprice Viennois* and *Liebesfreud,* which he initially announced were written by the old masters, though he later acknowledged he had written them himself.

Costliest Science-Fiction TV Show

LANDAU, MARTIN AND BAIN, BARBARA—At $275,000 for each of 24 episodes, *Space-1999* is the most expensive science fiction television series ever produced, and one of the 10 most expensive shows of any kind. Made in 1974-1975, the project stars the husband-and-wife acting team of Martin Landau and Barbara Bain, two television performers who have won Emmy awards for best acting in a dramatic show. They previously co-starred in the series, *Mission Impossible,* one of the highest rated shows in television history. *Space-1999* deals with a group of space pioneers who were on the moon when the planet broke away from earth's orbit. The British-made "sci-fi" series has been aired station-to-station in many parts of the United States in the 1976 season.

Biggest Rock Concert

LED ZEPPELIN—On May 5, 1973 at Tampa Stadium, Florida, the English rock group, Led Zeppelin, drew 56,800 people. The gross take of $309,000 for a single concert of the pop recording group is the highest on record.

Led Zeppelin, formed in 1968, includes Jimmy Page (guitar), Robert Plant (vocals), John Paul Jones (bass) and John Bonham (drums). Every record the group has made has sold more than one million copies.

Most Successful Songwriters

LENNON, JOHN AND McCARTNEY, PAUL—Lennon and Mc-Cartney collaborated (not only for The Beatles) on many songs between 1955 and 1969. From the formation of The Beatles group in 1962, until its disbandment in 1970, they composed 30 songs which sold more than one million copies, including such well-known titles as: *I Want to Hold Your Hand, Yesterday, Let It Be* and *Nowhere Man.* In one week in 1964, the songs of Lennon and McCartney held the first four positions on the American pop record charts.

Both war babies of lower middle-class English families, Lennon and McCartney grew up in the western industrial city of Liverpool, where they attended high school but had no formal musical training. Currently, they are pursuing solo musical careers, Lennon in America and McCartney in England and America.

First Cooperative Radio Broadcast

LEWIS, FULTON, JR.—In November of 1937, radio station WOL in Washington, D.C. broadcast a reading of the news by Fulton Lewis, Jr. (1903-1966). The program, directed by William B. Dolph, was the first radio news program broadcast on a co-operative basis; the sponsorship of the show was drawn from individuals in the listening area on a noncommercial basis. Lewis, who was well liked by the public, thus began a long radio career. He continued his regular newspaper column in which he offered commentary on current affairs.

A steady conservative, Lewis attacked F. D. Roosevelt and Harry Truman and supported Joseph R. McCarthy and Barry Goldwater.

First U.S. Private Railroad Car

LIND, JENNY—Soprano Jenny Maria Lind Goldschmidt (1820-1887), known as the "Swedish Nightingale," made her first appearance as a singer in the United States on September 11, 1850, at New York City's Castle Garden. This, her first tour of North America, followed successful engagements in her native Sweden, and throughout Europe. Jenny Lind is also known for something unrelated to her singing: the first private railroad car was designed specifically for her and was used during her tour of the United States.

Dean of Canadian Musicologists

MacMILLAN, ERNEST—Called "the Statesman of Canadian Music" in critical circles, Sir Ernest MacMillan was director of the Toronto Symphony Orchestra for 25 years. From 1942 to 1957, he directed the Toronto Mendelssohn Choir and was dean of the music faculty at the University of Toronto. He first accepted the latter position in 1927. MacMillan, the composer of numerous quartets, songs and other pieces, was also active in promoting the arts in Canada. He was knighted by King George V in 1935.

Composer of Longest Symphony

MAHLER, GUSTAV—In 1895, Gustav Mahler wrote his Orchestral Symphony No. 3, in D minor. The piece, requiring two choirs, a contralto, an organ, and a full symphony orchestra, is one hour 34 minutes long—the world's longest symphony.

Born in Bohemia in 1860, this Austrian composer and conductor studied under Bruckner and became director of the Vienna Opera in 1897. In his later years, he conducted the Metropolitan Opera Orchestra and the New York Philharmonic. He died in 1911.

First to Print Greek Alphabet

MANUTIUS, ALDUS—As soon as word that a movable type machine had been perfected reached Aldus Manutius (1459-1515) in Venice, the printer opened his own shop. The Aldine Press became famous when Manutius produced Greek editions of the works of Homer and Virgil, which he sold to scholars and students for low prices. In so doing, he became the first printer to use the Greek alphabet, Gutenberg and others having printed in Latin and European tongues. Manutius is also credited with having been the first to employ the *italic* style of print.

Record Television Contract

MARTIN, DEAN—Dino Paul Crocetti (born on June 17, 1917) was offered a rather unusual contract for a weekly hour-long variety show by the National Broadcasting Company. Dino (alias Dean Martin) was to act as the show's master of ceremonies, sing three songs, and play in several skits each week. He would earn $34,000,000 as part of the three-year, no-option contract—a record for the television industry. Before Martin accepted the contract in 1968, he was already earning $5 million a year.

Upside-Down Painting Record

MATISSE, HENRI—For 46 days, from October 18 to December 4, 1961, an estimated 116,000 people passed through the gallery of the Museum of Modern Art in New York City. Not until the forty-seventh day did anyone notice that *Le Bâteau*, the work of the great French painter, Henry Matisse, was hanging upside down. Needless to say, the discovery was a source of great embarrassment to the museum's staff.

Matisse (1869-1954) is possibly best known for the wall decorations and stained-glass windows he designed for the chapel of Sainte Marie de Rosaire. Some of his better-known canvases include: *Odalisque, Woman with Turban, The Three Sisters* and *Italienne*.

Ventriloquist's Dummy Awarded Degree

McCARTHY, CHARLIE—Edgar Bergen, the popular stage and radio ventriloquist, hosted an hour-long NBC program, originating from Chicago, in the 1930s. Bergen and his two dummies, Charlie McCarthy and Mortimer Snurd, quickly became audience favorites. Listeners found McCarthy's wit and intelligence utterly delightful, as is evidenced by the fact that Northwestern University conferred a degree upon the dummy on August 28, 1938. In a special ceremony in NBC's Chicago studios, Dean Ralph Dennis of the School of Speech awarded Charlie a "Master in Innuendo and Snappy Comeback" degree.

Bergen, who still occasionally makes television appearances, is the father of film actress and photographer Candice Bergen.

First Animal Cartoon Character

McCAY, WINSOR—Winsor McCay introduced Gertie the Trained Dinosaur in an animated cartoon in 1910 as a surprise for his friends. He would "instruct" Gertie to perform stunts, and, by the newly-discovered art of animation, she would pull up trees and heave boulders in a timed sequence. McCay, famous for his Sunday comic strips of "Little Nemo in Slumberland," is credited with having created the first animal cartoon character. *Little Nemo* is the only comic strip to have been the subject of an exhibit at the Metropolitan Museum of Art in New York City.

Born in Spring Lake, Michigan, in 1871, McCay worked for the old *Life* magazine, the *Cincinnati Times Star* and *Harper's Weekly*, among other publications. He died in 1934.

First Assassination of Record Compiler

McWHIRTER, ROSS—Ross McWhirter, who with his twin brother, Norris, edited the world's most successful record book, *The Guiness Book of World Records,* was shot to death by two gunmen on November 27, 1975 in his London home. McWhirter, a conservative, had openly denounced the Irish Republican Army and offered a $100,000 reward for the (presumably IRA) bombers who had brought death or injury to more than 200 Londoners and caused millions of dollars in property damage. The motive for McWhirter's slaying seems to have been related to the announcement of that reward. The McWhirter brothers had been collecting records since they were 10 years old, and Norris assures the public that publication of the *Guiness Book* will continue and that the reward money still stands.

Most Successful Art Forger

MEEGEREN, HANS VAN—The poor Dutch painter, Hans van Meegeren (1889-1947), was so expert at reproducing the works of Vermeer that, in the years preceding World War II, he was able to sell each of his forgeries for upwards of a quarter of a million dollars. When the Nazis occupied the Netherlands in 1940, Van Meegeren was able to sell his "Vermeers" to high-ranking German officials, including Herman Goering. After the war, to prove that he was not a traitor for selling to the Nazis, the impostor admitted the forgeries. No one believed him, so he painted his last work of art for the court, and died in jail.

First Gold Record Award

MILLER, GLENN—On a Chesterfield broadcast on February 10, 1942, Glenn Miller was recognized for having sold one million copies of a recording of "Chattanooga Choo Choo." He was presented with a master copy of the song sprayed with gold, the first such award given.

"Chattanooga Choo Choo" was first heard in the movie, *Sun Valley Serenade,* in 1941 and a recording of it made by RCA Victor reached the million sales mark within a few months. Miller made another successful musical film, *Orchestra Wives,* and several Broadway shows, including *Strike Up the Band, Girl Crazy* and *Whoopee.* One of the best-loved band leaders of the 1930s and 1940s, Miller was killed while flying to an engagement in Paris with his American Expeditionary Force Orchestra on December 15, 1944.

Inventor of Montessori Schools

MONTESSORI, MARIA—At the age of 24, Maria Montessori (1870-1952) became the first woman in Italy to receive a medical degree. Four years later, she became director of the Rome Ortho‑ pedic School, where she began working with feeble-minded children. Maria developed a revolutionary approach to teaching and, encouraged by the success of her method, she founded the first Montessori school in a Roman slum in 1907. The Montessori method stresses training of the child's senses and aims at self-education by guiding rather than controlling the child's activity. A pacifist, she fled Italy after the rise of Mussolini in 1922 and spread her teachings to other parts of Europe and America. Her approach to teaching has been widely accepted as an alternative method.

Inventor of Music Synthesizer

MOOG, ROBERT—A music synthesizer was first demonstrated in 1953 when the bulky RCA synthesizer at Columbia University produced tapes of Chopin's Polonaise in A flat. But the RCA synthesizer, and others by Don Buchla and Al Parlemon, were not produced commercially.

In the 1960s, Robert Moog, an electronics professor at Cornell University, New York, was able to reduce the size of several of the synthesizer's bulkier components and make a machine that would fit into the back of a station wagon. The portable Moog synthesizer was put on sale to the general public. The machine was capable of reproducing virtually any sound and modulating it to an appropriate pitch electronically.

Moog regrets that his machine is often used to duplicate existing music. His intention was to develop an instrument that could be used to create new and unique electronic music.

Highest Paid TV Interviewer

MOORE, GARRY—In 1963, television interviewer Garry Moore, host of *The Garry Moore Show*, was earning a greater salary than any talk show interviewer in history—$43,000 a week, or $2,236,000 a year. Moore made additional salaries as the host of a television game show, *To Tell the Truth*, and a nationally-syndicated radio program. Other TV talkers, Johnny Carson, Jack Paar and David Frost included, have earned huge salaries, but Moore (real name: Thomas Garrison Morfit) has been the most consistently highly paid.

Highest Priced Living Sculptor

MOORE, HENRY—Born in Castleford, West Yorkshire, England on July 30, 1898, Henry Moore is one of the most respected sculptors of the twentieth century. His wood carving, *Reclining Figure*, 75-inches in height, was sold for $260,000 in 1968 at an auction at Parke-Bernet Galleries in New York City, the highest price ever paid for the work of a living sculptor. Moore is known for his large outdoor sculptures in stone and metal which decorate plazas, parks and gardens. Among them is the sundial of the *London Times* building.

Speediest Classical Composer

MOZART, WOLFGANG AMADEUS—Born in 1756, Austrian composer Wolfgang Amadeus Mozart was a child prodigy who began to compose music at the age of five. By the time he was nine years old, he had published his first compositions.

Mozart emerged as one of the world's leading operatic composers and, by the time of his death at age 35, he had written more than 600 operas, operettas, symphonies and shorter pieces, only 70 of which were published in his lifetime. Some of his better known titles include: *The Marriage of Figaro, The Magic Flute* and his Symphonies in E^b and G Minor.

Mozart is regarded as the speediest and most prolific of classical composers. Almost as if to prove his right to the title, he wrote the opera, *The Clemency of Titus,* in only 18 days.

Designer of World's Tallest Columns

NERVI, PIER LUIGI—In the early 1950s, sixteen 82-foot-tall concrete and steel pillars, as designed by Pier Luigi Nervi, were constructed for the Palace of Labor and the attendant Exhibition Hall in Valentino Park in Turin, Italy. The 16 columns, the largest in the world, were built in only eight days. The entire Nervi-designed complex took somewhat longer to complete.

Nervi, born on June 21, 1891, had designed many monumental government and civil structures—including the Pirelli office building in Milan and the UNESCO Buildings in Paris—in Italy and other European countries. His structures feature bold designs and the use of his own substance ("fevro-cemento"). He is considered the pioneer in the architectural use of reinforced concrete.

Most Curtain Calls

NUREYEV, RUDOLF AND FONTEYN, MARGOT—In October of 1964, at the Vienna Staatsoper (State Opera), Austria, Rudolf Nureyev and Margot Fonteyn received a record 89 curtain calls. The duo had just completed a performance of *Tchaikovsky's Swan Lake*.

Nureyev, born near Irkutsk, U.S.S.R. on March 17, 1938, defected to the West because, he said, he was not allowed to dance as much as he wanted. He made his break on June 17, 1961, while the Leningrad Kirov Ballet was on tour in Paris. Initially, he sought asylum in France. Soon thereafter, he joined Britain's Royal Ballet, where he danced with Fonteyn, Britain's *prima ballerina assoluta*.

Fonteyn, Dame Peggy Arias, was born in Reigate, England, on May 18, 1919. She made her triumphant American debut at New York's Metropolitan Opera House in *The Sleeping Beauty* on October 9, 1949.

Most Gold Records in One Year

OSMOND BROTHERS—During a 12-month period (1973-74), the Osmond family of Utah recorded 11 albums whose sales exceeded one million dollars, earning a record number of gold records in a year for a recording group. The Osmond Brothers, who began their careers on television's *Andy Williams Show* in 1962, have recently added a sister, Marie, to their line-up. The Mormon family of singers includes Jimmy (the youngest), Marie, Donny, Merrill, Wayne, Jay and Alan; they perform in varying combinations. The children live with their mother, father and two nonsinging brothers, near Provo, Utah, and denote a percentage of their income to the Church of the Latter-Day Saints.

Highest Paid Concert Pianist

PADEREWSKI, IGNACE JAN—The multitalented Ignace Paderewski (1860-1941) was a pianist, composer, statesman, and prime minister of Poland from 1919 to 1921. As a concert pianist, he amassed a fortune of over $5,000,000. During the 1922-1923 season alone, he earned in excess of half a million dollars; for a single concert at Madison Square Garden in New York City in the 1920s, he was paid $33,000—both record-makers.

At the outbreak of the Second World War, Paderewski resumed interest in Polish politics, and served as premier of the Polish government in exile in 1940.

First Successful U.S. Tabloid

PATTERSON, JOSEPH MEDILL—*The New York Daily News,* which today has the largest circulation of any daily in the country, was the first successful tabloid-type newspaper in America. Founded in 1919 by Joseph Medill Patterson, "the Picture Newspaper" has a daily circulation of over three million. Patterson came to New York after working with the *Chicago Tribune,* of which he was part owner.

Husband-Wife Religious Broadcasters

PEALE, NORMAN VINCENT AND RUTH—Ordained a minister in the Methodist Episcopal Church in 1922, Norman Vincent Peale has devoted his life to the idea that religion and psychology were compatible disciplines. With this notion as his trademark, he founded the Religio-Psychiatric Clinic in 1937. In 1951, it was replaced by the American Foundation for Religion and Psychiatry.

Dr. Peale has written numerous books discussing religion and psychiatry, the sales of which have exceeded seven million. On October 1, 1952, Peale and his wife, Ruth, became the first husband and wife to broadcast a program of a religious nature when they began a television series, called *What's Your Trouble?,* on CBS. He is currently pastor of the Marble Collegiate Church in New York City.

Largest Painting in Existence

PHILIPPOTEAUX, PAUL—It took French muralist Paul Philippoteaux and 16 assistants two and one-half years to complete the largest painting in the world—a 410-foot-long painting of a scene from the American Civil War's Battle of Gettysburg. The 70-foot-high, 11,800-pound canvas is housed in the Cyclorama, a circular building at the site of the Battle of Gettysburg in southern Pennsylvania. Called *The Battle of Gettysburg,* the painting depicts the decisive moment in Pickett's Charge when the Confederates attempted to overrun the Union emplacements during the second and third days of the battle. Philippoteaux's work of art had been held in storage until the Cyclorama was built in 1965. Until that time no suitable place for display could be found.

Queen of Soap Opera

PHILLIPS, IRNA—In 1930, Irna Phillips began her career as a radio actress. She soon realized that scriptwriting was of greater interest to her, and she embarked on a new career. By 1943, Irna was "radio's number one author by volume" with three radio dramas running concurrently five days a week. The original author of *As the World Turns, The Guiding Light, Young Doctor Malone* and *The Road of Life,* Phillips was called the "Queen of the Soap Opera." She is said to have originated the "tease technique" of radio scripting, which leaves audiences cliff-hanging until the next episode. She died in 1973.

Highest Price Paid Living Painter

PICASSO, PABLO—In December, 1967, $1,950,000 was paid for two of Spanish painter Pablo Picasso's (1881-1973) oil paintings: *Two Brothers* (1905) and *Seated Harlequin* (1922). This, the largest sum for the paintings of an artist while he was still alive, was paid by the Basle City Government.

At the time of Picasso's death in 1973, his total work was estimated to be worth $750 million. He is considered to be the greatest painter of the twentieth century, his work having had a monumental impact on modern art.

Founder of the First University

PLATO—The student of Socrates, teacher of Aristotle, and possibly the greatest of all philosophical writers was Plato (427-347 B.C.). A constant companion of Socrates until the master's execution, the 35 surviving *Dialogues* of Plato are written in the voice of Socrates. Plato traveled throughout Greece and Egypt, eventually returning to Athens, where, in 387 B.C., he founded the Academy as a school of philosophy. This oldest of known universities was a flourishing center of learning until it was closed by the Roman emperor, Justinian, in 529 A.D. Plato, whose greatest work, the *Republic,* discusses the nature of justice in an ideal state, profoundly influenced the Christian Church, particularly St. Augustine.

First Detective Story

POE, EDGAR ALLAN—Edgar Allan Poe (1809-1849), the American-born poet, critic, mystery and suspense writer, published his first book, *Tamerlaine and Other Poems,* in 1827. In April of 1841, he published *The Murders in the Rue Morgue,* which was the first detective story to achieve popularity. It appeared in *Graham's Magazine* of Philadelphia, Pennsylvania. His famous poem, *The Raven,* was published with other poems, in 1845. Poe's wife died in 1847 and he himself died two years later, never fully recovering from the shock of her death.

First Black "Best Actor" Award

POITIER, SIDNEY—For his portrayal of a construction worker who finds faith in *Lilies of the Field*, Sidney Poitier became the first black to win an Academy Award for Best Actor. At the thirty-sixth annual Academy of Motion Pictures Arts and Sciences Awards ceremony in Santa Monica, California on April 13, 1964, Poitier received his Oscar.

Born in Miami in 1924, Poitier has starred in over 20 motion pictures and has more recently turned to directing. His first directorial efforts were *Uptown Saturday Night* and its sequel, *Let's Do It Again*, with Bill Cosby.

First Copyrighted Choreographic Score

PORTER, COLE—Originally a student of law, American composer Cole Porter (1893-1964) served with the French Foreign Legion in World War I as he was beginning his career as a writer of popular songs. Cole wrote many Broadway musical comedies, beginning with *See America First* in 1916. In the 1950s, he scored many movies. His musical comedy, *Kiss Me, Kate*, based on Shakespeare's *Taming of the Shrew*, became the first choreographic score to be copyrighted when it was registered in the Rudolf von Laben notation on February 25, 1952, three years after its premiere at the Century Theatre in New York.

Some of the many hit musicals by Porter (he wrote both music and lyrics) are: *Anything Goes* (1934), *Can-Can* (1953) and *Silk Stockings* (1955). Among his songs are "Begin the Beguine" and "Night and Day."

Most Gold Records

PRESLEY, ELVIS—Since 1958, when the Record Industry Association of America began issuing gold records for either sales of one million copies, or for one million dollars in sales, Elvis Aron Presley (born in 1935) has earned 120 such awards, more than any other performer. The Tupelo, Mississippi rock and roll singer (now living in Memphis, Tennessee) has recorded 67 "gold" songs, which have brought him 104 gold disc awards, some records "going gold" more than once. He also has 16 long-playing "gold" albums.

Throughout the world, Presley's recordings have sold an estimated 160,000,000 copies, the equivalent of 300 million singles. Since his first gold record, the superstar has never played to a less-than-capacity audience.

Black Country/Western Singer

PRIDE, CHARLIE—In an industry dominated by white southerners, Charlie Pride, a southern black singer, has successfully broken the racial barrier and made a significant contribution to the country/western music world. A former professional baseball hopeful with the Milwaukee Brewers, Pride is also very popular in Australia, where he has received five gold discs for record sales.

Born in 1938 in Sledge, Mississippi, Pride has made over a dozen long-playing albums and won country music's highest awards as Best Male Vocalist and Entertainer of the year in 1971. He has won Grammy awards for his hit singles, "Did You Think to Pray?" and "Let Me Live."

Writer of the Longest Sentence

PROUST, MARCEL—*The Cities of the Plain,* by Marcel Proust (1871-1922), contains a sentence of 958 words. The sentence can be found in the fourth book of Proust's extraordinary seven-volume opus, *Remembrance of Things Past,* written between 1913 and 1927. This work, a monument to memory and childhood experience, explores the psychological attitudes of Proust's time.

In addition to *Remembrance of Things Past,* Proust, regarded as one of the three greatest writers of the twentieth century, wrote essays and translated the works of Ruskin. The Frenchman died after a life-long illness in 1922.

Record Payment for Modern Art

RENOIR, PIERRE AUGUSTE—The Norton-Simon Foundation of Los Angeles, California purchased *Le Pont des Arts* by the great French Impressionist, Pierre Auguste Renoir (1841-1919), for $1,950,000, a record price for the work of a modern artist. The transaction was made at the Parke-Bernet Galleries, New York City, on October 9, 1968.

Renoir met painters Monet and Sisley upon entering art school. After a period of experimentation, his unique and warm style was noticed in conservative art circles: a painting of his was accepted for the Salon of 1879. In his later years, Renoir, plagued by illness until his death in 1919, painted with a brush strapped to his weakened arm.

Most Highly Paid Drummer

RICH, BUDDY—The highest-paid jazz drummer in the world is Buddy Rich. Rich, born in Brooklyn on June 30, 1917, began as a child musician in the big bands of the thirties and forties. Among the music greats with whom he worked were Harry James, Tommy Dorsey, Artie Shaw, Count Basie and Josephine Baker. He later formed a band of his own. Always a perfectionist, Rich was known as the fastest "kid" drummer in his youth. Later, he desired to be the most successful big band leader, and he was. He is now the most respected old-time jazz drummer, an "all-star" who played a command performance for the Queen of England in November, 1969. Rich earns a minimum of $75,000 per year as a drummer from tours and club dates. In 1975, he opened a night club of his own, called "Buddy's Place," in New York.

Black Scholar, Actor and Athlete

ROBESON, PAUL—A Phi Beta Kappa in his junior year at Rutgers University and class valedictorian upon graduation, Paul Robeson (1898-1976) won varsity letters in basketball, baseball and track, and became the first black football All-American. He played professional football while studying law and drama in New York City and later appeared in the original productions of several Eugene O'Neill plays. He popularized the song "Ol' Man River" when he played on Broadway in Jerome Kern's *Showboat*. After playing *Othello* successfully in London, the play was brought to Broadway in 1943 where it ran for 295 performances, a record for a Shakespearean play on Broadway. Robeson was blacklisted in the 1950s for his socialist views and he traveled extensively in Europe and the Soviet Union from 1958 to 1963. He died in 1976 at the age of 77 in Philadelphia, having appeared in public very infrequently during the last decade of his life.

Fastest Backward Runner

ROBINSON, BILL "BOJANGLES"—Bojangles Robinson, a vaudeville and stage dancer during the 1920s and 1930s, was known for his ability to tap dance on sand. He appeared in *Stormy Weather,* a movie which featured talented black performers who had hitherto received no film attention. Robinson set the record for "backwards" running: he ran 100 yards backwards in 13.5 seconds.

Inventor of the Saxophone

SAX, ADOLPHE—In 1840, Adolphe Sax (1814-1894), a nineteenth-century Belgian instrument maker, invented a new type of brass instrument, the *saxophone*. Sax came up with the idea while experimenting with a clarinet mouthpiece on a brass instrument called the *ophicleide*. His new, valved, wind instrument had a full, even tone and wide range. Sax prospered as the supplier of the French army with instruments. He became famous for the new brass saxophones and won honors at the Expositions of 1844, 1849, 1851, 1855 and 1867. Sax is also known for his invention of the *saxhorn* in 1842, which is still used in European bands, and the *saxo-tromba* in 1850, which is a legitimate ancestor of the tuba.

Creator of the Padded Shoulder

SCHIAPARELLI, ELSA—An Italian-born French citizen, Elsa Schiaparelli started her first clothing salon in Paris in 1927. She immediately created a color revolution among designers with her introduction of such bold and unknown shades as "shocking pink" and "ice blue." In 1932, "Schiappe" introduced the padded shoulder to women's clothing, which became a required look for 20 years. She brought her shop to New York City in 1949 and continued as a leader of high fashion. Her uncle, Giovanni Schiaparelli, discovered the "canals" of Mars.

Most Popular Comic Strip

SCHULZ, CHARLES M.—Born in Minneapolis, Minnesota on November 26, 1922, Charles Schulz created one of the most successful comic strips of the twentieth century. Entitled "Peanuts," the strip is based on the reaction of a group of three- and five-year-olds to the frustrations of modern life. It first appeared in 1950 and is today syndicated in 1,000 United States newspapers, with a readership totalling approximately 90,000,000.

The "Peanuts" comic strip, which originally carried the name "Li'l Folks," introduced the now famous character, Charlie Brown, who became the inspiration for television specials and for the off-Broadway stage production, *You're a Good Man Charlie Brown* (1967).

First Historical Novel

SCOTT, WALTER—The first historical novel set in the identifiable past, *Waverly*, published by Constable of Edinburgh on July 7, 1814, was written by Scotsman Sir Walter Scott (1771-1832). *Waverly*, Scott's first novel, met with immediate popular success. His poems and stories soon received growing acclaim and, in 1820, Scott was made a baronet. In *Ivanhoe,* published that year,

Scott dedicated himself to reconstructing history through his writings. His subsequent efforts, including *The Talisman* and *The Abbot of Kenilworth,* followed that pursuit.

Discoverer of Lithography

SENEFELDER, ALOYS—Aloys Senefelder, a playwright born in Prague in 1771, is assured of a place in history: the work that he did between 1796 and 1799 culminated in the discovery of what he called "a new way of printing." The new way of printing was *lithography,* a process of printing from a flat sheet of limestone drawn upon with a grease-based crayon or pencil. Water is applied to the surface of the limestone, and is absorbed, *except* where the design has been drawn. When printer's ink is applied, the drawing (greasy) is affixed to the ink (greasy) and the background (water-soaked stone) remains clear. When on the stone, a reverse image of the design is produced. The method was first used in the publication of the works of Mozart. The first artists to employ the method were Benjamin West and Henry Ruseli in 1803 in England.

Senefelder died of typhoid in 1834 in Munich.

American Indian Written Language

SEQUOIA—The great Cherokee educator, Sequoia, was the first of all American Indians to develop a written language for his people. Living in Oklahoma at the beginning of the nineteenth century, Sequoia labored from 1809 to 1821 to produce a large series of painted designs and inscriptions on pieces of bark. Angered one night by Sequoia's lack of ambition with tribal affairs and crop planting, his wife threw the bark writing into the fire. It took Sequoia two more years to perfect his language, which he taught to his daughter in a week.

The 86 characters of the Cherokee alphabet were used in the first Cherokee newspaper, their first Bible, the first written book of Cherokee laws and the Cherokee constitution. The language is still taught today, 150 years after its invention.

Longest Long-Playing Record

SHAKESPEARE, WILLIAM—A 137-record set of recordings of the complete works of Shakespeare constitutes the longest long-playing recording ever made. The 1,337 records, produced by Britain's Odeon Records and completed in 1957, took seven years to make and sell for $729.75 per set.

Shakespeare (1564-1616), the pre-eminent English dramatist

and poet, wrote 38 full-length plays, including comedies, tragedies and histories. As an indication of his unparalleled fame and popularity, autograph collectors estimate that if an authenticated signature of the Bard were to become available to the public, its sale price would set a record.

Father of Modern Dance

SHAWN, TED—Co-founder of the "Denishawn" Schools of Dance with his wife, Ruth St. Denis, Ted Shawn is called the "father of modern dance." From the so-called Denishawn Era of modern dance in the 1920s emerged such notables as Martha Graham.

Shawn founded the first all-male dance troupe in the United States and, in 1932, established the Jacob's Pillow Dance Festival, with its teaching center, one of America's most respected artistic institutions. Shawn and St. Denis stressed the importance of ethnic dances and classical ballet, in addition to the modern dance they have credit for establishing.

Painter of the Largest Mural

SIQUEIROS, DAVID ALFARO—*The March of Humanity,* completed in 1968 by David Siqueiros (1898-1974), is a 54-panel mural in the Olimpico Hotel in Mexico City. Covering an area of more than 48,000 square feet, it is the largest mural in the world.

Born in Chihuahua, Mexico in 1898, David Siqueiros' life and art have been concerned with vehement social protest. He was an officer in the Mexican Army and, as a result of what he learned from his military travels and experiences, organized a movement referred to as "people's art." In 1938, Siqueiros fought in the Spanish Civil War. His murals depicting social struggle can be found throughout Mexico. Subjects of his and other "people's artists" included the struggle of the Indian peoples against the Spanish, the peons against the French and the workers against the military governments which successively controlled Mexico after it had achieved independence.

Largest Brass Musical Instrument

SOUSA, JOHN PHILIP—American bandmaster and composer John Philip Sousa (1854-1932), known as the "March King," constructed a contrabass tuba that stood 7½ feet tall. The tuba, with its 39 feet of tubing and a bell three feet four inches wide, is the largest brass instrument ever built. It was used during

Sousa's world tour of 1897, and is still being used today by a circus promoter in South Africa.

Sousa's most memorable musical compositions are "Stars and Stripes Forever," "Semper Fidelis" (the U.S. Marine Corps song), and "The Washington Post March." He also wrote several comic operas.

Best-Selling Nonfiction Book

SPOCK, BENJAMIN—*The Common Sense Book of Baby and Child Care,* first published in May, 1946, had sold over 25 million copies by February, 1974; it holds the distinction of being the best-selling nonfiction book of all time. The name of Dr. Benjamin Spock, born in New Haven, Connecticut on May 2, 1903, became a household word shortly after the publication of *Baby and Child Care,* which is still considered the bible of child rearing by millions of young American mothers.

Spock is also noted for his activism and outspokenness during the last years of the Vietnam War. Many of the babies who had been raised on his book were fighting and dying in that Asian conflict.

First Three-Dimensional Feature Movies

STACK, ROBERT AND PRICE, VINCENT—*Bwana Devil,* starring Robert Stack, was the first three-dimensional movie ever made. The black-and-white film, which was released in February, 1953, required that audiences use Polaroid viewers to get the 3-D effect. *House of Wax* was the first color 3-D movie, released two months later, and was the first major motion picture to use the new Polaroid technique. This Vincent Price horror picture was a remake of 1933's *Mystery of the Wax Museum.* Stack went on to star in television's *The Untouchables,* a top-rated crime series. Price has made over 100 motion pictures, mostly of the horror genre.

Inventor of the Calliope

STODDARD, JOSHUA C.—Patent #13,368 on a steam-motivated pipe musical device was issued to Joshua C. Stoddard on October 9, 1855. The *calliope,* named after the chief Greek muse and patron of eloquence and poetry, is arranged with keys like an organ and was useful in circuses and outdoor entertainment for its attractive and loud tones. Stoddard's American Steam Music Company of Worcester, Massachusetts gave the first nautical performance of the calliope on August 6, 1856 aboard the side-wheeler, *Union.*

The Most Valuable Violin

STRADIVARI, ANTONIO—The greatest violin craftsman of all time is Antonio Stradivari, born in 1644 in Cremona, Italy. During his 93 years, he hand-produced over 1,000 instruments, including violas, cellos, bass violins, guitars and mandolins.

The earliest violin bearing the Stradivari label is dated 1666; the last is dated 1737, the year of his death. His finest violin, called Alard, was made (for the Alard family) in 1715. The most valuable—and the one that brought the highest price on record—was made for Lady Anne Blunt (and was called the Blunt) in 1721. In 1971, it sold at auction, in England, for 84,000 English pounds—approximately $200,000.

Inventor of the Stroh Violin

STROH, CHARLES—The *Stroh violin* was created in England, in 1901, specifically to be used in making records. Previously used stringed instruments had been very hard to capture on acoustic recording devices. Accordingly, Charles Stroh (1866-1925) replaced the wood of a violin with a resonating piece of metal. For further amplification, he installed a horn, similar to those used in gramophones. The Stroh violin soon became used extensively in concert recordings of the early twentieth century.

Top-Selling Novelist

SUSANN, JACQUELINE—Jacqueline Susann's *The Valley of the Dolls*, published in March, 1966, has sold over 17 million copies in nine years. When the novel, which revolved about Hollywood and drugs was released in paperback, it sold 6.8 million copies in its first six months. Other books by Susann, such as *The Love Machine* (1969) and *Once is Not Enough* (1973), garnered her multimillion dollar film and paperback contracts.

Because of her exposure in the media—television, radio, newspapers, periodicals—Jacqueline Susann has been called "the most instantly recognizable woman writer in literary history." She even made several movie and television cameo appearances. This top-selling novelist, a victim of cancer, died an untimely death in 1974.

Most Turns in Ballet Choreography

TCHAIKOVSKY, PYOTR ILYICH—In *Swan Lake*, a ballet by Pyotr I. Tchaikovsky (1840-1893), the composer calls for 32 turns, or *fouettés rond de jambe en tournant*, the greatest number in classical dance repertory.

Tchaikovsky, the great Russian composer of the nineteenth century, was also the composer who first conducted his own work (in 1891) at Carnegie Hall in New York. His most notable compositions are *The Sleeping Beauty*, written in 1889; *The Nutcracker*, written in 1891 and later rearranged as a suite; and *Romeo and Juliet*, written in 1870. He also composed 11 operas, but they never achieved a popularity equal to his symphonies and concertos. Tchaikovsky died of cholera in 1893.

Most Prolific Classical Composer

TELEMANN, GEORG PHILIPP—German composer Georg Telemann was born in 1681 and died in 1767. Experienced in all forms of the music of his day, Telemann wrote 40 operas—such as *Pimpinone, Der gedultige Socrates* (1721) and *Miriways* (1728)—and nearly 700 orchestral suites. For the church, he composed 12 complete sets of services (and a cantata every Sunday) for a one-year period; he also wrote 78 services for special religious occasions, and 44 Passions.

Telemann, the composer of concertos and chamber music as well, was a very well-rounded musician besides being the most prolific. He engraved most of his published works with his own hands.

Youngest Millionaire

TEMPLE, SHIRLEY—The youngest millionaire not born to his or her wealth is the child film actress Shirley Temple. Born in April, 1928, the pictures she made for Twentieth Century-Fox between 1934 and 1939 netted her one million dollars before her tenth birthday. Among them were: *The Little Colonel, Curly Top, Dimples* and *Heidi*. Her last film was *A Kiss for Corliss* in 1949.

When Shirley married Mr. Charles Black in December, 1950, she abandoned her film career. In 1969, she was appointed a United States delegate to the United Nations by President Nixon, a position she held until 1972. In 1974, Shirley Temple Black was appointed U.S. Ambassador to Ghana and, in 1976 was appointed the first female Chief of Protocol for the United States by President Gerald Ford.

Poet Laureate Record Holder

TENNYSON, ALFRED LORD—Publishing his first book of verse at age 21 in 1830, Alfred Tennyson did not achieve recognition until 1842 when "Morte d'Arthur" and a collection of his other poems were published. In 1850, at the age of 41, Tennyson was named Poet Laureate of England, probably in no small part because of his successful elegies of Arthur Henry Hallam, a former laureate. Tennyson held the honor until his death, 41 years later, the longest any man has been poet laureate. In 1884, he was selected for England's peerage and was made the first Baron Tennyson.

Tennyson's lyric poems are generally regarded as his best, although his longer works, including "The Charge of the Light Brigade," have achieved greater fame over the years. He died in 1892.

Creator of the Largest "Old Master"

TINTORETTO—Between the years 1587 and 1590, *Il Paradiso* was painted on a wall of the Sala del Maggior Consiglio in the Palace of the Doges in Venice. Seventy-two feet two inches long by twenty-three feet high, it is the largest extant work of an "Old Master." The work by Jacopo Robusti (1518-1594), also known as "Il Tintoretto," contains over 100 human figures. Influenced by Titian and Michelangelo, this great Venetian Renaissance artist is renowned for his cycle of religious paintings in the Scuola di San Rocco in Venice.

The Heaviest Brain on Record

TURGENEV, IVAN SERGEYEVICH—A Russian author born into the landholding class in 1818, Ivan Turgenev grappled with social issues in his novels, short stories and dramatic work. His most notable novel is *Fathers and Sons,* in which he discusses the conditions of serfdom in Russia and expresses sympathy for the peasant revolts in Europe.

When Turgenev died in 1883, the physician who performed his autopsy discovered that his brain registered the heaviest weight ever recorded—four pounds 6.96 ounces.

First Typewritten Manuscript

TWAIN, MARK—Samuel Langhorne Clemens (1835-1910) has often been called the greatest American novelist and humorist of all time. Using the pseudonym, Mark Twain, he wrote many books, including *The Adventures of Tom Sawyer* and *Life on the Mississippi.* Both were typed on a Remington typewriter, the first manuscripts for publication ever typed. Twain had long been intrigued with the idea of circumventing long-hand drafts and, in 1875, first used the new machine. Quite coincidentally, he was born and died under Halley's Comet.

Highest Auctioned Painting

VELAZQUEZ, DIEGO RODRIGUEZ DE SILVA—*The Portrait of
Juan de Pareja* (also known as *The Slave of Velazquez*), painted
by Velazquez in 1649, was sold for $5,544,000 to New York's
Wildenstein Gallery in 1970. The Spanish painter is said to have
painted it as an exercise prior to painting his very famous portrait
of Pope Innocent X.

Velazquez (1599-1660), court painter to King Philip IV in
Madrid, was deeply influenced by Rubens, Titian and Tintoretto.

First Met Televised Opera

VERDI, GIUSEPPE—Giuseppe Verdi (1813-1901) is the nineteenth-
century, Italian composer who is considered to have brought
Italian opera to its peak. Verdi was commissioned to write *Aida,*
one of his most famous works, by the khedive (the Turkish
viceroy) of Egypt for the official opening of the Suez Canal in
1869. One of his last works, *Otello,* was the first opera to be
performed for television at New York's Metropolitan Opera
House on November 29, 1948, 47 years after the composer's
death. Verdi, who was once refused admittance to the prestigious
Milan Conservatory because the directors thought he lacked
sufficient musical ability, is today one of the world's best-loved
Italian operatic composers.

The Longest Opera

WAGNER, RICHARD—German composer Richard Wagner's (1813-
1883) *Die Meistersinger von Nurnberg* requires five hours 15
minutes to perform in its uncut version. When *Die Meistersinger*
was first performed in 1868, it was well received as a comic-opera,
and had greater appeal than Wagner's more masterful, more difficult works. Among the latter are *The Flying Dutchman, Tann-
hauser,* and *The Ring of the Niebelung.*

Fastest Playwright

WALLACE, EDGAR—Edgar Wallace, born in Greenwich, England
in 1875, authored more than 150 novels of the detective and
thriller genre. Sales of his books have sometimes exceeded five
million copies in a single year.

Wallace was also a playwright—and the fastest on record.
In 1931, he wrote *On the Spot,* a melodrama about the life of
gangster Al Capone, in less than four days. Wallace wrote *The
Three Oaks Mystery,* a novel, in a similar period of time. He
died in 1932.

First Outdoor Filmed Movie

WALSH, RAOUL—Released in January of 1929, *In Old Arizona* was the first full-length sound movie filmed outdoors. Directed by Raoul Walsh, 90% of the feature was shot in the national parks of Utah and California. Previously, all adventure stories had been shot in studios because of lighting difficulties. *In Old Arizona* marked Walsh's directorial debut, beginning a successful 35-year film career.

Born in New York in 1892, Walsh began his career as an assistant and actor for D. W. Griffith. Among his most significant directorial contributions are: *The Roaring Twenties* (1939), *High Sierra* (1941) and *Background to Danger* (1943). His most recent film is *A Distant Trumpet* (1964).

Four Stars Longest Film

WARHOL, ANDY—Warhol's film, "* * * *," ran for 24 hours. Not surprisingly, it is the longest film ever released. When it was distributed in its uncut form in 1967, the film was a failure. But when it was rereleased a year later in 90-minute segments, including *The Loves of Ondine*, and *International Velvet*, it fared better.

Born in Pittsburgh, Pennsylvania in 1928, Andy Warhol began his career as an artist by executing the drawings for *Amy Vanderbilt's Book of Etiquette* in the late 1950s. His works of "pop art" in the 1960s brought him a great deal of success, financially and otherwise.

Greatest Movie Box-Office Attraction

WAYNE, JOHN—Born Marion Michael Morrison in 1907, he was nicknamed "Duke" after his pet airedale. The first of Morrison's more than 200 films was *Hangman's House*, a 1928 production directed by John Ford, with whom he did some of his best work. The name of John Wayne was given to him by director Raoul Walsh shortly after the 1930 release of *The Big Trail*, the first sound, 70mm feature film. Wayne perfected the choreographed barroom brawl scene and performed the first such staged confrontation before the cameras. He won an Academy Award nomination in 1949 for *Sands of Iwo Jima*, one of the few non-western pictures he ever made. After many years of unprecedented film success, Wayne's performance in *True Grit* finally earned him the Oscar for Best Actor in 1969.

ARTISTS AND THE ARTS • 83

First Sponsored Color TV Series

WEBB, JACK—The WNBC-TV hit show, *Dragnet*—the first regularly scheduled, sponsored television program to be shown in both color and black-and-white—was first presented on December 24, 1953 outside of New York City.

The National Broadcasting Company-affiliated police program featured Jack Webb as Sergeant Joe Friday, and Ben Alexander as Detective Frank Smith. It was a huge commercial success. The show has since been revived with Harry Morgan as Friday's partner and Los Angeles as their new "beat."

The First Epidemiologist

WEBSTER, NOAH—The author-lexicographer of the *American Dictionary of the English Language* was, quite naturally, a serious student of various academic fields. Noah Webster's (1758-1843) pioneer study of diseases of America, *A Collection of Papers on the Subject of Bilious Fevers* . . . , published in 1796, followed by a long, general treatise on epidemic disease, are reckoned to be the first serious studies of their kind ever printed.

Webster was also an active political figure, advocating the Federalist position with Alexander Hamilton. His stand for a strong central government was shown in his desire to see the Uniform Copyright Act become national law.

First Keyed Trumpet

WEIDINGER, ANTON—A Viennese instrument maker, Anton Weidinger (1766?-1814?) is credited with the invention, in 1801, of the first trumpet with keys. Trumpets in use today are identical to Weidinger's design except for the addition of rotary valves in 1832. The valves increased the range of the trumpet and made it more easily controllable. Blumel's piston valve of 1815 was another improvement on Weidinger's design.

First Award for Best Picture

WELLMAN, WILLIAM—On May 16, 1929, when the first motion picture Academy Awards were presented in Hollywood, the award for Best Picture between the years 1927 and 1928 went to *Wings*, directed by William Wellman (1896-1976) at Paramount Studios. (*Sunrise*, by F. W. Murnau, also received a Best Picture award; two pictures were eligible that year.) *Wings*, which starred Clara Bow and Gary Cooper as a World War I pilot, featured daring stunt men in dogfight sequences over the Western Front.

Wellman, who had made seven other films in 1927 and 1928, had himself been a fighter pilot with the Lafayette Flying Corps during the war.

American President of Royal Academy

WEST, BENJAMIN—Born in Pennsylvania in 1738, American painter Benjamin West moved to Italy in 1760 to further his studies. In 1764, like his fellow expatriate John Singleton Copley, he moved to London, where he lived for the rest of his life. West became court historical painter to King George III in 1772. Copley and other American painters, Charles Wilson Peale and Gilbert Stuart included, were greatly influenced by West's panoramic historical paintings and portraiture. He helped found the Royal Academy of London and became its president in 1792. West, the first American elected to what was to become a very exclusive British society, died in 1820.

This American Realist painter, who was also influenced by the Romantic trend of the time, is known for such canvases as *Death on the Pale Horse* (1802), *Penn's Treaty with the Indians* (c. 1771), and *Saul and the Witch of Endor* (1777).

First Black Author in America

WHEATLEY, PHYLLIS—Brought from Africa as a slave, Phyllis (1753?-1784) was sold to John Wheatley of Boston in 1761. He taught her English and encouraged her to write poetry. In 1778, she married John Peters, but died just six years later.

Phyllis Wheatley's first book of poems, entitled *Poems on Various Subjects, Religious and Moral,* was much admired in London, where it was published. Other of her well-received volumes included *An Elegiac Poem on the Death of George Whitfield,* published in 1770.

First Magnetic Videotape Show

WINTERS, JONATHAN—The first high definition magnetic videotape recording was made in the laboratories of the Bing Crosby Enterprises Inc. electronics division on October 3, 1952. A one-inch wide magnetic tape was used; one of its 12 tracks carried the sound and the other 11 carried the picture.

On October 23, 1956, WRCA of New York City broadcast *The Jonathan Winters Show* from magnetic videotape. Telecast in color and black-and-white, the program marked the beginning of the end for "live" television. Tapes could now be instantaneously replayed, edited, in the production studio, and set aside for future airing.

Winters, an Indiana-born comic, has created many classic comic characters such as "Maude Frickert" and "Elwood P. Suggins."

Largest Recording Contract

WONDER, STEVIE—On August 5, 1975, black recording artist Stevie Wonder signed a contract with Motown Records. The record-making seven year agreement gave Wonder $13 million and a royalty of at least 20%, both unprecedented figures, Wonder's deal topped the contracts previously signed by Elton John and Paul McCartney, both $8 million agreements.

"Little Stevie Wonder" (1951-), as he was known in his child star drummer/singer days, has been a pioneering force in contemporary music for a decade. The blind singer turned composer in the late 1960s and made several million-selling albums. Born in Detroit's ghetto, Wonder's first album was released in 1963 under the title, "Twelve-Year-Old Genius." Other of his popular titles include: "Uptight," "I Was Made to Love Her," and "Sunshine of My Life."

Oldest English Poet Laureate

WORDSWORTH, WILLIAM—William Wordsworth (1770-1850) was the English poet who, by calling attention to common things and defying the conventional poetic subject matter, was responsible for launching the Romantic Movement in English literature. In 1843, at the age of 73, he received the bay (wreath of honor) of poet laureate, succeeding Robert Southey and becoming the oldest man to be so honored. Wordsworth served for seven years, until his death in 1850.

Longest Kiss on Screen

WYMAN, JANE AND TOOMEY, REGIS—In a 1940 film, *You're in the Army Now,* Jane Wyman and Regis Toomey performed a 185-second kiss, the longest ever filmed for a feature motion picture.

Jane Wyman, born Sarah Jane Fulks in St. Joseph, Missouri in 1914, received the Academy Award for Best Actress in the 1948 film, *Johnny Belinda.* Regis Toomey was, like Wyman, a Warner Brothers Pictures contract actor, and played opposite Humphrey Bogart, Clark Gable, and Walter Brennan before moving on to television.

First New World Algebra Book

ZENGER, JOHN PETER—John Peter Zenger, a journalist who emigrated from Germany to New York City in 1710, found employment as a printer. In 1730, he published Pieter Venima's *Arithmetic, or the art of ciphering, according to the coins, measures and weights of New York, together with a short treatise on Algebra.* Venima's book was the first algebra book printed in the New World.

Zenger later began the *New York Weekly Journal,* for which he was arrested by the British for sedition and libel. In his paper, he had printed facts concerning a corrupt British official. He was acquitted of the charges, the judge stating that one cannot be held responsible for printing statements about an individual, as long as those statements are the truth. The judge's ruling was a coup for freedom of the press in America.

DAILY LIFE AND BUSINESS

Origin of the Goldfish Industry

AMMEN, DANIEL—One of America's most popular house pets was unknown before Commodore Matthew Perry opened up Japan to the West in the 1850s. One of his naval colleagues, Daniel Ammen (1819-1898), who later became a rear admiral in the United States Navy, brought the first goldfish back from Japan in 1878. Ammen originally presented them as an ichthyological curiosity to the United States Fish Commission. But as the goldfish proved to be responsive to breeding in captivity, offspring were given as gifts to Washington D.C. government officials and the goldfish boom began. It reached a bizarre height of popularity in the 1930s when goldfish were eaten by college students in competition.

First Video Recorder

BAIRD, JOHN LOGIE—In 1928, Englishman John Logie Baird made the first video recordings. The recordings, made on a 78 rpm record, were fed through a Baird Televisor. It was the first step in the development of video tape recordings used on news and sports programs today. This invention utilized the advances Baird had made two years earlier when, in giving the first demonstration of true television, he had modulated light waves (using electricity) which he directed towards the receiver. The record enabled him to duplicate that electrical modulation and replay it. In 1956, Alexander Poniatoff, using Baird's work as a basis, demonstrated a process of prerecording for television that was soon adopted by American television networks.

Surveyor of Washington, D.C.

BANNEKER, BENJAMIN—He had never seen anything but a sundial and a watch, yet he constructed a clock which kept time for over twenty years. This, the first clock made in America that "struck the hours," was built entirely out of wood by 23-year-old Benjamin Banneker (1731-1806?) in 1754. Banneker went on to become a distinguished scientist and engineer who made accurate land surveys of the area surrounding his Elkbridge Landing, Maryland home. In 1790, he was chosen to survey the land for the new capital of Washington, D.C.

American Red Cross Organizer

BARTON, CLARA—During the Civil War (1861-1865), Clara Barton organized the distribution of medical supplies to Northern forces. At its conclusion, she coordinated a search for soldiers missing in action. From 1870 to 1871, during the Franco-Prussian War, Barton served the International Red Cross in Europe. The assistance and guidance she received from the founder of the society, Jean Henry Dunant, helped her in organizing an American branch. On May 21, 1881, in Washington, D.C., Clara Barton's dream came true: she founded and became the first president of the American Red Cross.

Inventor of the Telephone

BELL, ALEXANDER GRAHAM—On March 9, 1876, Alexander Graham Bell (1847-1922) patented the first telephone, an instrument that was capable of "carrying" voices over a distance. On the following day, Bell, using his new invention, successfully transmitted a message to his assistant, Thomas Watson: "Come here, Watson, I want you."

Two years earlier, Bell had stated the correct principle for telephone transmission thusly: "If I could make a current of electricity vary in intensity precisely as the air varies in density during the production of sound, I should be able to transmit speech telegraphically."

First Successful Automobile

BENZ, KARL—In 1885, his Mannheim, Germany firm, Rheinische-Gasmotorenfabrik Karl Benz (1844-1929) was the first to successfully manufacture and market a gasoline-engined automobile. The single cylinder, 560-pound, ¾-horsepower vehicle had three wheels. Benz's car was patented on January 29, 1886, but the first practical demonstration of the revolutionary device did not attract many customers. Rheinische-Gasmotorenfabrik Karl Benz later combined with the firm of Gottlieb Daimler to develop a very profitable venture. Despite their long and continued success, Benz and Daimler never met.

Developer of Bessemer Steel

BESSEMER, HENRY—Sir Henry Bessemer's (1813-1898) landmark treatise, *The Manufacture of Malleable Iron and Steel Without Fuel*, was first made public on August 4, 1856. In it, the English engineer and inventor explained the *Bessemer process*, a method of making steel by forcing a blast of air through molten iron to remove carbon and impurities. Through his process, Bessemer thought he was manufacturing a form of wrought iron; actually he was producing what is now called "mild steel." Mild steel, easier and cheaper to produce, soon replaced wrought iron in industrial use. The extremely valuable Bessemer converters were used in steel-making until 1973. Bessemer, knighted by Queen Victoria for his accomplishment, helped launch the Industrial Revolution.

Inventor of Deep Freezer

BIRDSEYE, CLARENCE—Clarence Birdseye was traveling in Labrador in 1919 when he first noticed that it was the quickness of freezing rather than the degree of coldness that made for the most successful preservation of meat and produce. In 1923, he began experimenting with principles of refrigeration and opened a New Jersey factory in which foods were frozen by pressing them between refrigerated metal plates. The first retail frozen foods were sold in 1930 in Springfield, Massachusetts. Birdseye, whose company is one of the largest frozen food concerns in the world, died in 1956 at the age of 70, with 300 patents to his name.

Inventor of the Ballpoint Pen

BIRO, LADISLAO AND GEORG—Ladislao Biro (1916-) was a printer's proofreader; his brother, Georg (1918-), was a chemist. Both needed a long-lasting pen that would not smudge. First experimenting in their native Budapest, they emigrated to Argentina in 1943. There, they found financial backing from an Englishman, Henry Martin, who set up a factory in England to manufacture pens to be used by Royal Air Force pilots at high altitudes. The company was later bought by the French firm of Bic, who created a huge mass market for a pen with a throwaway design.

Inventor of Bloomers

BLOOMER, AMELIA—Amelia Bloomer (1818-1895) was editor of the *Lily*, a newspaper devoted to feminism and reform. In 1851, she adopted the short skirt and baggy pantaloon trousers (which later became known as "bloomers") as the dress of the reformed woman. She sported them on her lecture tours.

The *Lily*, first published in Seneca Falls, New York, was also devoted to temperance. Bloomer advertised her revolutionary costume in the newspaper and encouraged that all liberated women adopt it as their own in their struggle for equality.

Salvation Army Founder

BOOTH, WILLIAM—In East London, England a charitable organization called the Christian Mission was founded in 1865 by William Booth (1829-1912). In March, 1880, Booth brought his idea to the United States, which since 1878 had been called the Salvation Army. Booth's emissary, Commissioner G. S. Railton, and seven women arrived in New York City on March 10. In Castle Garden, they conducted their first religious services. The group soon began holding services in the streets and between performances of *Uncle Tom's Cabin*, which was being staged at Harry Hill's Gentleman's Sporting Theatre.

In addition to spiritual guidance, the Salvation Army offered food and housing to the most destitute so that they might then be more receptive to Christianity.

Code for the Blind

BRAILLE, LOUIS—The first raised letter type for the use of the blind was invented by Valentine Hauy in 1784. (Hauy later organized the Royal Institute for Young Blind Persons.) Soon thereafter, Captain Charles Barbier developed a code of raised dots that became the basis of the system devised by Louis Braille in 1829. Barbier had discarded the idea of making three-dimensional versions of the alphabet for the blind to feel. He favored a simpler code, which Braille standardized and simplified still further.

Braille (1809-1852), himself blind since the age of three, taught his system at the Royal Institute for most of his adult life. His system, commonly referred to as "Braille," was adopted as standard by France in 1854. Standard English Braille was accepted world-wide in 1932.

First Hydraulic Jack

BRAMAH, JOSEPH—Using the principles of weight-lifting fluids developed by Simon Stevin and Blaise Pascal, Joseph Bramah (1748-1814) did experimental work in hydraulics in the late 1700s. He invented the *patent lock* and the *water closet*, and, in 1795, the first *hydraulic press* and *hydraulic balance*. He incorporated hydraulics in further developing the water closet, and, in an 1812 patent, first suggested that a telescoping hydraulic pack might be used to lift weights. Bramah died two years later, without fully realizing the significance of his idea.

Inventor of Cellophane

BRANDENBERGER, JACQUES EDWIN—Jacques Brandenberger had been in search of a protective and waterproof covering for food and other perishable goods. In 1912, he invented a thin, pliable film made with viscose: *cellophane*. After World War I, DuPont used the Swiss chemist's license to manufacture the transparent material on a grand scale. Cellophane led to the DuPont company's 1936 invention of nylon.

First Coin-Operated Machine

BROWNHILL, R. W.—In 1887, English inventor R. W. Brownhill patented the first successful coin-operated machine, a gas meter whereby customers received a pennysworth of gas after feeding a coin slot. The development of coin-operated machines was propelled by the need for pay telephones and meters of all kinds. Brownhill's invention was the forerunner of all such devices.

Inventor of Sideburns

BURNSIDE, AMBROSE E.—A veteran of the Mexican War, at the outset of the Civil War Ambrose Everett Burnside (1824-1881) recruited a regiment of volunteers for the Union. By 1862, he had taken over command of the Union Army of the Potomac. As one of a number of militarists-turned-politicians after the war, Burnside was elected governor of Rhode Island for three terms (1866-1875). From 1875 until his death in 1881, he served as a senator from that state. Burnside was elected the first president of the National Rifle Association, organized in 1871 in New York City. Styling facial hair on either side of the face down to the jawline in the shape of muttonchops was introduced by Burnside. After him, the muttonchops were called "sideburns."

First Adding Machine

BURROUGHS, WILLIAM—William Seward Burroughs (1857-1898) marketed the first adding machines. He obtained a patent for the machine he had invented on August 21, 1888 and incorporated his St. Louis, Missouri business under the name of American Arithmometer Corporation. In 1905, the company was acquired by the Burroughs Adding Machine Company, also his organization. His son, named after him, is the author of the novels, *Naked Lunch, Junkie,* and others.

Modern Baby Carriage Designer

BURTON, CHARLES—In 1848, at his factory in New York City, Charles Burton (1822-1881) made the first modern baby carriage. Of the many modes of transporting infants used until that time, Burton's use of springs, canopies and other modifications made his unique. Burton moved to England following protests in the United States that baby carriages were repeatedly, although perhaps accidentally, running into pedestrians. His idea was widely accepted in Europe, however, and noted among his customers were Queen Victoria of England, Queen Isabella II of Spain and the Pasha of Egypt.

Developer of the Jeep

CANADAY, WARD—While employed by the Willys-Overland Motor Corporation for 37 years, Ward Canaday developed and produced the Jeep, a small, rugged automotive vehicle with a ¼-ton capacity and a four-wheel drive. The company for which Canaday worked had been founded by John N. Willys, and was the world's first corporation to sell automobiles on a time-payment basis. During the years of the Second World War, Willys produced more than $700 million worth of war vehicles, mostly Jeeps. In 1945, Canaday left Willys and amassed a fortune in the credit and investment business. He later served under the Truman and Eisenhower administrations as one of the directors of an economic development agency in the Virgin Islands. He died in 1976.

Most Money Earned in One Year

CAPONE, AL—In 1931, Al Capone was imprisoned for income tax evasion. One of the interesting bits of evidence revealed in the course of his trial was that, in 1927, he "earned" the most money in one year ever earned by an individual. His take-home pay that year was $105,000,000.

Known by his subordinates as "Scarface," Capone was born in Naples, Italy in 1899 and was reared in New York City. His predilection for lawlessness and brutality quickly earned him a ferocious reputation. In 1920, Capone migrated to Chicago, where he became a lieutenant to John Torrio, a notorious gangster. After spending eight years in Alcatraz for income-tax evasion, he was released in 1939 due to ill health. He died seven years later from venereal disease.

Inventor of Nylon

CAROTHERS, WALLACE HUME—Working with E. I. DuPont de Nemours & Company, Dr. Wallace Carothers (1896-1937) produced a synthetic material called *nylon*. The highly elastic, very strong material was derived from coal, air and water. A patent issued in February of 1937 covered the process of making nylon as well as the synthetic polymers that were made into pliable fibers. Bristles for brushes, stockings and parachutes were the first products produced by Carothers' process. Carothers, who had been an employee of DuPont since 1928, had also co-invented several synthetic rubber substances.

Creator of the Synthetic Perfume

CHANEL, GABRIELLE BONHEUR—In 1914, Gabrielle Bonheur "Coco" Chanel (1883?-1971) opened her first clothing shop in Deauville, France. During her five-decade long career, she immeasurably influenced the world of women's fashions. Coco's styles, of almost spartan simplicity, were designed to be comfortable, a concept which challenged men's ideas of what women "'should" wear to make them more appealing. In the 1920s, when Chanel introduced her "No. 5" perfume, the first synthetic scent ever produced, she began to firmly establish what would become a multimillion dollar fashion empire. Until that time, organic scents from animal products—musk (musk deer), civet (civet cat), ambergris (sperm whale) and castor (beaver)— and scents from parts of plants—blossoms, bark, leaves, fruit and seeds—were used.

Inventor of the Canal Pound Lock

CHIAO, WEI-YO—To overcome great changes in water level, the flash lock was invented. The device enabled a boat to pass through dangerous bodies of water with abrupt changes in water level. In 983 A.D., Chiao Wei-Yo put two of these flash locks 80 yards apart, creating the pound lock, which allows the water to rise *gradually* and insures *safe* passage. Chiao built his first pound lock on the West River section of the Grand Canal of China, situated near the town of Huai-yin. A pound-type lock was first used in Europe near Bruges, Belgium in 1396.

Inventor of First U.S. Passenger Train

COOPER, PETER—The *Tom Thumb*, the first United States passenger train, was designed and built in Baltimore by Peter Cooper in 1830. On August 28 of that year, it carried passengers for a distance of 13 miles on the Baltimore & Ohio Railroad track. Cooper (1791-1883), an insightful and daring industrialist, inventor, reformer, and philanthropist, made his fortune from a glue factory, the transatlantic cable, a wire factory, and an iron mill. He won the Bessemer Medal in 1870 for rolling the first iron for fire-proof buildings. Cooper founded and became the first president of Cooper Union College in 1854, the first institution of higher learning which banned discrimination on the basis of race, creed or color, and which provided educational opportunities for working class New Yorkers.

Inventor of the Flush Toilet

CRAPPER, THOMAS—Although many inventors, including Sir John Harrington (from whose name the bathroom euphemism "john" may have originated), have claimed to have worked on the development of the modern toilet, most historians agree that Thomas Crapper (1854-1912) deserves the most credit. His device, the *Valveless Water-Waste Preventer,* was introduced at the British Empire Health Exhibition of 1884, where he demonstrated it before Queen Victoria. Crapper successfully flushed a sponge, a dozen apples and other assorted vegetables down his contraption. The water tank with rubber ball developed by the ingenious Crapper is still in use today. When the toilet is flushed, water is emptied from the bowl, and fresh water enters the bowl from a tank above. As that tank refills, following the theory of equilibrium, so does the bowl. The first toilets were installed by Crapper's company for King Edward II.

Designer of the Brassiere

CROSBY, CARESSE—Also known as Mary Phelps Jacobs, this outgoing American heiress first patented the brassiere in November of 1914. Many claims have been made to its invention, but Caresse Crosby, descended from inventor Robert Fulton, said she invented a brassiere because she objected to corsets. Caresse and her French maid fashioned the garment from two handkerchiefs and some pink ribbon sewn together with thread. They named it the "backless brassiere." The patent was sold to Warner Brothers Corset Company for $15,000, beginning an industry that is today worth over $15 million.

First Commercial Photographic Process

DAGUERRE, LOUIS J. M.—Louis Daguerre's (1789-1851) contribution to the new technique of photography was to reduce exposure time from about eight hours to between 15 and 30 minutes. Previously, photography had been condemned by the artistic community as a lazy man's way of painting still lifes. The new daguerrotype method was successfully marketed and subsequently improved upon. Daguerre's process utilized copper photographic plates covered with silver salts. When light was exposed to the plate, it would darken the salts in the pattern on which the light had been focused. Sodium thiosulfate dissolved the undarkened salts, leaving a permanent image.

First Motorboat and Motorcycle

DAIMLER, GOTTLEIB—In 1885, Gottleib Daimler (1834-1900) a pioneer in automotive design, invented the Daimler motor car. It contained a high-speed, one-cylinder internal combustion engine. (A two-cylinder version was developed in 1889.) In August of 1885, Daimler introduced a single-cylinder, four-stroke motorcycle, the first ever made. His son, Paul, took the two-wheeled vehicle on a six-mile test drive.

The following year, in August of 1886, he launched the first gasoline-driven motorboat in the River Nektar in Germany. Daimler began commercial production in 1890; one of his first customers was Otto von Bismarck, former chancellor of Germany.

Inventor of the Miner's Lamp

DAVY, HUMPHRY—As an electrochemistry researcher, Humphry Davy (1778-1829) won a professorship in London in 1801. In 1815, Davy devised the Davy Safety Lamp, after which all miner's lamps are modelled. It ensured that the flame-lit beacon of the lamp would not ignite flammable or toxic gases that might be present in a mine.

In 1820, he began his tenure as president of the Royal Society. Sir Humphry discovered and identified potassium, sodium and aluminum oxide, proved that diamonds are composed of carbon, and described and demonstrated the nature of chlorine and other elements.

First American Drugstore

DeLEON, DAVID C.—A veteran in the Army Medical Corps during the Seminole and Mexican Wars, Dr. David Camdem DeLeon was a prominent Charleston, South Carolina physician at the outbreak of the Civil War. Summoned by the Confederacy to come to their aid, the former Surgeon General of the Union Army became the first Surgeon General of the Confederate forces. In 1864, he established the first store in America in which prescriptions for drugs and essential medicines could be processed and purchased. A full-time staff of druggists was employed to explain the latest techniques in pharmaceutics. DeLeon, who returned to private practice after the war and frequently contributed to drug and medical journals until his death in 1872, is remembered as the "father of the modern drugstore."

The Dewey Decimal System

DEWEY, MELVIL—As acting librarian at Amherst College in 1874, Melvil Dewey (1851-1931) devised a system for classifying library books according to subject. He numbered them from 000 to 999, using decimal points to classify them more specifically. As librarian at Columbia University in the 1880s, Dewey founded the first School of Library Science, and founded another such school in Albany in 1905. Considered the father of the American Library Association, Dewey also founded the New York State Library Association, and the *Library Journal*, an important librarians' periodical.

The Diesel Engine

DIESEL, RUDOLF—An avid student of thermodynamics, young Rudolf Diesel (born in 1858) wanted to invent an internal combustion engine that would maintain cylinder temperature, with the result that more heat would turn into power. After 14 years of hard work, Rudolf was able to patent the idea and, in 1893, the Krupp Works financed his first model.

Diesel never saw the revolutionary effect that his engine would have on such vehicles as trucks, buses, small ships and railways. He jumped off an English Channel steamer in 1913, driven to suicide by his financial condition.

Inventor of the Addressograph

DUNCAN, JOSEPH SMITH—Patented on April 28, 1896, J. S. Duncan's addressing machine, called "Baby O," was the first addressograph ever made. The machine worked on the following principle: a multisided globe with an address on each facet revolved to stamp addresses on envelopes. Put into production in 1893 in a one-room plant in Chicago, Illinois, Duncan marketed his product to most Chicago businesses and began a very profitable venture.

The Pneumatic Tire

DUNLOP, JOHN—A tube inflated through a valve and protected by a rubber-impregnated outer case—this was the first pneumatic tire. John Dunlop (1840-1921), a Scotsman practicing veterinary medicine in Ireland, designed it in 1888 to protect his son's tricycle wheels from cobblestone roads. Dunlop, aware of the significance of his invention, established the Dunlop Rubber Company. Racing enthusiasts were thrilled by the fact that the pneumatic tire enabled them to drive faster and more smoothly. But it wasn't until after a substantial passage of time that the product became accepted by the public at large.

First Hand-Held Camera

EASTMAN, GEORGE—George Eastman's (1854-1932) invention of the roll film camera, the first camera not requiring a supportive stand, made photography a hobby for millions after its first appearance in September of 1888. It was lightweight and produced instantaneous exposures. Eastman's now world-famous firm, Eastman Kodak Company, which opened in Rochester, New York in 1880, later produced the first transparent film for movies and a process for making sensitive, dry gelatin photographic plates. In addition to his substantial photographic supplies business, Eastman founded the Eastman School of Music in 1921.

Most Prolific Inventor of Modern Age

EDISON, THOMAS ALVA—Edison was born in Milan, Ohio in 1847 and, through his accomplishments, earned the title as greatest inventor of the Industrial Age. He improved upon the invention of the telegraph, making it possible to send six messages on one line. He invented the phonograph, and later improved it. He invented the incandescent light bulb, a primitive motion picture machine, a storage battery, the mimeograph machine, and patented the first radio.

Edison served the United States government as organizer and director of the Naval Consulting Board during World War I. He died in 1931.

Introduction of the Fork

ELIZABETH I—Aside from her role in bringing England to world power in the late sixteenth and early seventeenth centuries, Elizabeth I (1533-1603), the daughter of Henry VIII and Anne Boleyn, was an innovative and trend-setting monarch. Her continued backing of English exploration led to the creation of vast colonial lands and wealth. Her idea of using the fork for eating outraged the clergy of the day but the idea caught on in the New World and forks have been with us ever since.

The First Outboard Motor

EVINRUDE, OLE—In 1909, Scandinavian emigrant Ole Evinrude perfected the first outboard motor at his shop in Milwaukee, Wisconsin. The 40-pound, gas-powered engine was able to propel a small boat several knots with its 1½-horsepower thrust. The single-cylinder, two-stroke design was started by a battery and worked up to 1,000 revolutions per minute. Ole first tested it on Lake Michigan.

Discoverer of Saccharin

FAHLBERG, CONSTANTINE—The treatise, entitled *On the Liquid Toulenesulphochloride*, was published on February 27, 1879 in the *American Chemical Journal*. Constantine Fahlberg discovered the substance while conducting laboratory experiments at Johns Hopkins University in Baltimore. He found that the coal-tar derivative, some 450 times sweeter than cane sugar, was neither fattening nor dangerous to people monitoring their glucose intake. Saccharin has been used by the government during sugar shortages, although it does not possess any food value.

Inventor of the Ferris Wheel

FERRIS, GEORGE W.—The first *Ferris wheel*, named after its inventor, George Ferris (1859-1896), was erected in 1893 at Chicago's World's Fair at a cost of $300,000. With a diameter of 250 feet, and weighing 1,070 tons, it carried 1,440 passengers in 36 cars, each seating 40 customers. In 1904, eight years after Ferris' death, the wheel was moved to St. Louis and was sold as scrap for $1,800.

The First Cocktail

FLANAGAN, BETSY—Betsy Flanagan, a barmaid at Halls Corners Tavern in Elmsford, New York, was responsible for decorating the bar with rooster tail feathers. In 1776, as the story goes, Halls Corners was a regular meeting place for boisterous young revolutionaries wishing to let off steam and drink to independence. One intoxicated patriot demanded "those cocktails" and Betsy Flanagan obligingly served him a tall drink, out of which protruded a feather.

Inventor of the Screw Auger

FRENCH, WALTER—The invention of the screw auger by Walter French (1779-1841) in 1810 did much to improve furniture construction and large scale building. The forerunner of the modern bit and brace, the screw auger is a center bit used to bore holes, employing threads like those of a normal wood screw, to facilitate the drilling of straight, even holes. French's shop in Seymour, Connecticut produced the tool in quantities sufficient to aid the rapid urban expansion taking place in the United States during the 1800s.

First Steam-Driven Warship

FULTON, ROBERT—An expert gunsmith during the American Revolution, Robert Fulton (1765-1815) later became interested in landscape painting. While touring with his paintings in England, he became fascinated with the mechanics of John Fitch's steam-driven boat, and studied the mechanics of underwater torpedoes and submarines.

Upon his return to the United States, Fulton was contracted by Robert R. Livingston to build a steamboat to travel along the Hudson River. Called the *Clermont*, it became the first commercially successful steamboat to navigate American waters. In 1814, he designed the *Demologos* for the United States Navy, the first steam-driven warship.

First Description of a Pencil

GESNER, KONRAD VON—An important Swiss writer and lecturer in the field of natural science, Konrad von Gesner (1516-1565) was known as the "German Pliny" in the intellectual circles of the sixteenth century. In 1565, Von Gesner published a treatise on fossilized animal and plant remains. It contained the description of a writing instrument consisting of a piece of lead in a wooden case, the first known description of the modern-day pencil. Gesner's work, *Historia Animalium* (1551-58), is considered to be the basis of modern zoology.

Richest Man in the World

GETTY, JEAN PAUL—Born in Minneapolis, Minnesota on December 15, 1892, J. P. Getty lived in a Tudor mansion in England where, reports have it, pay telephones are installed for the use of guests. In May, 1968, *Fortune* magazine, a business periodical, *estimated* Getty's personal wealth at $1,338 billion; his true wealth, made mostly from oil, is thought to be much greater. Jean Paul Getty was the richest man in the world, but Howard Hughes and Daniel K. Ludwig trail not far behind.

Inventor of the Safety Razor

GILLETTE, KING CAMP—The inventor of the disposable bottle cap, William Painter (1855-1932) advised young King Camp Gillette of Fond du Lac, Wisconsin to invent something functional that could be easily discarded. Gillette took the advice and, in 1895, invented the safety razor. Not until 30 years later was his brain-storm produced commercially.

First Modern Department Store

GIMBEL, ADAM—After immigrating to the United States from Bavaria in 1835, Adam Gimbel (1817-1896) bought a supply of household goods and headed up the Mississippi Valley from New Orleans to eventually settle in Vincennes, Indiana. There, he started a retail department store which is said to have been the first of its kind. Known for its wide variety, bargain prices, and large stock, Gimbel and his sons soon established other store branches in Milwaukee, Philadelphia and New York, where in the early 1860s Roland H. Macy had opened a similar department store. From his first Indiana store, founded in 1842, Gimbel and his seven sons developed one of the largest retail chains in the country, known for its innovative marketing techniques. The Gimbels also established a foundation respected for its philanthropic works.

Inventor of Barbed Wire

GLIDDEN, JOSEPH F.—Patented on November 24, 1874, barbed wire became a principal tool used in taming the wild American West. Joseph Farwell Glidden's (1813-1906) invention, which he began manufacturing in 1873 in DeKalb, Illinois, was used extensively by western cattle and sheep ranchers for sectioning off great tracts of land needed for grazing and herding. Originally made from sheet metal which was cut into strips and twisted around two pieces of wire, the sharpness of the barbed wire served to keep livestock from wandering.

The Long-Playing Record

GOLDMARK, PETER—While working for the Engineering Research and Development Department of the Columbia Broadcasting System, Dr. Peter Goldmark and his associates produced the first long-playing phonograph record. The first experimental 33⅓ rpm record was produced in 1945. Three years later, Columbia Records began mass production. The new long-playing records rendered the 78-rpm records obsolete: it was now possible to record entire concerts or operatic pieces without interruption.

The Aerosol Spray Cannister

GOODHUE, LYLE DAVID—The aerosol spray, a cannister filled with a pressure-packed fluid, was invented in 1941 by Lyle David Goodhue, an American scientist. For an aerosol spray to work, the fluid used must be alcohol-solvent; alcohol serves as the dispensing medium as the fluid is changed to a spray. Several of the chemicals now used as components of aerosol sprays are suspected to be harmful to the earth's ozone layer, and yet aerosol sprays are still extremely popular in most parts of the world.

Originator of the Graham Cracker

GRAHAM, SYLVESTER—A nineteenth century temperance lecturer, Sylvester Graham (1794-1851) advocated healthful living and whole wheat bread as a means of discouraging consumption of alcohol. He was one of the original contenders that whole wheat bread was healthier than white. Followers of Graham, including publisher Horace Greeley and poet Ralph Waldo Emerson, lived in commune-like boarding houses, following his dietary regimen, abstaining from drink and exuding a cheerfulness at the dining table. Graham devised a food product—the Graham cracker—which he claimed contained all essential nutrients and was a cure for alcoholism.

Inventor of the Pay Telephone

GRAY, WILLIAM—In 1888, a Hartford, Connecticut inventor, William Gray (1860-1922), patented a coin box which could be attached to a telephone. When money was inserted into the box, the telephone would become functional. The first pay telephone was installed in the Hartford Bank the following year, the profits being divided between the telephone company (65%), Gray (25%) and the bank (10%). The immediate success of the invention led Gray to establish the Gray Telephone Pay Station Company, working in conjunction with the Southern New England Telephone Company. His firm is still in business, although Bell now earns a larger share of the profit.

First Dental Drill

GREENWOOD, JOHN—John Greenwood (1760-1819) was a sailor aboard an American colonial privateer from Boston. After the American Revolution, he moved to New York where he became a dentist. Greenwood achieved fame in 1789 by making a set of false teeth out of elephant and hippo tusks for President George Washington. In 1790, Greenwood came upon an idea to power a dental drill utilizing the action of a spinning wheel; it resulted in the invention of the first "dental foot engine." Dentists did not pay much attention to the device, possibly due to Greenwood's unprofessional background, but his dentist son improved upon it and, with the coming of the motor age, it was perfected.

Inventor of the Cork Life Preserver

GUERIN, NAPOLEON E.—On November 16, 1841, a New York City inventor, Napoleon Guerin (1812-1869), applied for a patent on his life preserver. The buoyant, vest-like device, made of 19 quarts of grated cork, was a great contribution to water safety. Not until 30 years later was such a jacket federally approved. The occasion of its approval by the Board of Supervising Inspectors was the sinking of the SS San Francisco in the Pacific in 1877. The 287 survivors all had been wearing the Guerin-inspired cork life preservers. That was enough to convince the government of the significance of the invention.

Originator of the Guillotine

GUILLOTIN, JOSEPH I.—In ancient Persia and in Western Europe during the Middle Ages, instruments of beheading were often used to end the lives of condemned men. In France, in the year 1789, Dr. Joseph Ignace Guillotin advocated the use of such instruments—consisting of a heavy blade dropped between two grooved uprights—to the French Constituent Assembly. Dr. Guillotin, who was a deputy of the Assembly, proposed the idea as a quick and painless method of ridding revolutionary France of its enemies in the nobility and upper classes. Designed by a German named Schmidt, the *guillotine* was first called a *louison* or *louisette,* after the king of France who was to become its victim. The name was later changed to honor the patriotic doctor who had advocated its use.

First European Movable Type

GUTENBERG, JOHANN—Craftsmen in Korea first developed the technique of printing with movable type cast in molds. Johann Gutenberg (1398?-1468), the first European to use this method, perfected the technique in Strasbourg, France and produced the bulk of his printing in the German city of Mainz after 1438.

Gutenberg's most famous work was the printing of 300 Bibles. Forty-eight copies of the Bible, now called the Gutenberg Bible, are known to have survived the centuries. Complete copies of it are priceless. Gutenberg is also credited with having printed the first calendar in 1454.

Inventor of the Sextant

HADLEY, JOHN—An associate of Edmund Halley and a Fellow of Britain's Royal Society, John Hadley (1682-1744) invented a reflecting quadrant, which was soon developed into an instrument called the *sextant.* The sextant, an arc capable of measuring one-sixth of a circle, was adopted by the admiralty in 1732 as a vital tool for maritime navigators. Hadley also improved upon the recently developed reflecting telescope (1719) and was a leading astronomer and scientific mind in England.

The Cigar-Rolling Machine

HAMMERSTEIN, OSCAR—Cigar-smoking Oscar Hammerstein was an opera impresario residing in New York City between 1847 and 1919. On February 27, 1883, he patented the first practical cigar-rolling machine and, although many maintained that hand-rolled cigars were much superior, Hammerstein's invention made possible the production of a "five-cent cigar." Hammerstein was the grandfather of Oscar Hammerstein II, the Oscar-winning musical comedy librettist.

Founder of Automation

HARDER, DELMAR S.—In 1946, Delmar Harder devised a system of assembly line production for the making of Ford automobiles. The completely automatic assembly system was able to produce an entire engine in 14 minutes, a process which had previously taken 21 hours. Harder, whose machines are able to adjust themselves to yield the best possible performance, is credited as the founder of automation.

Largest Vintage Car Collection

HARRAH, WILLIAM—William Harrah (1920-) owns property in Reno and Lake Tahoe, Nevada and runs several hotels and gambling casinos. Outside of Reno, he maintains a complex of airplane hangars and prefab buildings fully equipped with climate and temperature controls. On this property is housed the largest antique automobile collection in the world. Harrah's full-time staff of automotive experts repairs and services his 1,440 cars, whose estimated worth is more than $3,000,000.

Most Expensive Private Dwelling

HEARST, WILLIAM RANDOLPH—The Hearst Ranch overlooking the Pacific Ocean at San Simeon, California (south of San Francisco) took 17 years to build. Its estimated cost upon completion in 1939 was $30 million. The complex, originally owned by newspaper magnate William Randolph Hearst (1865-1951), contains over 100 rooms, including an 83-foot-long assembly hall, a 104-foot-long heated swimming pool, and a garage large enough to house 25 automobiles. Relics and artifacts were transported from all over the world to furnish and decorate this most expensive private dwelling ever constructed. Sixty servants were required to maintain it.

Most Successful Hotel Entrepreneur

HILTON, CONRAD—Conrad Hilton (1887-) began buying hotels in Texas and New Mexico after World War I, expanding to California in 1929, and to New York in 1943. In 1945, he bought the Stevens Hotel in Chicago, then the largest hotel in the world, and changed its name to the Conrad Hilton. Hilton Hotel Systems was formed in 1946 and, in 1948, the company went international, building first in Berlin, Tokyo, Madrid and Istanbul. Today, the name Hilton is a household word in every major world capital.

Inventor of the Burglar Alarm

HOLMES, EDWIN T.—On February 21, 1858, Edwin Thomas Holmes installed the first electric door alarm in a Boston house.

The principle of the home protection system was simple: upon opening the door, a short circuit was created, tripping an alarm. In 1872, the Holmes Burglar Alarm Company of New York was the first to hook up such alarms to a central office.

Inventor of the Sewing Machine

HOWE, ELIAS—Born in Spencer, Massachusetts in 1819, Elias Howe, following ideas developed by French tailor Thimmonier, built America's first sewing machine in 1846. He traveled to England to patent his invention, but on his return to America found others manufacturing sewing machines of their own. Howe filed suit against the major companies, including Isaac M. Singer and was awarded royalties from all future sales. He died in 1867.

The Pin Manufacturing Machine

HOWE, JOHN I.—In 1832, a Derby, Connecticut machinist, John I. Howe (1793-1876), patented a machine that could mass produce pins. For this contribution, he received the silver medal at New York's American Institute Fair. To market the apparatus, Howe formed the Howe Manufacturing Company, which was for many years the nation's leading producer of straight pins. He later bought the patent rights to the *Poughkeepsie pin,* a pin with a solid head. He expanded his enterprise by creating the *rotary pin machine,* which produced these solid head pins at a steady and quick rate.

Inventor of the Alarm Clock

HUTCHINS, LEVI—The man responsible for waking most Americans up each morning is Levi Hutchins, the maker of the first alarm clock. In 1787, in his Concord, New Hampshire home, Hutchins constructed a device that would consistently awaken his sound-sleeping wife. The device was set at a fixed time and could not be altered by those desiring a few extra winks. The 29-inch by 14-inch clock was encased in a pine box, with a mirror affixed to the door for shaving.

The Paper Drinking Cup

JENKINS, CHARLES FRANCIS—One of America's most overlooked and important inventors is Charles Francis Jenkins. In 1895, Jenkins developed a movie projector with an intermittent flickering movement, the forerunner of the present-day projector.

For the newly-invented airplane (1903), he produced an altimeter and air brake (1911). He invented the first engine selfstarter for the formerly crank-started automobile (1916). Around the turn of the century, Jenkins devised the first paper drinking cup, conical in shape and dispensed from a metal tube attached to a drinking fountain or sink. Jenkins went on to do important work in radio-movies (movies transmitted by radio waves), radio-photography and television. He died in 1934.

The First Zipper

JUDSON, WHITCOMB L.—A Chicago engineer, Whitcomb L. Judson, was the first to patent the *slide fastener*. The fastener, which later became known as the zipper, was first used on high-buttoned shoes; it was found to be unreliable. Two decades later, in 1913, Gideon Sundback made the necessary improvements.

Inventor of Instant Coffee

KATO, SATORI—Around 850 A.D., an Abyssinian goat-herd discovered the use of the coffee bean. More than 800 years later, in 1652, Europe's first coffee house was established in London, England, introducing the beverage to Western civilization. In 1832, interest in an "instant" coffee, or coffee substitute, started to grow, but it was not until 1901 that a Japanese chemist named Satori Kato developed the first powdered instant coffee in Chicago. The product was first put on sale at the Pan American Exposition in Buffalo, New York, the site of President William McKinley's assassination. But Kato was unsuccessful in marketing the product; only during the First World War did instant coffee, in a refined composition, begin to sell.

Flaked Breakfast Cereal

KELLOGG, JOHN—In the February, 1895 issue of *Food Health* magazine, Dr. John Kellogg (1852-1943), a physician at the Battle Creek Sanatorium in Battle Creek, Michigan, announced the invention of his "Granose Flakes." Kellogg's cereal was so successful that he went into the cereal business with his brother, William, the following year. The company, based in Battle Creek, was called the Sanitas Food Company. The name was later changed to Kellogg's, today the largest cereal company in the world. William Kellogg introduced the famous Corn Flakes in 1898.

First Traffic Signal

KNIGHT, J. P.—The first traffic signal was erected by J. P. Knight, a British railroad signal engineer, in front of the English House of Parliament in London in 1868. Looking much like a railway semaphore signal, it had the familiar red and green lights. Gas lamps were lighted at night, and semaphore arm signals were used in the daytime. One night, the traffic signal exploded, killing a policeman. The signals did not reappear on London streets until after the invention of the automobile a century later.

First Steam-Operated Printing Press

KÖNIG, FRIEDERICH—Having immigrated to London in the early 1800s, Friedrich König and his chief mechanic, Friedrich Bauer, set up a printing shop and began work on a steam-operated printing press. They received early financial backing from John Walter II, son of the *London Times'* founder, and, on November 29, 1814, the morning issue of the *Times* was printed on the revolutionary new press. The König-Bauer printing press was able to print 1,200 sheets per hour, compared to the 300 sheets per hour the *Times* had been able to produce. The steam-powered operation controlled many aspects of printing: inking, sheet laying, pressing and rolling.

Inventor of Instant Photography

LAND, EDWIN—In 1947, Edwin Land (1909-) invented the Polaroid Land Camera. The new camera was able to produce positive prints without it being necessary to remove negatives from the camera for developing. The invention was immediately adopted by police departments for ID pictures. Today, it is used world-wide in a much improved form. The original camera was loaded with a double roll of film with sealed developing chemicals between the layers. At the proper moment, the chemicals were released and developing automatically began.

Highest Paid Woman Executive

LAWRENCE, MARY WELLS—As chairman of the New York advertising firm of Wells, Rich, Green, Incorporated, Mary Wells Lawrence (1928-) earned $385,000 in 1973. She is believed to be the highest paid female executive in the world. Her firm achieved advertising fame for its handling of such accounts as Volkswagen and Avis Rent-a-Car, and is known for the use of satire in its advertising. Her husband, also reputed for his business acumen, is Harding L. Lawrence, chairman of Braniff Airways of Texas.

First Internal Combustion Engine

LENOIR, ETIENNE—The first working *internal combustion engine* was produced in 1860 by Etienne Lenoir (1822-1900). The engine was a fuel guzzler, its source of energy being a coal-derived illuminating gas. The engine developed only one horsepower at 100 rpm. In addition, its rough running tended to produce violent shocks. The engine was improved with the introduction of the four-stroke cylinder principle, which saved gas, limited emission, and provided for a smoother running engine.

World's Longest Ship Canal

LESSEPS, FERDINAND DE—French diplomat Ferdinand de Lesseps (1805-1894) designed and supervised the building of the Suez Canal, which, at approximately 100 miles in length, is the longest ship canal in the world. The 197-foot-wide canal, built by 8,213 men and 368 camels, joined the Mediterranean and Red Seas through the Isthmus of Suez. Empress Eugenie was present at the opening of the artificial waterway on November 16, 1869. The Suez Canal is now owned by Egypt.

Originator of Macadam Roads

MACADAM, JOHN—A Macadam road contains granite which has been broken into small chips to form a smooth surface. It is named after its inventor, John Macadam (1756-1836), who was striving to render the various layers of small stones impervious. He succeeded in 1820. Macadam was a contemporary of Thomas Telford, who had been experimenting with layers of different-sized stones.

The Rubber Raincoat

MACINTOSH, CHARLES—Rubber was used by the Maya and Aztec civilizations hundreds of years before it was discovered by the Western world. In 1824, Scottish inventor Charles Macintosh (1766-1843) developed the rubber raincoat, or macintosh, and set up a small firm for the item's manufacture. Years later, Charles Goodyear (1800-1860), a developer of the vulcanizing process, contacted the firm in the hopes of forming a merger. But, Macintosh and his partner, Thomas Hancock, were able to duplicate Goodyear's formula and patent it in Britain in 1844, a few days before Goodyear. The business became an instant financial success.

Inventor of the Bicycle

MACMILLAN, KIRKPATRICK—The invention of the bicycle was the result of the work of many men throughout the centuries, all of whom shared the belief that a man could ride on a two-wheeled vehicle. The first steerable machine, much like a scooter, was produced in 1817 by Karl von Drais. But the first real bicycle, one that could be pedalled, was invented by Kirkpatrick Macmillan in Great Britain in 1839. The rear wheel was driven by cranks attached to the pedals.

First Parking Meter

MAGEE, CARL C.—Carl Magee, frustrated by parking problems in Oklahoma City, Oklahoma, applied for a patent for the first automatic parking meter in December of 1932. But before it was mass produced in 1936, he changed the original design to the oval shape that is still manufactured today.

Inventor of the Wireless

MARCONI, GUGLIELMO—On June 22, 1896, Guglielmo Marconi (1874-1937), an Italian-Irish Marchese, was awarded patent number 12039 for a communications system employing electromagnetic waves. Marconi established the first permanent wireless station in November, 1896 on the Isle of Wight, off Hampshire, England. In 1901, he received the first transatlantic wireless signals at Cornwall, England.

Most Dangerous Typhoid Carrier

MALLON, MARY—Typhoid fever, an acute infectious disease caused by a bacillus and characterized by fever and intestinal disorders, can be "carried" by a person who shows no symptoms of ill-health.

Mary Mallon was the source of an outbreak of 1,300 cases of typhoid fever in New York City in 1903. "Typhoid Mary," as she came to be called, kept eluding health authorities by assuming false identities. All the while, she continued to seek and gain employment in restaurants and food handling places where she would pass on the disease. Finally captured in 1915, Mary was placed in hospital detention until her death in 1938.

Inventor of the Mechanical Reaper

McCORMICK, CYRUS H.—Although invented in 1831 and patented in 1834, not until 1844 was American Cyrus McCormick's (1809-1884) mechanical reaper recognized as a truly revolutionary agricultural device. In its first demonstration in 1831, McCormick's machine reaped, in half a day, what six men could have reaped by hand in the same period. Mass production did not begin until 1847, but, once it had, the widespread use of McCormick's reaper became a major contributing factor to the Industrial Revolution.

Father of the Typewriter

MILL, HENRY—Queen Anne of England granted a patent to Henry Mill (1683?-1771) for what became the forerunner of all modern typewriters. Mill presented a specimen of his invention on January 7, 1714. The machine was equipped with keys marked with letters of the alphabet; when a key was pressed, the letter on the key was printed on paper inserted in the machine. There is no surviving model of Mill's original typewriter. Not until the mid-1800s were typewriters used on a mass scale.

First Telegraph Cable in the U.S.

MORSE, SAMUEL F. B.—On October 18, 1842, American inventor Samuel Finley Breese Morse (1791-1872) laid an insulated copper wire between the Battery and Governors Island in the harbor of the City of New York. The next day, the cable was destroyed when it became entangled in the anchor chain of a ship. Another cable was laid for commercial use in 1842 by Samuel Colt, inventor of the revolving breech pistol. Colt's cable was insulated with cotton yarn, beeswax and asphalt.

Morse has other accomplishments to his credit. In 1840, he obtained a patent for the telegraph. In 1843, he received an appropriation from the United States Congress to build the first telegraph line. He sent the message "What hath God wrought?" in 1844 from Baltimore to Washington using a system of short and long signals he devised, called the *Morse Code.*

Highest Sustained Lecture Fee

NADER, RALPH—At $4,000 an hour, or $66.66 a minute, Ralph Nader (1934-) commands the highest lecture fee on a sustained basis. Boxer Muhammad Ali sometimes receives a higher fee, but the proceeds are always donated to the Muslim Church. Several of the Watergate conspirators, John W. Dean III included, have commanded greater fees, but these were only for short periods of time.

Nader, a consumer protection advocate, has been lecturing at the $4,000 fee for more than 12 years. The range of topics discussed includes the hazards to consumers of automobiles, food products, insecticides and industrial pollution.

Inventor of the Steam Hammer

NASMYTH, JAMES—Francis Humphries, engineer of the Great Western Railways, asked James Nasmyth (1808-1890) to design a forge hammer powerful enough to shape the heavy metal parts of a giant new steamship Great Western was planning to build. Nasmyth, a Manchester machine tool manufacturer, designed a steam-operated hammer that would accomplish the task, but the ship plan was scrubbed and his idea lay idle until 1842 when a French manufacturer built a prototype of his plans. Nasmyth immediately patented his invention and began production.

First Steam Engine

NEWCOMEN, THOMAS—The Earl of Dudley's Coneygre Colliery was in need of a water pump in 1712 and Thomas Newcomen (1663-1729) erected a steam engine that did the job effectively for 30 years. Newcomen's invention, installed at Tipton, Staffordshire, was the world's first practical steam engine. It was innovative in that steam had never before been used to create a vacuum which, in turn, caused a piston to be driven. James Watt improved upon it later in the century.

Inventor of the Safety Elevator

OTIS, ELISHA—At the 1853 Crystal Palace Exposition in New York, Elisha Otis (1811-1861) demonstrated the first safety elevator. He raised himself up in the elevator, cut the cable and, remaining suspended, shouted, "All safe, gentlemen, all safe." Though Louis XIV owned a crude, hand-operated, one-person elevator in the eighteenth century, and the Englishmen Frost and Strutt built a primitive elevator called the "Teagle" in 1835, Otis and his company developed and marketed the first steam-propelled elevator. With Otis' invention, it became possible for builders to consider construction of buildings more than five stories high.

Inventor of the Bottle Cap

PAINTER, WILLIAM—On February 2, 1892, William Painter (1838-1906) received a patent for a new invention—the bottle cap. The device consisted of a disc of tin, corrugated at the edges, with a piece of either natural or composition cork inserted in the middle. Painter sold his invention at his Crown Cork and Seal Company of Baltimore. Ingenious man that he was, Painter advised King Camp Gillette that if he could invent something disposable he would make a fortune. Gillette went on to produce the first disposable safety razor.

Painter had invented many things previously. Among his 85 patents are: the railroad fare box, the car seat and couch (1858), counterfeit coin detector (1862), the kerosene lamp burner (1863), and the wire-retaining rubber stopper (1885).

Inventor of the Steam Turbine

PARSONS, CHARLES ALGERNON—In 1894, the first steam turbine ship, the *Turbinia,* was launched by Charles Parsons (1841-1931), and steam travel was revolutionized. When the 100-foot, 2,000-horsepower vessel was first demonstrated to the public in 1897, it reached a speed of 34.5 knots. Ships traveling at this rate of speed were unheard of at that time and Parsons was encouraged to set up the Parsons Marine Turbine Company the following year. He was knighted in 1911 for his contributions to steam travel and aviation, and for improvements made on the phonograph and the automobile tire.

Inventor of the Lawn Mower

PLUCKNETT, THOMAS—The first *lawn mower*—"a machine for mowing corn, grass, etc."—was invented by Thomas Plucknett in 1805. The mower, a pair of carriage wheels fitted with a gear to revolve a circular blade parallel to the ground, was clumsy; it would not function over even the slightest bumps. Edwin Budding sought to improve Plucknett's creation with a rotating bin of blades and a catch bag. Budding's mower was the first to be widely distributed and was manufactured by Ransome of Ipswich after 1832.

First Teaching Machine

PRESSEY, SYDNEY L.—While working at a teacher's training college in the 1920s, American-born Sydney L. Pressey developed a teaching machine with which students could test themselves and correct their mistakes without the help of teachers. The device consisted of a cardboard sheet with question and answer holes to be drilled with a pencil tip. Only the correct answer would penetrate both sides of the cardboard.

Inventor of the Pullman Sleeping Car

PULLMAN, GEORGE—With his partner, Ben Field, George Mortimer Pullman (1831-1897) assembled *Old Number 9* (a railroad car) in Chicago and demonstrated the invention on September 1, 1859. Made entirely of wood, except for the wheel assemblages, the revolutionary Pullman car slept 20 in double-tiered sleeping areas, was lit by candle, and had a water fountain. The first transcontinental rail trip, from Boston to San Francisco in 1870, utilized eight new Pullman cars. Pullman's *Maritana* of 1875 was the first parlor car ever produced. Pullman created the first all-steel model in 1907.

The Collapsible Tube Container

RAND, JOHN GOFFE—The convenient container used to hold oil paints, toothpaste, hair cream and glue was invented by John Rand (1801-1873). Rand was a New Hampshire-born portrait painter who exhibited at the Boston Athenaeum (1828-1829), in New York City (1833) and at the London Royal Academy (1840). When he took out his first patent on September 11, 1841, he forever simplified the storage and application of liquids, fluids, and semisolids for which there had previously been no acceptable receptacle. Rand's collapsible lead tube was first used for his oil paints. Then, as now, the tube would empty its contents gradually by being slightly pressured on its sides. The unused contents of the tube could easily be capped and stored without fear of spoilage.

The First Billionaire

ROCKEFELLER, JOHN DAVIDSON—The term "billionaire" was invented in 1861, and the person it was invented to describe was John D. Rockefeller (1839-1937). His absorption of smaller oil concerns into his giant Standard Oil Company in the late 1800s gave him control of 90% of all American refineries. He also held sizable interests in railroads, banks, and steel. As a philanthropist, he established the University of Chicago and numerous foundations.

Inventor of the Electric Razor

SCHICK, JACOB—Jacob Schick was a retired American Army lieutenant colonel when he conceived the idea of affixing several thin strips of sharpened steel to an electric motor to create an electric shaver. In 1928, he patented the device, which had a shearing head over reciprocating blades, and, in 1931, marketed it through his Schick Razor Company. The invention of a process to sharpen thin strips of steel was devised by William Nickerson of the American Safety Razor Company in 1901.

World's Largest Retail Store

SEARS, RICHARD W.—In 1886, Sears, Roebuck and Company was founded in a railway station in North Redwood, Minnesota by Richard Sears (1863-1914). By 1974, the sales of Sears, Roebuck had exceeded $12.3 billion; its assets were valued at $10.4 billion. The enterprise, with 840 retail stores and 2,785 mail order offices in 15 countries, is the largest general merchandising firm in the world. Much of its trade is conducted through the use of a telephone book-like mail order catalogue.

Fathers of the Transistor

SHOCKLEY, WILLIAM; BARDEEN, JOHN; BRATTAIN, WALTER—Working for the Bell Telephone Laboratories in 1948, Shockley (1910-), Bardeen (1908-) and Brattain (1902-) developed the first *transistor*. Possibly the most revolutionary discovery of the electronic age, the transistor consists of huge numbers of components reduced to the size of a pinhead. Transistors are made of silicon and germanium elements, known as *semiconductors,* and have virtually replaced the old-style radio valves. For their monumental contribution, the Americans Shockley, Bardeen and Brattain were awarded the 1956 Nobel Prize in Physics.

Non-Poisonous Love Apple

SICCARY, LUCIUS—The *Lycopersicon esculentum* was classified and brought back to Europe soon after its discovery by North American settlers in the seventeenth century. Called the "love apple," the fruit was used strictly for ornamental purposes in European homes, because it had been deemed to be poisonous.

In 1733, Dr. Lucius Siccary (c. 1690-1749), a colonial physician living in Virginia, proved that the love apple was not poisonous, and that, to the contrary, it was tasty and healthful. Dr. Siccary spent the rest of his life singing the praises of the love apple or, as it is more commonly called, the tomato.

Inventor of the Locomotive

STEPHENSON, GEORGE—George Stephenson (1781-1848) was in the mining business. His invention of the coal-carrying engine, "The Blucher," convinced him of the future of rail travel and, in

1829, he designed "The Rocket," a freight and passenger-carrying locomotive which was capable of traveling at nearly 30 miles per hour. "The Rocket" was sold to the Liverpool and Manchester Railway, which became the first railroad to rely completely on steam haulage.

Creator of the Drinking Straw

STONE, MARVIN C.—A piece of hand-rolled manila paper coated with paraffin—the first drinking straw—was patented in 1888 by Marvin Chester Stone (1851-1899) of Washington, D.C. Although reed and rye straws had been used previously, Stone's invention was the forerunner of the modern straw. In 1905, Stone's company perfected mass production of the straws, which had previously been rolled by hand.

First Blue Jeans

STRAUSS, LEVI—In 1850, San Francisco miners complained that their cloth pants wore out too quickly. So Bavarian immigrant Levi Strauss made a toughened fabric, now called denim, and went into business. In 1874, after a miner showed him how his pants had been riveted by a blacksmith so that he could carry rock samples in the back pockets, Levi began using rivets for extra strength. "Levis" are being manufactured in San Francisco to this day.

First Fire Department

STUYVESANT, PETER—In 1647, the Dutch West India Company sent their governor in Curacao, Peter Stuyvesant (1592-1672), to New Amsterdam (now New York City) to administer its burgeoning Dutch immigrant population. In 1659, Stuyvesant distributed hooks, ladders, and leather buckets to form the first American fire department. In 1654, he created the first orphanage for the town's foundlings.

Earliest User of Shorthand

TIRO, MARCUS TULLIUS—Around 63 B.C., the first organized system of shorthand notetaking was developed by Marcus Tullius Tiro. Tiro desired to record the speeches of the members of the Roman Senate, particularly his friend, Cicero. These *notae* were based on Roman letters, which Tiro, a freedman, had learned in schools set up by the emperor. The system omitted vowels and used consonants at various angles to denote the missing vowels. Tiro's shorthand system became the basis of systems that are still in use more than 2,000 years later.

First Post Box

TROLLOPE, ANTHONY—The pillar-type corner mailbox was first employed by the British Postal Service upon the suggestion of Anthony Trollope (1815-1882). Trollope, a novelist, served in the post office from 1834 to 1867 and rose to the rank of inspector. He traveled widely while in the employ of the Postal Service and wrote travel books based on his experiences. Among his 50 novels, Trollope's best known are the Barchester series about life in a cathedral town.

First Effective Seed-Drill

TULL, JETHRO—Jethro Tull (1674-1741) was an eighteenth-century magician who took to farming when he found himself unable to make a living as a musician or lawyer. A clever man and a fast talker, Tull devised the *seed drill*, a machine which greatly reduced the number of farmer hours required for planting. He removed the sounding board and tongue from an organ mechanism and was successful in achieving a steady flow of seed into holes which were mechanically poked into the ground.

Inventor of the Rotary Engine

WANKEL, FRITZ—By changing the up-and-down movement of an engine cylinder to a rotating one, Fritz Wankel (1903-) revolutionized the automobile industry. In the late 1950s, he worked out the basic design of the Wankel rotary engine and, by 1968, the first rotary-engined cars had been produced by Audi and Mazda.

Rotary cylinders are round; their pistons are triangular rotating discs. Rotary engines are relatively light and this, coupled with their efficient use of gasoline, have prompted industry spokesmen to state that, by 1980, eight out of 10 General Motors cars will be rotary engine-equipped.

Father of Anarchy in America

WARREN, JOSIAH—In 1827, Josiah Warren (1798-1874) opened a general store in Cincinnati, Ohio in the hope of proving his theory of "labor for labor." In his "time store," he sold his wares at cost, adding 7% to cover handling and the salary of a clerk.

Warren advocated the abolition of government and the assumption of its duties by private persons. Though not a violent anarchist, Warren was the first radical, anti-government figure in American history.

Inventor of the Fountain Pen

WATERMAN, LEWIS EDSON—Early pens were dipped into ink reservoirs to fill their tips with a writing fluid. But the ink never flowed smoothly on to paper and, in 1884, American insurance salesman Lewis E. Waterman (1837-1901) developed a capillary feed action pen—ink was squirted into the pen with an eye dropper—to solve the problem. In 1908, a lever action was introduced to facilitate loading. Waterman left the insurance business to patent his pen and market it. He established an ink business which parlayed the Waterman safety pen into a fortune. He also started a magazine called *Pen Prophet.*

Cotton Gin Inventor

WHITNEY, ELI—A farmer's son from New England, Eli Whitney (1765-1825) journeyed to South Carolina after graduating from Yale University in 1792 to become a tutor. In need of money, Whitney devised a machine that separated cotton fibers from its seeds. In so doing, he revolutionized the industrial South. The device was patented in 1793 and Whitney made a fortune, all of which was spent on defending the device in court. He later made still more money by mass producing small fire-arms, but it is his invention of the cotton gin that has ensured Whitney a place in history.

First to Manufacture Acetylene

WILLSON, THOMAS L.—The owner of the Willson Aluminum Company of Spray, North Carolina, Thomas L. Willson was the first to manufacture acetylene, a gas derivative of carbide. He first noticed, on May 4, 1892, that a mass of melted-down lime and coal tar emits a gas. The gas was later identified as acetylene, which is used as the starting material in the synthesis of many organic compounds, for lighting, and, with oxygen, in a blow-torch. Acetylene had been manufactured in a laboratory earlier, but Willson was the first to notice its potential as an industrial tool, and the first to market it.

Inventor of Esperanto

ZAMENHOF, L. L.—Esperanto is the most popular "artificial" language ever developed. Ancient Greek, modern French and German thinkers have all experimented with the idea of universal language. But it was Dr. L. L. Zamenhof (1859-1917), a Russian Pole, who published the first manual on Esperanto in 1887.

Esperanto is based on word bases common to the main European languages: it has self-evident parts of speech (all nouns end in -*o*, all adjectives end in -*a*, etc.), a single and regular conjugation of verbs, and a few simplified inflections. The language thrived in turn-of-the-century Western intellectual circles. Although scientific papers are still presented in Esperanto today, it is rarely spoken, except at conventions of Esperanto enthusiasts.

POLITICS, RELIGION AND THE MILITARY

First U.S. Ambassador to England

ADAMS, JOHN—The first vice-president of the United States, John Adams (1735-1826), was a leader in Massachusetts and colonial politics and one of the Sons of Liberty in revolutionary Boston. He represented the United States in the Court of London in 1785 as the first American ambassador to England. During his term as second president of the United States between 1791 and 1801, Adams founded the Marine Corps (1798) and launched the first U.S. naval vessel (1797). He died on July 4, 1826, the same day as his rival and former vice-president, Thomas Jefferson, and exactly 50 years after they had signed the Declaration of Independence.

First Monotheistic Religion

AKHENATON—The Pharaoh Amenhotep IV ruled as king of Egypt from 1374 to 1358 B.C. Early in his reign, he changed his name to Akhenaton and his religion to the worship of a single sun deity, Aton. When the Pharaoh changed his religion, his subjects followed. And all over Egypt, laborers were put to work defacing and demolishing all reminders of the old polytheistic religion and replacing them with icons to Aton. This is the earliest instance of monotheistic (one-god) worship in recorded history, and the sculpture and painting of Akhenaton's period are among the finest in ancient history. Unfortunately for theologians and art historians, when Akhenaton died in 1358, the religion reverted back to the worship of the old gods and, with few exceptions, all religious art of the period was destroyed.

Speediest Canonization

ANTHONY OF PADUA—The thirteenth of June has been set aside to honor Anthony of Padua, patron saint of Portugal and Padua. On that date in the year 1231, St. Anthony died. Just 352 days later, on May 30, 1232, he was canonized. During his lifetime, Anthony was known as a "hammer of heretics" for his fearless preaching of Bible sermons among non-believers.

Anthony, born in 1195, served in the Augustinian Order from 1210 to 1220. He then joined the Franciscans and was sent to work as a missionary among the Moslems in Morocco. St. Anthony is revered as a miracle worker and finder of lost articles.

American Woman in British Parliament

ASTOR, NANCY WITCHER LANGHORNE—Born in Virginia in 1879, Nancy Witcher Langhorne married Waldorf Astor, a British politician, at the turn of the nineteenth century. When her husband, a member of the House of Commons, succeeded to the title of viscount, she ran for his Commons seat and won, serving from 1919 to 1945. Representing Plymouth, Lady Astor was a conservative who advocated women's rights. She also espoused the notion of temperance and, at parties held in her Clivedon estate before World War II, she proposed policies of appeasement towards Hitler and Mussolini. Lady Astor died in 1964.

First Casualty of American Revolution

ATTUCKS, CRISPUS—In Boston, Massachusetts, on March 5, 1770, British soldiers, angered by taunts and snowballs being hurled at them, fired gunshots aimlessly into a crowd. Five citizens were killed, Crispus Attucks, a black man, being the first to die. Attucks, 47 years old at the time of his death, was the leader of the group that was protesting taxes imposed on the citizens of Boston by the British. The Boston Massacre is traditionally considered the first major skirmish in the struggle for the establishment of a free country in the New World.

Founder of the Boy Scouts

BADEN-POWELL, ROBERT—For 12 days in the summer of 1907, Lieutenant General (Sir) Robert Baden-Powell (1857-1941) invited 20 boys to attend a camp and try out his "Game of Scouting." They were divided into four patrols, received badges bearing insignia similar to that of the Fifth Dragoon Guards, and learned various frontier skills that Baden-Powell had acquired in his soldiering days.

The movement developed widely after Sir Robert began publishing *Scouting for Boys* in 1908. The first troop, the First Glasgow, was started in that year. By 1964, its membership had exceeded 10 million. The Boy Scout organization is the largest secular voluntary organization in the world.

Submarine Circles Globe

BEACH, EDWARD L.—The *U.S.S. Triton* left the New London, Connecticut Submarine Base on February 16, 1960 and returned on May 10, 1960. Under the command of Captain E. L. Beach (1918-   ), the vessel, after traveling 30,708 miles, became the first submarine to circumnavigate the globe.

Captain Beach, an attack submarine commander in World War II and a career Navy man, had previously written a best-selling book, *Run Silent, Run Deep*, about heroic submariners in the Pacific.

Youngest Pope

BENEDICT IX, POPE—Benedict IX served a total of three terms as head of the Roman Catholic Church. His longest reign as pope spanned the years 1032 to 1044. When he was elected head of the Church in 1032, Benedict's "extreme youth" (as the Catalogue of Popes referred to it) did not interfere with his efficiency. Historians have estimated that he was a mere 11 years of age at the time. Benedict IX's second papal term, to which he was elected in the spring of 1045, was of one month's duration; his third term lasted eight months, from November, 1047 to July, 1048. Benedict was a lay citizen at the time of his death in 1056.

Father of Modern Israel

BEN-GURION, DAVID—David Ben-Gurion (1886-1974) was born in Plonsk, Poland and emigrated to Palestine, then a part of the Ottoman Empire, in 1906. He was one of the founders and staunchest defenders of the State of Israel; he proclaimed Israeli independence in 1948 and stirred international controversy when he equated Judaism with Israeli nationality. As premier of Israel, and later as its defense minister, Ben-Gurion organized Israel's

Labor Party and remained a powerful national figure for 25 years. The father of modern Israel, as he came to be regarded, retired from the Knesset (Parliament of Israel) in 1970 and died in 1974.

English Monarch Never Saw England

BERENGARIA—The politically advantageous marriage of the daughter of Sancho VI of Navarre to Richard I (1157-1199) of England brought peace between Spain and England. Ironically, although Sancho's daughter, Berengaria (?-1230?), was Queen of England, she never set foot on English soil. She was content to follow Richard on the Third Crusade (1191), and waited in Italy and France (1192-1194) for the return of her husband by the kidnappers, Duke Leopold of Austria and Holy Roman Emperor Henry VI. When he was freed, Berengaria joined him in his campaigns against Philip II of France, until his death in battle in 1199. She remains the only English monarch never to visit the country which she ruled.

Longest Wait for Canonization

BERNARD OF TIRON—Also known as St. Bernard of Abbeville, St. Bernard of Tiron (1046-1117) lived as a hermit for many years before becoming abbot of St. Cyprian's Abbey in about 1100. As abbot, Bernard was the head of the monastery, teaching monks and administering all spiritual and temporal duties of his abbey. He resigned after a quarrel with the abbot Cluny and retired to a forest in Tiron, France (also called Thiron) where he built a monastery. The Benedictine monastery, of which he became prior, was called Saint Sabinus. Bernard died in 1117.

Seven hundred forty-four years—a record period of time—elapsed between the time of Bernard's death and his canonization in 1861. St. Bernard should not be confused with Bernard of Clairvaux, who lived around the same time and who was a noted theological writer, or Bernard of Montjoux, after whom the passes in the Alps and the dog are named.

Lost Congressman Elected

BOGGS, HALE—Thomas Hale Boggs, a congressman from the State of Louisiana and the Democratic House Majority Leader, had served his constituents for 14 elected terms when he decided to run again in 1972. His November victory seemed assured when, in October, an airplane in which he was flying was reported lost over Alaska. When election day arrived, although Boggs was still listed as "missing," he was overwhelmingly reelected. The Louisiana congressman, two colleagues who were with him, and the plane's pilot were eventually listed as dead. Boggs' wife, Corinne C. "Lindy" Boggs, was designated to serve in his stead. She took office on March 20, 1973.

First Conference of American Republics

BOLÍVAR, SIMÓN—The Liberator, as he was called, was a South American revolutionary leader whose triumphs over Spain led to the independence of Venezuela, Colombia, Panama, Ecuador, Bolivia and Peru with the help of the Argentinian freedom fighter, José de San Martín. Simón Bolívar's (1783-1830) great victory over the Spanish at Ayacucho in 1824 led him to convoke the General Congress of South American States in December of that year. The United States sent delegates to the conference, but they arrived after it had already adjourned. Bolívar died poor and unnoticed in 1830 following his forced resignation by political rivals.

First Jewish Supreme Court Justice

BRANDEIS, LOUIS D.—A Boston lawyer known for defending liberal causes, Louis Dembitz Brandeis (1856-1941) presented the first proposal for savings bank life insurance to the Massachusetts legislature in June of 1907. His renown as a barrister increased after his successful arbitration of the 1910 New York City garment workers' strike.

Brandeis was appointed an associate justice of the Supreme Court on January 28, 1916, the first Jew to hold the position; He served for 23 years. Brandeis was president of the Zionist Organization prior to accepting the Supreme Court nomination.

First Black Senator

BROOKE, EDWARD W.—The first black United States senator was elected by the Commonwealth of Massachusetts on November 8, 1966 by a margin of approximately 440,000 votes. Senator Edward W. Brooke (1919-) was seated at the 90th Congress on January 10, 1967 and, in 1972, was elected to a second six-year term. Before serving in the Senate, Brooke, a Republican, served as Attorney General of Massachusetts.

The Only Bachelor President

BUCHANAN, JAMES—The fifteenth president of the United States was perhaps the most individualistic of all to hold that office.

When James Buchanan (1791-1868) was inaugurated in 1857, he was a bachelor. At the end of his four-year term, he stated that he was "heartily tired" of being president. When the Civil War erupted one month after he left office, Buchanan joined the Confederate Army.

Buchanan, the first president to hail from the state of Pennsylvania, had served as a congressman (1821-1831), a senator (1834-1845), secretary of state to James Knox Polk, and in several diplomatic posts in Russia, Britain, France and Spain before becoming president. Buchanan's vice-president, John Breckinridge of Kentucky, only 36 at the time of inauguration, was the youngest man to serve the nation in that office. Like Buchanan, Breckinridge later joined the Southern forces.

First Black Nobel Prize Winner

BUNCHE, RALPH—For his role as mediator in the 1949 armistice negotiations between Israel and the Arab states, Ralph Bunche (1904-1971) was awarded the 1950 Nobel Peace Prize. The first black to be thus honored, Bunche helped organize the United Nations and joined the permanent United Nations Secretariat in 1947. During World War II he worked with the Joint Chiefs of Staff and the Office of Strategic Services (later the Central Intelligence Agency). The Detroit-born Bunche was a professor of government at Harvard from 1950 to 1952. He was an undersecretary of the United Nations between 1955 and 1971 and was director of the body's peacekeeping missions in the Suez (1956), Congo (1964) and Cyprus (1964).

First Colonial Secret Service

BURR, AARON—Aaron Burr (1756-1836) is remembered chiefly as a talented American statesman, vice-president of the United States from 1801 to 1805, and as the man who killed Alexander Hamilton in a duel. What is rarely mentioned is that Burr, with the help of Major Benjamin Talmadge, established a secret service for the United Colonies in June of 1778. Called the Headquarters Secret Service, the organization was the first organized intelligence unit of the Army of the United Colonies. One month after the founding of the organization, General George Washington appointed Burr head of the Department for Detecting and Defeating Conspiracies.

Inventor of the War Submarine

BUSHNELL, DAVID—A Saybrook, Connecticut patriot, David Bushnell (c. 1742-1824), served under General George Washington between 1779 and 1783, and rose to the rank of Captain of the Army Corps of Engineers. He presented a novel idea to the Continental Army in 1776, hoping that it would revolutionize naval warfare. Bushnell's invention, *The American Turtle,* was the first submarine built specifically for warfare. The hand-operated vessel, which could carry only one person, was first used to torpedo the British *Eagle* in New York harbor. The attempt was unsuccessful: the explosive floated away from the vessel at the last moment and no damage occurred. Bushnell then developed the idea of floating kegs of gunpowder, which would explode upon contact with a ship's hull. In his first attempt, against the frigate *Cerberus* in 1779, four sailors were killed, but the ship was left undamaged.

Formulator of Calvinism

CALVIN, JOHN—One of the most important religious movements of the past three centuries, Calvinism, was developed by the French theologian John Calvin (1509-1564). Converted to the Reformation in 1532, Protestant reformer Calvin began preaching his doctrine of the predestination of all souls to either Heaven or Hell and salvation solely by God's grace. In 1533, to avoid persecution, he fled to Switzerland, where he published his new teachings and gradually acquired a following of Swiss, Scots and French Huguenots. Both the Dutch and the German Reform Churches, which were established during the European Reformation of the seventeenth century, are based on Calvinism, as was the English nonconformist group, the Puritans. Since 1875, the worldwide Calvinist institution has been known as the Alliance of Reformed Churches Throughout the World Holding the Presbyterian System.

Western Hemisphere Communist Country

CASTRO, FIDEL—On January 2, 1959, Fidel Castro assumed command of the Cuban armed forces and became leader of what is today the only Communist/Marxist country in the Western Hemisphere. Possessing both a law degree and a doctorate, Castro was imprisoned and later exiled for attempting to overthrow the right-wing government of Fulgencio Batista. Castro returned from secret training camps in Central America in 1958 and began waging guerrilla war with Batista's troops, many of whom secretly supported Castro's cause. When Castro assumed power in 1959, he was quick to accept military and financial aid from the Soviet Union. In January of 1961, Castro formally severed diplomatic relations with the United States.

League of Women Voters

CATT, CARRIE CHAPMAN—As president of the National American Woman Suffrage Association (1900-1904) and the international Women's Suffrage Alliance (1915-1920), Carrie Chapman Catt (1859-1947) was the leader of the drive which finally brought women the right to vote in the United States. The national suffrage amendment was added to the United States Constitution in 1920, and Catt founded the League of Women Voters that same year. The League has worked for increased voter registration of women and has lobbied for legislation to equalize salaries and benefits for employed women.

Inventor of Snooker Pool

CHAMBERLAIN, NEVILLE—The son of British statesman Joseph Chamberlain, Neville Chamberlain (1869-1940) served as Britain's prime minister from 1937 to 1940.

Sir Neville, best known for his futile negotiations with Hitler at Munich in 1938, was also the inventor of snooker pool, a game he devised while a subaltern (a low British rank) in the Devonshire Regiment in India. The word "snooker" was originally used to refer to a young cadet at the Royal Military Academy; hence, the name of the game. Snooker pool, a modification of pocket billiards, combined with elements of carom (or three-cushion) billiards, became the rage in India and was brought back to England in 1885.

Originator of Yachting Races

CHARLES II, KING—On September 1, 1661, Charles II (1630-1685) of England bet his brother James, Duke of York, £100 that he could sail from Greenwich to Gravesend faster. This was the beginning of the sport that we know today as yacht racing. The 23-mile course on the Thames River is still being used for racing. The sport, popular enough to be included in the Olympic roster, is divided into classes according to size and construction style.

Charles, King of England, Scotland and Ireland from 1660 to 1685, fled his home as a youth after the defeat of his father, Charles I, in the civil war with the Scots and Puritans. He was tutored by the philosopher Thomas Hobbes until finally ascending to the throne in 1660. Charles' reign was marked by several Dutch wars, an increase in parliamentary power, and great advancements in New World colonization and trade.

Face on the $10,000 Bill

CHASE, SALMON P.—The $10,000 bill was last printed in June of 1944; there are now an estimated 400 bills of that denomination still in circulation. The face of neither a president nor a son of liberty adorns that currency. Rather, it is the face of Salmon Portland Chase (1808-1873), governor of Ohio, antislavery lawyer, United States senator, and secretary of the treasury under Abraham Lincoln.

As treasury secretary, Chase established the national banking system. Later, Lincoln appointed him Chief Justice of the Supreme Court.

First Black Woman in Congress

CHISHOLM, SHIRLEY—When the Congressional districts of Brooklyn, New York were restructured in 1968, a new district—the 12th—in the Bedford Stuyvesant section was created. The field was wide open for candidates of many racial and ethnic backgrounds of that working class area to seek their political fortune. A black woman and a Democrat, Shirley Chisholm (1924-), won the election and became the first of her race and sex to be seated in the United States Congress. She was sworn in on January 3, 1969, and subsequently won reelection in 1970, 1972 and 1974.

Honorary U.S. Citizen

CHURCHILL, WINSTON S.—A veteran of the Indian, Sudanese and Boer Wars, British statesman Winston Churchill (1874-1965) was Lord of the Admiralty and Minister of Munitions during World War I. In May, 1940, he became prime minister of Great Britain and inspired the British to sustain their courage during the German bombings of 1940 and 1941. Defeated after the war in a reelection bid, Churchill was returned to power in 1951; he served in that capacity until 1955. Sir Winston won the Nobel Prize for Literature in 1953 and, on April 9, 1963, he was made an honorary United States citizen by an act of Congress.

Father and Son Attorneys General

CLARK, RAMSEY AND TOM—Thomas C. Clark was appointed assistant attorney general in 1937 by Franklin Delano Roosevelt. He served as attorney general from 1945 to 1949 under Harry S. Truman. The Dallas lawyer left the post in 1949 to become a justice of the Supreme Court, where he formed part of the conservative wing of that body. His son, William Ramsey Clark, joined the administration of Lyndon B. Johnson on March 10, 1967. Also serving as attorney general, the Clarks are the only father and son to have both held that position. Ramsey served until Richard Nixon became president in 1969, and is generally regarded as having been a liberal chief law enforcer. He ran for the United States Senate from the State of New York in 1972, but was defeated.

Victim of Poisonous Toadstool

CLEMENT VII, POPE—A Medici and a man of great personal integrity, Clement VII (1478-1534) was a patron of Michelangelo, Raphael and Cellini. He was pontiff during the time of the Reformation, the heresy of Henry VIII of England and the rise of Lutheranism. Clement VII was struck down at age 56 by *Amanita phallotides,* the world's most poisonous fungus, which brings death between six and 15 hours after invasion of the body.

President Elected to Nonconsecutive Terms

CLEVELAND, GROVER—As mayor of Buffalo and governor of New York State, Grover Cleveland (1837-1908) fought the corrupt political machine in New York. He was elected the twenty-second president of the United States in 1884, but was defeated for reelection in 1888 by Benjamin Harrison. In 1892, he was elected to an unprecedented second, but nonconsecutive, term as the twenty-fourth president. His tenure was marked by efforts at civil service reform. In 1894, Cleveland deployed federal troops to move the mail during a railroad strike by pullman workers.

First Agriculture Secretary in U.S.

COLMAN, NORMAN JAY—The post of secretary of the Department of Agriculture, newly created by an act of Congress in 1889, was given to Norman J. Colman (1827-1911). Colman, a former professor at an upstate New York agricultural college, had been commissioner of agriculture on the federal level from April 4, 1885 until his appointment by Grover Cleveland. The department, formerly a branch of the Patent Office, and, later, under the jurisdiction of the Department of the Interior, became the eighth executive department. Colman served as secretary of agriculture from February 13, 1889 to March 5, 1889, when a new administration was sworn in and new cabinet appointments were made.

First Patented Revolver

COLT, SAMUEL—While at sea aboard the SS *Corlu*, 16-year-old Samuel Colt (1814-1862) whittled a wooden model of what was to become the first pistol with a revolving breech. Colt patented his invention in 1835 and formed his own corporation to manufacture the weapons. The .34-calibre "Texas" model was first produced in 1836. His Colt .44 and Colt .45 models became standard weapons used by peace officers in the West for a century.

Colt's firm produced the first electric underwater torpedo. President John Tyler witnessed a demonstration of the torpedo in action as it blew up three ships in 1841.

First U.S. President on Radio

COOLIDGE, CALVIN—The thirtieth president of the United States, Calvin Coolidge (1872-1933), ascended to the presidency on August 3, 1923 upon the death of Warren Harding. In Vermont, where he received news of Harding's passing, Coolidge was sworn into office by his father, who was a judge. When he won the election of 1924, Coolidge was sworn in by former president and Chief Justice William Howard Taft, a unique swearing-in of one chief executive by another.

Coolidge's arrival on the political scene at the time of the advent of radio established him as the first president to speak, be inaugurated and send photographs using the medium of radio. Coolidge, a former governor and political leader from Massachusetts, was also the first candidate to be shown on a newsreel.

Largest Indoor Banquet

DALEY, RICHARD J.—On March 3, 1971, a $15-a-plate dinner was held as a campaign fund-raising event for the mayor of Chicago, Richard J. Daley (1902-). It was the largest indoor banquet ever held: 10,158 people gathered at the McCormick Place Convention Hall on the Lake in support of Chicago's Democratic mayor and party leader.

First American Admiral

DEWEY, GEORGE—Born on Christmas Day, 1837, George Dewey saw action as a naval officer in the American Civil War, rising quickly in rank. He was, successively, chief of the Bureau of Equipment and president of the Board of Inspection and Survey. In 1896, he reached the rank of commodore. Through a political connection with Assistant Navy Secretary Theodore Roosevelt, Dewey became commander of the Asiatic Squadron. When the Spanish-American War erupted in 1898, he sailed for Manila, capital of the Spanish-owned Philippines, defeated the enemy squadron, and captured the city. He was given a hero's welcome upon his return to America and the newly-created post of Admiral of the Navy was bestowed upon him. Dewey died in 1917.

First Woman Congressional Lobbyist

DIX, DOROTHEA—Dorothea Dix (1802-1887) was considered such an important and influential lobbyist in Washington, D.C. that a special alcove in the Capitol Library was designated for her use in research and discussion with members of Congress. Dix, who lobbied for the erection of buildings to house the mentally ill, helped influence the passage of numerous prison reform bills. Born in Hampden, Maine, she pursued a lifelong career in social work and served in the Civil War as supervisor of a corps of nurses for the Union.

Founder of the Dominican Friars

DOMINIC—Pope Innocent III sent Dominic (1170-1221) to France to preach against the Albigenses sect. As part of his campaign against the heretics, Dominic set out to found the Friars Preachers, based on Augustine's dicta. This powerful group of anti-heretical monks, founded in 1215, became known as the Dominican Order. Although they were ascetics, the Dominicans, who attained great political influence in thirteenth-century Spain, were responsible for a large amount of the suffering inflicted upon Protestants and Jews as part of the Spanish Inquisition. England knew them as the Black Friars; the French knew them as the Jacobins.

America's Four Highest Decorations

DONOVAN, WILLIAM JOSEPH—Lieutenant Colonel William Joseph Donovan, cited for meritorious conduct in combat, won the Congressional Medal of Honor, the Distinguished Service Cross and the Distinguished Service Medal as an officer with the American Expeditionary Force in France during the First World War. From June 1942 until the end of the Second World War, "Wild Bill" Donovan served as the director of the Office of Strategic Services, for which he received the National Security Medal in 1957. He is the only American to win all four of his country's highest decorations. The OSS later became the base for the formation of the Central Intelligence Agency.

Inventor of the Periscope

DOUGHTY, THOMAS—During the Civil War, Acting Chief Engineer of the United States Navy Thomas Doughty was stationed in the Red River aboard the monitor, *Osage*. To counteract the incessant harassment of naval vessels by Confederate snipers, Doughty devised the first *periscope*: a tube of sheet iron affixed with mirrors. By looking into the mirrors, the shoreline could be safely observed from the engine room below.

First Black Politician in the U.S.

DOUGLASS, FREDERICK—A slave until his escape at the age of 21, Frederick Douglass (1817?-1895) became an active abolitionist, publishing an anti-slavery periodical and lecturing in Europe and the northern United States. In 1866, he became the first black delegate to the National Loyalists' (an anti-slavery party) Loyal Union Convention. In 1872, Douglass was the first black vice-presidential candidate (for the National Women's Suffrage Association). In 1888, he was nominated for the presidency at the Republican convention but was later defeated by Benjamin Harrison. Douglass also served as the American consul general of Haiti.

Youngest Head of State

DUVALIER, JEAN-CLAUDE—Nineteen-year-old Jean-Claude Duvalier succeeded his father, Papa Doc Duvalier, on April 22, 1971, becoming the youngest nonroyal head of state in the world. So that he would meet the qualifications for the job, a special act of Haiti's National Legislature declared him to be two years older than he actually was. Like his father had been, Jean-Claude was named "president for life" of Haiti.

Haiti, the oldest republic in Latin America and the first black-governed republic in the world, won independence from France in 1804. The country is considered to be the poorest in the Western Hemisphere and the 14-year dictatorship of Papa Doc did little to alleviate the nation's condition. Since Jean-Claude assumed power, conditions have improved somewhat, though the former law student is considered to be a puppet controlled by his ministers.

Resignation of Vice-Presidential Candidate

EAGLETON, THOMAS F.—Nominated by the Democratic Party as the vice-presidential running mate of Senator George McGovern in 1972, Missouri Senator Thomas F. Eagleton (1929-)

resigned the nomination less than one month later, the first such candidate to do so in the history of American politics. Reports that Eagleton had been hospitalized for mental disturbances in his recent past led to press speculation as to his ability to handle the vice-presidency, if elected. Under great pressure, Eagleton resigned. Robert Sargent Shriver of Maryland replaced him on the Democratic ticket.

First Christian Scientist Church

EDDY, MARY BAKER—An invalid for many years, Mary Baker Eddy (1821-1910) became convinced, through the teachings of Dr. Phineas Quimby, that the Bible contained the key to mental healing. In 1874, she founded the Christian Science movement in Boston, Massachusetts and, four years later, set up the First Church of Christ, Scientist. Eddy wrote many volumes on the subject and is principally known for *Science and Health, and Key to the Scriptures,* written in 1880, which is her church's chief text.

The First Gun

EDWARD III, KING—In 1362, young King Edward III (1312-1377) of England had a treatise written and compiled. The treatise, called *On the Duties of Kings,* contains a picture of a gun mounted on a bench. The gun is being fired by a hot iron applied to the touchhole, loaded with a four-headed arrow. The illustration is not mentioned in the text, but it is considered the first authenticated reference to a firearm. Speculation has it that such weapons were in general use during the Hundred Years War (1337-1437).

Opposition Party in Congress

EISENHOWER, DWIGHT D.—Although a very popular president (his 1956 victory then was the biggest popular presidential landslide in history), Dwight David Eisenhower (1890-1969), a Republican, faced a Democratically-controlled Senate and House for a record three consecutive sessions.

At age 62, Eisenhower was one of the oldest U.S. presidents at the time of his inauguration in 1953. (W. H. Harrison was older.)

Long-Distance Naval Signal Lamp

EVANS, ROBLEY D.—In 1876, career Navy man Robley D. Evans perfected the long-distance naval signal lamp. His method of affixing mirrors and lenses to an earlier model filled the need for a steady beam with a consistent on-off mechanism. He was one of the prime movers in changing the United States Navy over to steel warships, and, as a steelmaking expert, was made chief inspector of steel in 1886. "Fighting Bob" Evans fired the opening United States shot in the Spanish-American War in Santiago in 1898. He became a rear admiral in 1901. Evans was commander of the Great White Fleet of 1907, which circled the globe; midway through the journey, he took ill and had to be replaced.

First Appointed U.S. President

FORD, GERALD RUDOLPH—In 1973, President Richard Nixon appointed Congressman Gerald R. Ford to replace the former vice-president, Spiro Agnew, who had resigned from office. Ironically, Ford was sworn in on August 9, 1974 to replace Nixon, who was forced to resign from the presidency the day before because of his involvement in the Watergate scandals. On that day, Ford became the first American president not to have been popularly elected. Ford later appointed Nelson A. Rockefeller as his vice-president, thus placing the United States in the unique position of not having elected either of its two highest officials.

Ford immediately set out to cut the federal budget and curb economic inflation by rejecting nearly every money-spending bill passed by Congress. In so doing, he set a presidential record for the greatest number of vetoes issued by any single administration. As of January 28, 1976, Ford had vetoed 44 bills, eight of which were overridden by Congress.

First Grand Dragon of Ku Klux Klan

FORREST, NATHAN BEDFORD—The Ku Klux Klan was organized as a social group in Tennessee in 1865. By 1869 it had decayed into a lawless gang of thugs, white supremacists and terrorists. The noted Confederate war general, Nathan Bedford Forrest, was elected as the Klan's first Grand Dragon in 1867. To his credit, when acts of violence and arson began to outweigh social functions, he resigned and called for the Klan's breakup. The organization emerged again in the 1920s.

Inventor of Bifocal Glasses

FRANKLIN, BENJAMIN—Benjamin Franklin (1706-1790), early American statesman, scientist, inventor and writer, was responsible for many novel discoveries:

He invented the Franklin stove, an open iron stove, similar to a fireplace, which greatly improved the quality of colonial life.

On June 15, 1751, he flew a kite to which a metal key was attached, demonstrating that lightning is a form of electricity. The demonstration was so significant that an account of it was read before London's Royal Society.

Franklin was the first man to experiment with electrocution. In 1773, he demonstrated his conclusions by killing a 10-pound turkey, a lamb, and many chickens.

In 1785, Franklin found a way of combining two lenses into one, thereby making the first pair of bifocal glasses.

First Senate Trial

GALLATIN, ALBERT—The noted banker, Albert Gallatin (1761-1849), was denied a Senate seat to which he had been elected on grounds that he had not been a United States citizen for the required nine years. In 1794, the protesting Swiss émigré, who later served for 14 years as secretary of the treasury (1801-1814), was placed on trial before the Senate in its first public hearing. Gallatin was denied his seat, but later served as a congressman from the State of Pennsylvania. Gallatin, seemingly to prove that his Senate ouster had been unfair, went on to become an important statesman in the diplomatic corps, negotiating an end to the War of 1812 and representing the United States in London and Paris for eight years. He also founded the American Ethnological Society, and the first glass factory west of the Alleghenies, in New Geneva, Pennsylvania in 1794.

Inventor of the M1 Rifle

GARAND, JOHN C.—The standard infantry weapon used by the United States Army and Marine Corps during World War II was the Garand M1 semi-automatic rifle. Its inventor, John C. Garand (1888-1974), granted the rights to the invention to the government, accepting no royalties or fees. Although the Canadian gunsmith first demonstrated the rapid-firing, .30-caliber gun in 1923, it was not patented until 1934. The weapon, which weighed 9¼ pounds, had 75 parts. General George S. Patton called the Garand rifle "the greatest battle implement ever devised."

First President to Use a Telephone

GARFIELD, JAMES A.—The twentieth president of the United States is remembered by many as the second of four presidents to be assassinated in office. James Abram Garfield (1831-1881), who only served seven months of his term before meeting an untimely death, was the first president to use the newly-invented telephone while in office. He had had one installed in 1878, while still a member of Congress, and continued to use the device as president. Garfield's mother was the first to watch a son inaugurated and was also the first presidential mother to live in the White House. Garfield was the first president to campaign in a foreign language, using German on many occasions in an attempt at wooing the immigrant vote. He was also the first left-handed chief executive.

First Adjutant General of the Army

GATES, HORATIO—A $125-a-month brigadier general, Horatio Gates (1728?-1806) was nominated by John Hancock in June of 1775 to fill the newly created post of Adjutant General in the Continental Army. Congress established the post as part of its military preparedness plans. Gates went on to command the Northern Army at the outset of the Revolution, but, despite his victory over Burgoyne at Saratoga, was transferred to the Southern Army, where he was defeated and relieved. By war's end, Gates had been reinstated to a field command.

Inventor of Rapid Fire Machine Gun

GATLING, RICHARD JORDAN—Student of medicine and inventor Richard Jordan Gatling (1818-1903) is primarily remembered for the invention of the *Gatling gun*, a kind of machine gun consisting of a cluster of barrels arranged parallel with and around an axis, designed to be successively discharged when rotated by a crank. Capable of firing 250 rounds per minute, it was used extensively by the United States Army since its invention in 1866. The gangster slang term, "gat," is synonymous with "gun." The Gatling gun is now obsolete.

Only Reigning Monarchs to Visit U.S.

GEORGE VI AND ELIZABETH II—In June of 1939, the reigning monarchs of Great Britain, George (1895-1952) and Elizabeth (1900-   ), visited Niagara Falls, New York City and Washington, D.C. They were the first British royalty to so honor the United States. During that visit, while touring the New York World's Fair, they became the first monarchs to be televised. Queen Elizabeth's visit to Monrovia, Liberia was the subject of the longest continuous radio broadcast ever made: 14 hours, 20 minutes in duration on November 23, 1961.

First Congressional Filibusterer

GERRY, ELBRIDGE—The American statesman from Massachusetts, Elbridge Gerry (1744-1814), was a delegate to the Continental Congress, a signer of the Declaration of Independence, and a member of Congress from 1789 to 1793. On June 11, 1790, he instigated the first congressional filibuster when he stalled a decision to change the site of the nation's capital by speaking at length on various topics of regional interest. The term *gerrymandering* was coined following Gerry's strategic reshuffling of Massachusetts' electoral districts while governor. The redistricting was an effort to create voting blocs favorable to his party. Gerry served as vice-president under James Madison, but died after less than two years in office.

Initiator of Labor Day

GOMPERS, SAMUEL—In September, 1882, in New York City, the first Labor Day celebration was held. The man largely responsible for the celebration was Samuel Gompers (1850-1924), the most influential labor leader of his time. Gompers' family had come from England during the American Civil War to work in the New York tobacco industry. A member of the cigar maker's union, of which he had been elected a vice-president in 1881, Gompers salvaged the remnants of the Federation of Trades and Labor Unions to create the American Federation of Labor. In 1886, in Columbus, Ohio, Gompers was chosen first president of the new confederation of labor unions. He fought energetically to insure that the five million members of his organization would not be abused. One of his most important accomplishments—the eight-hour day—was achieved in 1924.

First Civil Service Commission

GRANT, ULYSSES S.—After serving the victorious Union forces during the Civil War, Ulysses Simpson Grant (1822-1885) was appointed the first general of the newly-reorganized United States Army on July 25, 1866. He held this position until March 4, 1869, when he was inaugurated as the eighteenth president of the United States.

During his term of office, Grant appointed the first Civil Service Commission. The seven-man board was sworn into office in March of 1871 and was voted by Congress to become effective on January 1, 1872. The commission was disbanded for lack of funds two years later, but was reestablished in 1883, its purpose being to set national standards of employment for federal workers.

Highest Priced Autograph

GWINNETT, BUTTON—Button Gwinnett was one of the three delegates representing the colony of Georgia at the Continental Congress between the years 1775 and 1777. As such, Gwinnett was one of the signers of the Declaration of Independence, which was one of the very few documents he ever signed.

In 1927, Gwinnett's holograph (autograph) was sold for $51,000 at auction; it would bring an estimated five times that amount if sold today. Gwinnett, born in Gloucestershire, England in 1735, was fatally wounded in a duel with his rival, Lachlan McIntosh, in 1777.

The Largest Aqueduct

HADRIAN, EMPEROR—During his reign (117-138 A.D.) as emperor, Publius Aelius Hadrianus ordered the construction of an 87.6-mile-long aqueduct in Carthage. The conduit was the largest in the ancient world, capable of carrying 8.4 million gallons of water per day. The emperor's reign was noted for its monumental constructions. Hadrian's Wall, which separated the Roman Britains from the Picts and Scots and stretched the width of England, still survives in part. The Pantheon in Rome, the Gate in Athens, and additions to the Forum are also contributions of Hadrian.

Most Highly Decorated Admiral

HALSEY, WILLIAM F.—Fleet Admiral William F. Halsey (1882-1959) was awarded the Navy's Distinguished Service Medal four times, more than any other United States Navy man. In World War I, he won the Navy Cross for his excellence as a destroyer commander. During World War II, he led the naval attacks on the Gilbert and Marshall Islands, made possible operations in the Solomon Islands, and became commander-in-chief of South Pacific Operations in October of 1942. When the Japanese finally surrendered to the United States on September 2, 1945, the documents were signed aboard Halsey's flagship, the USS *Missouri*, in Tokyo Bay.

First Treasury Secretary

HAMILTON, ALEXANDER—After distinguishing himself in combat during the American Revolution, prominent statesman Alexander Hamilton (1757-1804) formed the Federalist Party, which advocated a strong central government and financial organization, in 1788. He backed General George Washington for president and, after the election, Washington appointed him the first secretary of the treasury. While serving in that position from 1789 to 1795, Hamilton founded the Bank of the United States. The brilliance and spirit with which he opposed Thomas Jefferson and the Virginia Democratic-Republicans is said to have led to the formation of the two-party system, an important element in the makeup of the world's first democracy. Hamilton died from wounds inflicted during a duel with Aaron Burr in 1804. After his defeat in races for New York's governorship and the United States presidency, Burr had alleged that the elections had been rigged by Hamilton.

Only Posthumous Nobel Prize Award

HAMMARSKJOLD, DAG—Since 1901, the Nobel Prize has been awarded to those individuals who have made outstanding contributions to humanity's struggle for betterment. The hope of the Nobel Foundation has been that the prestige of the award and the prize money which accompanies it would encourage the winners to pursue their areas of endeavor even more seriously. It was, therefore, somewhat surprising when Swedish statesman Dag Hammarskjold, Secretary General of the United Nations from 1953 until his death in 1961, was awarded a Nobel Prize posthumously. For his assistance in negotiating treaties to end the Korean War and the 1956 Suez crisis, and for his attempts to achieve a settlement in the Congo crisis (he died in a plane crash in Africa while exercising such efforts), Hammarskjold was awarded the Peace Prize in 1961.

First to Sign the Declaration of Independence

HANCOCK, JOHN—John Hancock (1737-1793), elected the first governor of Massachusetts in 1780, was president of the Continental Congress of 1775-1777. As such, he was instrumental in persuading other delegates to sign the Declaration of Independence. To affix one's signature to the document was, in essence, to admit treason; the fact that Hancock was the *first* to sign his name and the boldness with which he did so was a testament to his bravery. The famous Battle of Lexington, the shots of which were "heard round the world," was originally intended by the British as an expedition to arrest Hancock and his fellow revolutionary Samuel Adams.

President and Wife Die in Office

HARDING, WARREN G. AND FLORENCE D.—The only United States President and his first lady to die while serving in those capacities were Warren Gamaliel and Florence D. Harding. The twenty-ninth president died on August 2, 1923 in San Francisco, California; the first lady, Florence Kling DeWolfe Harding, died on November 21, 1924 in Marion, Ohio, 10 weeks before her husband would have left office.

Harding was inaugurated on March 4, 1921 and was scheduled to serve until March 4, 1925. Upon his death, he was succeeded by Vice-President Calvin Coolidge, who won re-election to his own four-year term in 1924.

Creator of First Forest Preserve

HARRISON, BENJAMIN—Benjamin Harrison (1833-1901), grandson of William Henry Harrison, the ninth president of the United States, served as president between 1889 and 1893. Benjamin, who split Grover Cleveland's two terms, passed important legislation during his four-year term of office. In 1891, he created the Yellowstone Park Timberland Reserve, the first national park. The 52nd Congress, which convened during the last part of his term, was the first billion dollar Congress. During this congressional session, North Dakota, South Dakota, Montana, Washington, Idaho and Wyoming were admitted to the Union, the largest number of states admitted by any single administration.

First President to Die in Office

HARRISON, WILLIAM HENRY—Despite the fact that William Henry Harrison (1773-1841) served only 30 days in office, he was a record-setting chief executive. The ninth president of the United States was the first to die in office, succumbing on April 4, 1841 to pneumonia, which he had contracted at the inaugural ceremonies. Harrison was the last president born before the American Revolution and the only president who had studied to be a doctor. His was the only presidential father to have signed the Declaration of Independence and his grandson, Benjamin Harrison, was the only presidential grandson to become president himself. At the age of 68, William Henry Harrison was the oldest president to be inaugurated and the first to lie in state at the White House.

First to Use Word "American"

HAY, JOHN MILTON—The substitution of the word "American" for "United States" as an adjective in official government matters was initiated on August 3, 1904 on the recommendation of Secretary of State John Hay (1838-1905).

Hay had led a long and distinguished career in American government. At age 22, he became Lincoln's personal secretary, a position he held until the president's death. Based on his experiences, he wrote an incisive biography of Lincoln.

As Secretary of State from 1868 to 1905, Hay was responsible for America's Open Door Policy (1899) and the Hay-Pauncefote Treaty with Britain, which provided for the construction of the Panama Canal with United States control.

Founder of the Church of England

HENRY VIII, KING—Once named "Defender of the Faith" by Pope Clement VII, Henry VIII (1491-1547) was excommunicated by the same man for replacing his deputy, Cardinal Wolsey, with Sir Thomas More in 1529. The replacement was made so that Henry would be granted the right to divorce his wife, Catherine, on grounds that she did not bear him a son. After breaking with the papacy, Henry established the Church of England through a parliamentary Act of Supremacy in 1534, appointing himself head.

Much of the king's adult life was devoted to the search for a wife who could bear him an heir to the throne. In all, he had six wives: Catherine (mother of Mary Tudor); Anne Boleyn (mother of Elizabeth I and later beheaded); Jane Seymour (mother of Edward VI, who would become Henry's heir); Anne of Cleves; Catherine Howard (beheaded); and Catherine Parr.

First Japanese Emperor to Visit U.S.

HIROHITO—Emperor of Japan Hirohito (1901-), who began his reign on Christmas Day, 1926, is one of the longest-reigning monarchs in the world today. When he, accompanied by his wife, arrived in the United States in October of 1975, he became the first Japanese emperor to visit American shores. Included on the emperor's itinerary were a visit to the White House, a New York Jets' Football game, and a trip to Disneyland, where he was greeted by Mickey Mouse.

First Secretary of Health, Education and Welfare

HOBBY, OVETA CULP—President Dwight D. Eisenhower created the new cabinet post of Secretary of Health, Education and Welfare on April 11, 1953. Mrs. William Pettus Hobby (1905-) of Houston, Texas, the founder and head of the Women's Army Corps during World War II, was sworn into the cabinet as the new secretary. She was the second woman cabinet officer in history.

First Independent American Community

HOOKER, THOMAS—Thomas Hooker (1586?-1647) founded Hartford, Connecticut in 1636 after having been driven out of England and Holland for preaching a seventeenth-century version of "do your own thing." A clergyman, Hooker believed in a community's right to self-government. Any larger group, he argued, is too far removed to truly understand local problems. Hooker drew up the Fundamental Orders in 1639, a remarkable document, making Hartford the first American community to write its own laws without the guidance or consent of a larger or more powerful governing body. Hooker further proposed that all the colonies band together to drive away the indigenous New Englanders, the Indians.

Most Honorary Degrees Recipient

HOOVER, HERBERT—The thirty-first president of the United States, who defeated Democratic candidate Alfred E. Smith in the election of 1928, served in the White House from 1929 to 1933. The unique Herbert Hoover received more honorary degrees in his lifetime (89) than any other man. Most of these honors were awarded him after he lost the presidency to Franklin Roosevelt in 1932.

Hoover holds another unique record. In March of 1920, while involved in a food distribution program, he became the first future American president after whom an asteroid—Hooveria—would be named. He is also the only chief executive to hail from the state of Iowa.

Father of the U.S. Navy

HUMPHREYS, JOSHUA—Appointed in 1794 as the United States naval constructor, or "Master Builder," Joshua Humphreys (1751-1838) is considered to be the father of the American Navy. Distressed over troubles with pirates in Algiers, the Navy realized that its fleet was old and largely unseaworthy following the American Revolution. In response, Humphreys designed and built the 44-gun *United States*, which was radically different from traditional ships: all of its guns were on a single deck, making the vessel faster and more stable, and considerably influencing European shipmakers. Humphreys set up Navy yards in Philadelphia and Boston and built a series of vessels similar to the *United States*, all of which were well suited to battle. Between 1794 and 1801, he converted the United States into a truly modern naval power.

First President to Ride a Train

JACKSON, ANDREW—The seventh president of the United States is alleged to have fought in more than 100 duels before entering politics. On May 30, 1806, he killed Charles Dickenson for insulting his wife. The famous dueler, Andrew Jackson (1767-1845), was the first president to have been born in a log cabin and the first to marry a divorcee, Rachel Donelson.

On June 6, 1833, he rode the Baltimore and Ohio Railroad from Ellicott's Mills to Baltimore, Maryland, the first man to ride a train while president. During his presidential term (1829-1937), "Old Hickory," as Jackson was called, was very popular with the electorate. He was censured by Congress in 1834 for his financial and monetary decrees. In 1835, Jackson became the first chief executive to be the subject of an assassination attempt. The pistols of the house painter who wanted to take his life luckily misfired.

Creator of the Semaphore Code

JAMES II, KING—Visual signalling, a means of coded communication, has been employed by all pre-modern armies. When King James II (1633-1701) of England was Lord High Admiral in 1670, he devised a set of signals for the British Navy which is the earliest known semaphore code. A series of flags raised while rigging a ship, or the actual waving of these flags by a sailor, served to relay messages to those within visible proximity.

James, who had become Lord High Admiral upon his brother's ascension to the throne in 1660, resigned his commission upon his conversion to Catholicism in 1673.

First Secretary of State

JEFFERSON, THOMAS—As chairman of the committee which drafted the Declaration of Independence, Thomas Jefferson (1743-1826) can be considered one of the architects of American government. He was named the first secretary of state under George Washington in 1790, and served as vice-president under John Adams.

When Jefferson became the third president of the United States in 1801, his election was decided in the House of Representatives; the House chose him over Aaron Burr with whom he had tied in the electoral voting. Jefferson was responsible for the Louisiana Purchase, which brought an immense tract of land under American control in 1804.

Youngest Reigning King Today

JIGME SINGYE WANGCHUK—Born November 11, 1955, King Jigme Singye Wangchuk, the maharaja of Bhutan, is the youngest reigning monarch in the world. A relative, Jigme Doyi Wangchuk, ascended the throne in 1952, but, when Jigme Singye was born in 1955, the younger Jigme assumed technical control of the little mountain kingdom. Situated in the middle of the Himalaya Mountains in Asia, Bhutan is strategically located between India and Chinese-controlled Tibet, with Nepal and East Pakistan also close neighbors.

Organizer of First Teachers' Colleges

JOHN THE BAPTIST DE LA SALLE—While a student at Saint-Sulpice, John the Baptist de la Salle developed ideas on teacher-training. Ordained a priest in 1678, John devoted his life to teaching the French poor. In the 1680s, he set up the Brothers of the Christian Schools, and, around 1688, introduced the notion of Sunday School to Paris. His book, *The Conduct of Christian Schools*, became a basic text for parochial school teachers throughout the world.

Only Presidential Impeachment

JOHNSON, ANDREW—Abraham Lincoln's vice-president, Andrew Johnson (1808-1875), who took over upon Lincoln's assassination, was not a widely-liked politician. Struggles over how the South should be reconstructed led to his impeachment in 1868, but Johnson was *not* convicted of the conspiracy and abuse of power charges brought against him. The seventeenth president was the only chief executive to have had no formal schooling; he had been taught to read by his first wife at the age of 17. After his presidential term of office expired in 1869, Johnson was elected as a senator from Tennessee, the only president to later become a senator.

First Satellite Telephone Conversation

JOHNSON, LYNDON BAINES—The thirty-sixth president of the United States, Lyndon Baines Johnson (1908-1973), was the first person to place a telephone call using a communications satellite. On June 28, 1965, Johnson phoned the heads of state in London, Bonn, Berne, Paris and Rome and exchanged brief remarks. Little more than a year earlier, Johnson had been the first to use the trans-Pacific telephone cable in placing a telephone call to the prime minister of Japan in Tokyo.

Assuming the presidency in 1963 after the assassination of President John F. Kennedy, Johnson won election to the post in 1964, scoring a landslide victory over Republican-Conservative Barry Goldwater. His determined, hawklike policy in regard to the war in Vietnam may have led to his decision in March 1968 not to seek reelection.

First American Flag Flown on a Warship

JONES, JOHN PAUL—John Paul Jones (1747-1792), captain of the American man-of-war, *Ranger*, flew a flag from his naval warship on July 4, 1777. The flag, made from the gowns of young ladies, was hoisted to the *Ranger's* top mast while docked in Portsmouth Harbor, New Hampshire, waiting to sail for France.

Jones soon left for France, carrying news to the French court of Burgoyne's surrender. When he reached the harbor at Quiberon on February 14, 1778, the captain saluted the French flag with 13 guns; a nine-gun salute was returned, marking the first time an American flag was saluted by a foreign nation. The king of France had approved the tribute.

Founder of Rosicrucians in America

KELPIUS, MAGISTER—Reportedly founded by Christian Rosenkreuz around 1614, the Knights of the Rosy Cross are a philosophical order which principally follows ideas of mysticism, astrology, alchemy and secrecy. The ancient, mystical order of *Rosae Crucis* is the American branch of the group and was founded in 1693 by Magister Kelpius, who came from England with orders to set up the first New World chapter. The chapter opened a year later near Philadelphia. The national headquarters is located in Rosicrucian Park, San Jose, California.

Fastest-Talking U.S. President

KENNEDY, JOHN F.—Although United States presidents and politicians are generally known for their quick tongues, President John Fitzgerald Kennedy (1917-1963) topped them all when he delivered part of a December, 1961 speech at a rate of 327 words per minute.

Kennedy, originally a senator from Massachusetts, beat Republican candidate Richard M. Nixon in the election of 1960. He served two years and 10 months of his term before being assassinated on November 22, 1963 while riding in a motorcade in Dallas, Texas.

Only Presidential Candidate Assassinated

KENNEDY, ROBERT F.—In the 180-year history of United States presidential campaigning, only one candidate has ever been assassinated: Robert Francis Kennedy of New York. On June 6, 1968, after winning the important California primary, the junior senator from New York was shot and killed by Sirhan Bishara Sirhan, a Palestinian immigrant armed with a .22-caliber revolver. Although not considered the front-runner for the Democratic nomination at the time, Kennedy was providing a keen challenge to then-Vice-President Hubert H. Humphrey. Kennedy's older brother, John, had been the fourth American president to be assassinated when he was killed in Dallas on November 22, 1963.

Father of Modern Kenya

KENYATTA, JOMO—Because its politics are respected and its trade ties with the rest of the Central African states are powerful, Kenya is one of the most important nations in Africa. Becoming partially self-governing in 1953, there was a long and sometimes bloody struggle between blacks and whites for political control in this nation of ten million. Jomo Kenyatta (1893-), the founder of the progressive Kenya African Union in 1947, brought unity to black Africans after popular pressure forced his release from prison for allegedly leading the bloody Mau Mau revolt of the early 1950s. Kenyatta was the logical choice to become the country's first Prime Minister when Kenya became fully independent from Britain in 1963. And when Kenya became a republic in 1964, Kenyatta became its first president. His name and accomplishments are still revered throughout the Third World.

Only Vice-President Never to Serve

KING, WILLIAM RUFUS DE VANE—The only elected vice-president to serve in both houses of Congress was also the only one to never serve even a single day of his vice-presidential term. William Rufus De Vane King (1786-1853), elected to the office with Franklin Pierce, died on April 18, 1853, nearly eight months before the convening of the first session of the Congress at which he was to perform his duties. Since the principle duty of the vice-president at that time was to act as *president pro tempore* of the Senate, and inasmuch as the Senate was not scheduled to meet until the following fall, King had returned to his home in Dallas County, Alabama for a few weeks of recuperation from the election campaign. He died there without ever having occupied his new office in Washington, D.C. King had previously been a representative from North Carolina and a senator from Alabama.

First Foreigner Awarded Citizenship

LAFAYETTE, MARQUIS DE—A French statesman and general, Lafayette (1757-1834) came to the aid of General George Washington during the American Revolution. He lent his military expertise to the Continental Army through Cornwallis' surrender at Yorktown in 1781, and, for his immeasurable service to America, he was awarded honorary colonial citizenship in 1784. The grant was first made by Maryland, and then by the entire United States; citizenship was extended to all his heirs and descendants. In 1803, Lafayette was awarded 11,250 acres as a special land grant, the first to a foreigner. The Frenchman brought the first partridges to the New World in 1786 as a gift for his close friend and ally, George Washington.

First State Unemployment Insurance

LA FOLLETTE, PHILIP—On January 28, 1932, the first unemployment insurance law was passed in the state of Wisconsin. Governor Philip La Follette (1897-1965) signed the bill, which authorized that money from an employee's paycheck be automatically set aside against the time when he might become unemployed. The new law was a daring piece of New Deal Legislation.

Governor La Follette was a son of Robert Marion La Follette, the distinguished United States senator who served between 1906 and 1925, and who polled five million votes as a presidential candidate on the Progressive Party line in 1924.

First American Imprisoned in Tower of London

LAURENS, HENRY—A distinguished statesman from South Carolina and president of the Continental Congress in 1778, Henry Laurens was at sea, on his way to negotiate a treaty with the Dutch in 1780, when he was captured by the British and jailed for more than a year on suspicion of treason. He had to pay for his bed, board and jailer while in the Tower of London. The papers found with Laurens at the time of his capture were used by the British to declare war on the Dutch. He was released in 1781 in exchange of Lord Cornwallis, loser of the Battle of Yorktown. Laurens went on to draw up the treaty with Britain which ended the American Revolution.

Man with the Most Statues

LENIN, VLADIMIR ILYICH ULYANOV—Russian revolutionary
V. I. Lenin (1870-1924) became a social activist after the execution of his brother by Tsar Alexander III; consequently, in
1897, he was arrested and exiled to Siberia. Lenin went on to become a Marxist leader, organizer, and founder of the Bolshevik
(Communist) Party. He directed the revolution of 1917, and acted
as premier of the Soviet Union from 1918 to 1924. The survivor
of an assassination attempt, Lenin died from overwork and exhaustion. In his memory, a statue of the famous leader has been
erected in every Russian town.

Oldest Pontiff

LEO XIII, POPE—When he was elected pope on the third ballot
on February 20, 1878, Vincenzo Gioacchino Pecci began a reign
that lasted 27 years. One of the most vigorous and productive
of modern popes, Leo, a supporter of St. Thomas Aquinas,
founded many Catholic universities and schools for the study of
Catholic democracy. When he died on July 20, 1903, he was 93
years plus 140 days old—the oldest man ever to serve as pontiff.

First Secretary-General of U.N.

LIE, TRYGVE HALVDAN—Following World War II, the war-
weary nations felt that the time was ripe to establish an international forum for the airing and arbitration of differences. Thus,
in 1946, following a conference in San Francisco, the United
Nations was founded. The Norwegian patriot and statesman
Trygve Lie (1896-1968) had been a government official and
leader of his country's Labor Party from 1935 up to the Nazi
invasion. He became a member of the Norwegian government
in exile and, as a delegate to the first meeting of the United
Nations General Assembly, was elected as its first secretary-
general in 1946. Lie served until 1953.

First President to Be Assassinated

LINCOLN, ABRAHAM—Abraham Lincoln, sixteenth president of
the United States, was responsible for many firsts:
    1. He was the first president to grant amnesty, which he
did on December 8, 1963 and again on March 26, 1864.
    2. Born in Illinois in 1809, he was the first president not
to be born in one of the original 13 states.
    3. On May 22, 1849, Lincoln patented a device which en-

abled ships to cross treacherous shoals by means of inflated cylinders. He was the first president to receive a patent.

4. Lincoln was assassinated on April 14, 1865, the first of four American presidents to be shot while in office. He died the following day at the age of 56.

Three Presidential Assassinations

LINCOLN, ROBERT TODD—The oldest son of Abraham Lincoln, Robert Lincoln (1843-1926) was present at Ford's Theatre on the night of his father's assassination. Robert Lincoln had served on the staff of General Ulysses S. Grant in 1865 and was a corporate lawyer in Chicago when he was called to serve as President James Garfield's secretary of war in 1881. He was at the Washington railway station at the time Garfield was shot. Lincoln served as secretary of war until 1885, and, from 1889 to 1893, served as United States minister to Great Britain. In 1901, he was invited by President William McKinley to attend the Pan-American Exposition in Buffalo. When Lincoln arrived in Buffalo, he learned that the president had just been shot. Lincoln himself lived to be 83 years of age.

Father, Mother, Son Serve Senate

LONG, RUSSELL B.—Huey Long, known to his Louisiana constituency as "the Kingfish," was governor of that state from 1928 to 1931, and one of its United States senators from 1931 to 1935. When Huey was assassinated in Baton Rouge on September 8, 1935, his wife, Rose McConnell Long, was designated to fill the vacancy. In 1948, their son, Russell, was elected to fill an unexpired term in the Senate which he held for five consecutive terms. As such, he is the only senator whose father and mother held a senatorial seat before him. Russell Long has become as powerful in the Senate as his father, but most agree that he has obtained his power legitimately, unlike Huey who used political demagoguery and machine politics to achieve his ends. Russell Long's current Senate term expires in 1981.

Greatest Banquet Ever Staged

LOUBET, EMILE F.—Emile F. Loubet (1838-1929) was president of the French Republic from 1899 to 1906; his term was one fraught with social and political upheaval. The Dreyfus affair, a scandal involving the alleged passing of military secrets by a member of the French General Staff, reached its peak during his administration; he pardoned Dreyfus in 1900 to calm the situation.

Turn-of-the-century France was pre-occupied with an interest in the rise of the common man. Most unusual about Loubet was that to encourage cooperation with all French citizens, he threw the greatest banquet ever staged. It was held in the Tuileries Gardens in Paris on September 22, 1900. Every one of the 22,000 French mayors and their deputies were present.

Highest Priced Gun

LOUIS XIII, KING—Louis XIII of France had a flint-lock fowling piece made in 1615 by Pierre le Bourgeoys of Lisieux. On November 21, 1972, $312,000 was paid for it by London antique dealers F. Patridge & Co., a record sum for a single firearm on the open market. The flint-lock was sold by Sotheby & Co. of London from the collection of American gun collector William G. Renwick.

Louis XIII, who was king of France from the age of nine in 1610 until his death in 1643, turned over most of the affairs of state to his mother's protege, Cardinal Richelieu, in 1624, who became the power behind the throne. Richelieu advocated France's entrance into the Thirty Years' War (1618-1648), which it did and won, its victory re-establishing France as one of the strongest European powers.

First Passenger Elevator

LOUIS XV, KING—King Louis XV of France (1710-1774) needed a means of reaching the second floor apartment of his mistress, Mme. de Chateauroux, from his own on the first floor in the Petite Cour du Roy at Versailles. And so, "The Flying Chair" was installed in 1743. King Louis entered it from his balcony. Capable of being raised or lowered by hand, the elevator ran up the outside of the building, carefully sheltered by a courtyard.

The reign of Louis XV (1715-1774) was known as the Age of Reason, so called because of the flourishing of French intellectuals and philosophers and marked by the War of the Austrian Succession and the Seven Years' War.

Most Army Distinguished Service Medals

MacARTHUR, GENERAL DOUGLAS—General of the Army Douglas MacArthur (1880-1964) was awarded six Distinguished Service Medals—five by the United States Army and one by the

Navy—more than any other military man. MacArthur was also awarded the Congressional Medal of Honor for his defense of the Philippines at the outbreak of World War II. He was supreme commander of the Southwest Pacific for the duration of the war and commanded the United Nations forces during the Korean War. Relieved of the latter command by President Truman for allegedly trying to extend the war into Mainland China, MacArthur later became board chairman of the Remington Rand Corporation.

Father of the Dominion of Canada

MacDONALD, JOHN ALEXANDER—As George Washington is father to America, so is Sir John Alexander MacDonald to Canada. An Ontario legislator in 1844, MacDonald became Canada's premier in 1857. In 1867, in coalition with another statesman, George Brown, MacDonald helped create the confederation of Canada out of the loosely-associated colonies and territories of that huge land area.

Sir John was elected the first premier of the dominion of Canada in 1867. As premier, MacDonald oversaw the purchase of the Northwest Territories from the Hudson Bay Company and commenced the building of a rail system to tie together the world's second largest country. He was again elected premier in 1878 and served until his death in 1891.

President Who Faced Enemy Fire

MADISON, JAMES—On August 25, 1814, President James Madison (1751-1836), in an unsuccessful attempt to prevent the British from entering Washington, D.C., took command of the artillery battery of Commodore Joshua Barney near Bladensburg, Maryland. The Redcoats subsequently entered the city and burned the White House. Madison, the fourth president of the United States (1809-1817), was State Secretary under Jefferson and a distinguished delegate from Virginia to the Continental Congress. He was the last surviving member of the Congress who signed the Constitution. His wife, Dolley, was voted a seat of honor in the House of Representatives in 1844.

Only General to Receive Peace Prize

MARSHALL, GEORGE C.—A career military man, George Catlett Marshall (1880-1959) served in World War I, later became an aide to General Pershing, and served as chief of staff of the United States Army in World War II. He was appointed Secretary of State by President Harry Truman, a position he held from 1947 to 1949. He served as Truman's defense secretary in 1950-1951. During his tenure, Marshall formulated the European Recovery Plan, which gave millions of dollars in aid to the war-shattered nations of Europe. The program became known as the Marshall Plan. An active man until his death, the general was president of the American Red Cross in 1950 and was awarded the Nobel Peace Prize in 1953.

First Black Supreme Court Justice

MARSHALL, THURGOOD—President Lyndon B. Johnson appointed Thurgood Marshall as an Associate Justice of the Supreme Court on June 13, 1967. The first black to sit on the bench of the nation's highest court was sworn in as the ninety-sixth Supreme Court justice by Hugo L. Black on October 2, 1967.

Born in 1908, Marshall became the first black solicitor general of the United States in 1965, a position he held at the time of his appointment. As an attorney, Marshall had faced the Supreme Court in 1954 and had won a historic decision on the unconstitutionality of segregation in the nation's public schools, an issue which has caused heated debate as well as violent protest in both the North and the South.

First Paleontology Report in America

MATHER, COTTON—Cotton Mather (1663-1728), son of Boston clergyman Increase Mather and a participant in the Salem Witch Trials of 1692, prepared a report in 1713 to be read before the Royal Society of London the following year. The report described a 17-foot-long thigh bone and three teeth which had been excavated in Albany, New York in 1705. Mather concluded that they had belonged to a race of giants.

The American clergyman's report was very well received; in acknowledgement of the significance of the study, he was elected a member of the Royal Society, the first American to be so honored.

Founder of Army Ambulance Corps

McCLELLAN, GEORGE BRINTON—General George B. Mc-
Clellan (1826-1885) was commander of the Union Army for
much of the Civil War. On August 2, 1862, McClellan, then a
major general, created the first Army Ambulance Corps, which
was commanded by a captain. During the Peninsula campaign
in May of that year, McClellan used a field telegraph for the
first time in the history of warfare. He used it to communicate
with his advance guard of cavalry under the command of General George Stoneman near Mechanicsburg, Virginia. McClellan
ran for president in 1864 and, in 1878, became governor of New
Jersey.

First Income Tax

MEDICI, LORENZO DE—The Medici family produced three popes,
two queens of France, several cardinals and grand dukes—all
through skillful manipulation of family marriages and consider-
able banking acumen.

Lorenzo de Medici (1449-1492), labelled *Lorenzo Il Mag-
nifico* for his support of the arts, was a statesman, poet, scholar,
and prince of Florence. In 1451, he instituted the first income
tax, called the "Catastro" because of its unfairness. It was replaced shortly thereafter by a more progressive income tax called
the "Scala." At the hands of the powerful Medici family, the
income tax became a tool used for political blackmail. When the
Medici family was overthrown in 1492, the tax was immediately
repealed.

Founded First City in America

MENENDEZ, PEDRO DE AVILES—In 1564, Philip II of Spain-
entrusted seafarer and explorer Pedro Menendez de Aviles (1519-
1574) with the duty of colonizing the newly-gained territory of
Florida. Menendez proceeded to the eastern coast of Florida and,
in 1565, founded the town of St. Augustine, the first city in
America. Shortly thereafter, he instigated the first intercolonial
war in America by capturing the French-owned Fort Caroline,
which he renamed San Mateo. Menendez became governor of
Florida for life and was successful in securing Florida for Spain
for nearly 150 years.

Spoke Most Languages

MEZZOFANTI, GIUSEPPE CASPAR—From 1819, until his death in 1849, Giuseppe Mezzofanti was chief librarian at the Vatican Library in Rome, Italy. Mezzofanti, generally acknowledged to be the greatest linguist who ever lived, translated works from as many as 114 languages, including 72 dialects, during his 30-year tenure. In addition, the cardinal spoke 39 languages and employed an additional 11 languages when granting audiences and interviews.

Greatest Mass Wedding Ceremony

MOON, SUN MYUNG—The spiritual leader of the Holy Spirit Association for the Unification of World Christianity, the Reverend Sun Myung Moon, performed the largest wedding ceremony in history. In October of 1970, in Seoul, South Korea, he married 791 couples at one time.

Moon, who claims two million followers, was a Presbyterian before being "visited" by Jesus in 1936. He himself reportedly has been married four times, and is now commuting between Korea and the United States, where he is building a following, an international headquarters and a profitable business corporation. His activities are being financed by his $15-million personal fortune.

First U.S. Land Grant

MORRILL, JUSTIN—A congressional proposal made by Republican Justin Smith Morrill (1810-1898) of Vermont suggested that land be allotted in every state of the union for the erection of at least one agricultural college. The Morrill Act, as it was called, was signed by President Abraham Lincoln in 1862, after having been vetoed in 1857 by James Buchanan. This led to the formation of the first agricultural schools in the world.

Justin Morrill was first elected to the House of Representatives as a Whig from Vermont in 1854, and was reelected every two years until 1866. He then ran for a Senate seat and won, serving in that body for 32 more years, a record (at that time) for congressional longevity.

First Accountancy Law

MORTON, LEVI P.—The first act regulating the activities of public accountants was legislated in the State of New York on April

17, 1896 by Governor Levi Parsons Morton (1824-1920). On that date, the New York Board of Certified Public Accountant Examiners was established with Charles W. Haskins as its first chairman. The Board sought to ensure the integrity of public accountants by registering and bonding each as a Certified Public Accountant (C.P.A.).

Largest Sum Paid by Check

MOYNIHAN, DANIEL PATRICK—Daniel P. Moynihan (1927-) was the United States ambassador to India when the government of the United States wrote a check for 16,640,000,000 rupees to the government of India. In the history of banking no check had ever been written for so large a sum. The February 18, 1974 check, equivalent to $2,046,700,000, came from a transition account of the United States Disbursing Officer at the New Delhi embassy. Moynihan was the government official who handed the check to the Indian secretary of economic affairs.

Moynihan, a professor at Harvard University, served as a very outspoken United States ambassador to the United Nations for a six month period in 1975-76 before returning to his teaching duties at Harvard.

Founder of Universalist Church

MURRAY, JOHN—Englishman James Relly organized a Universalist Church in England in 1758. But, he met with much displeasure among that country's powerful clergy. His follower, John Murray (1741-1815), emigrated to the American colonies in 1770 to spread this doctrine of salvation for all, setting up the first Universalist Church in America at Gloucester, Massachusetts on Christmas Day, 1780. Murray is considered the father of organized Universalism because, under the less strict colonial religious laws, the sect was allowed to spread and flourish.

First Fascist Party

MUSSOLINI, BENITO—On the 23rd of March, 1919, Benito Mussolini founded the Fasci di Combattimento—the first fascist political party—in Milan, Italy. Born to socialist parents in 1883, Mussolini was himself an ardent socialist revolutionary until the outbreak of World War I. He was critically wounded on the battlefield and, after lengthy discussions with other war veterans, his politics took a 180-degree turn.

Mussolini was elected to the Italian Parliament in 1921; he took advantage of civic disorder to rise to positions of power in the cabinet, eventually becoming absolute dictator of Italy. He was executed in 1945 after a summary court-martial.

Largest Funeral

NASSER, GAMAL ABDUL—When Gamal Abdul Nasser died in 1970, an estimated four million people jammed the streets of Cairo, Egypt to witness the October funeral of their leader.

Born in 1918, Nasser had attended military school. As a young officer, he founded a Free Officers' Movement which, in 1952, successfully overthrew the monarchy of Egypt. In 1956, as premier, he nationalized the Suez Canal, provoking an invasion by French and British troops. In 1958, Nasser announced the unification of Egypt and Syria into the United Arab Republic.

First to Abolish Capital Punishment

NICHOLAS I—After the death of his brother, Tsar Alexander I, in 1825, Nicholas I (Nikolai Pavlovich 1796-1855) assumed power. The Decembrist Revolution erupted almost immediately, but was quickly squashed. Of the 579 Russians who were brought to trial, half were acquitted, the rest, excepting the five ringleaders who were hanged, were imprisoned. The public was amazed at the leniency of the punishment.

Soon thereafter, the tsar completely abolished capital punishment, opting instead for exile to Siberia except in cases of treason. Finland followed Russia's lead and also did away with the death penalty.

Christian Realist Philosophy

NIEBUHR, REINHOLD—Reinhold Niebuhr (1892-1971), a teacher at New York's Union Theological Seminary from 1928 to 1971, founded and developed the doctrine of Christian Realism. This outspoken Protestant theologian rejected both utopianism and cynicism, combining worldly pragmatism with the Biblical solution to problems brought about and ultimately resolvable by a fallible mankind. An influential spokesman for the non-Communist left wing in America, Niebuhr was the publisher of many books on Christian doctrine including a two-volume work, *Nature and Destiny of Man* (1943). In 1964, he was awarded the Presidential Freedom Medal by Lyndon B. Johnson.

First President to Resign

NIXON, RICHARD M.—During the Christmas of 1969, President Richard Milhous Nixon (1913-   ), and his wife, Pat, sent out an estimated 40,000 Christmas cards, a record as near as can be figured. Also in 1969, the most expensive automobile ever made was delivered to him at the White House. The specially-equipped and protected Lincoln Continental cost $500,000.

On August 8, 1974, the thirty-seventh president of the United States, disgraced by the Watergate scandals, became the first American president to resign from office.

First President of Ghana

NKRUMAH, KWAME—The African nation of Ghana, the first post-war independent African nation, was formed in 1957 by a merger of the Gold Coast and British Togoland. Instrumental in this effort was Kwame Nkrumah (1909-   ), prime minister of the Gold Coast from 1952 to 1957. He became prime minister of the new protectorate of Ghana in 1957 and, when it achieved full independence that year, became the new nation's first president. Deposed by a military coup in 1966, Nkrumah became a pan-African mediator and co-president of Guinea, a neighboring newly-independent state.

Only Pope to Visit U.S.

PAUL VI—The only pope ever to visit the United States was Pope Paul VI who, in the space of slightly more than 14 hours, arrived in New York City, visited with Francis Cardinal Spellman and President Lyndon B. Johnson, addressed the United Nations, gave a public mass at Yankee Stadium, visited the World's Fair and boarded a jet for his return to Rome. The New York visit was made on October 4, 1965. Approximately one million people saw the Italian head of the Roman Catholic Church in person; an additional 100,000,000 watched his public appearances on television. Paul, born Giovanni Montini in 1887, was archbishop of Milan and, later, became a cardinal before being elected pope in 1963.

Highest Price for Suit of Armor

PEMBROKE, EARL OF—In 1924, a record $125,000 was paid for a suit of armor allegedly made for the Earl of Pembroke. The earl for whom this suit was originally designed was quite possibly the third Earl of Pembroke, a patron of William Shakespeare, who lived from 1580 to 1630. A nephew of poet Sir Philip Sidney, he was an influential courtier in Queen Elizabeth's court. It is thought that the earl is the "Mr. W.H." to whom Shakespeare dedicated his sonnets, and that his mistress, Mary Fitton, was the Dark Lady of these sonnets. Shakespeare's 1623 First Folio was openly dedicated to the earl and his brother.

First New World Law Book

PENN, WILLIAM—William Penn (1644-1718), an English Quaker, was continually imprisoned because of his religious beliefs. The son of a British admiral, in 1681 Penn was given a tract of land in the New World on which to set up a colony free from religious persecution. The land was granted by the Crown as an inheritance claim filed by Penn, and the new colony was called Pennsylvania. In 1682, Penn laid out the plans for Philadelphia. In 1687, he authored the first law book published in America. Called *The Excellent Privilege of Liberty* . . . the 83-page book was printed by William Bradford of Philadelphia. Like most of Penn's works, this book discussed the legal foundations for free and liberal societies and advocated religious toleration. In 1698, the founder of Pennsylvania built the first stone bridge near Germantown.

First Woman Cabinet Member

PERKINS, FRANCES—Appointed secretary of labor by President Franklin D. Roosevelt, Frances Perkins (Mrs. Paul Caldwell Wilson (1882-1965) was sworn into the president's cabinet on March 4, 1933. The first female cabinet member remained in her post until June 30, 1945, which represented the longest continuous service for a United States cabinet officer up to that time. Mrs. Wilson, a sociologist who had been Industrial Commissioner of the State of New York, was ideally qualified to help carry out Roosevelt's New Deal.

First General of the U.S. Armies

PERSHING, JOHN J.—"Black Jack" Pershing (1860-1948), who commanded with distinction the American Expeditionary Force during the First World War, was unanimously approved by Congress as the first General of the newly-combined Armies of the United States. The appointment was ratified on September 4, 1919 under the "41 Statute L.283." Pershing, later Chief of Staff of the Army until his retirement in 1924, had served in the cavalry during the Indian campaigns in the American West, in the Spanish-American War and in the Philippines, where he waged a brutal campaign against the Moro Indians, annihilating them in 1913.

Longest Reign of a Monarch

PHARAOH PEPI II—Pepi II is thought to have lived between 2567 and 2473 B.C. and to have been a Pharaoh of Egypt for between 90 and 100 years. (It is difficult to determine exact dates because of the scarcity of VI Dynasty records.) Pepi II ruled successfully, largely because of his alliance with the Elephantine lords in the South, who waged victorious campaigns in Nubia and returned with many riches. Pepi negotiated advantageous trade agreements with Lebanon and Punt, and Egypt prospered during his very long reign.

First Secret Service Man

PINKERTON, ALLAN—President Abraham Lincoln formed the first Secret Service Bureau in 1861 and appointed Allan Pinkerton (1819-1884) as its first director. Before working in this position, Pinkerton, using the alias "Major Allan," had been a member of the staff of General George B. McClellan. Upon his retirement from the Secret Service, Pinkerton formed his own private detective agency, one of the first in the world. It still bears his name.

Longest Reigning Pope

PIUS IX—Of the 262 popes, the reign of Giovanni Maria Mastai-Ferretti was the longest. He reigned from June 16, 1846 until his death on February 7, 1878 at the age of 85. During his reign, Pius IX, in an attempt to regain power lost during the appropriation of the papal states, announced the doctrine of papal infallibility. He initiated the practice of retiring voluntarily as a prisoner of the Vatican Palace, a practice followed by all popes until 1929.

Greatest Ransom Demand

PIZARRO, FRANCISCO—The Spanish conquistador who conquered the Incas of Peru accomplished his mission in 1532 by kidnapping the Inca chief, Atahualpa, and holding him for ransom. Pizarro demanded a hall full of gold and silver worth an estimated $170 million. The demand was met, but the Inca was killed anyway.

Pizarro, born around the year 1470, came to the Americas in 1509 and was with Balboa when he saw the Pacific in 1513. He was assassinated in 1541 during a military squabble over the spoils of Peru.

First Dark Horse President

POLK, JAMES KNOX—When James Knox Polk (1795-1849) was nominated as the Democratic Party's presidential candidate on May 29, 1844, the news was relayed from Baltimore to Washington via telegraph. Never before had the telegraph been used in politics. The story of Polk's nomination was indeed extraordinary. The former governor of Tennessee and congressman for 14 years had not been mentioned at all on the first seven of the convention's ballots; on the eighth ballot he ran a distant third to Martin Van Buren (president 6 years before) and Michigan's Lewis Cass. On the ninth ballot, Polk was elected to the nomination unanimously. When Polk won the popular election in November, he became the first president to have previously been Speaker of the House of Representatives.

First to Import Camels to U.S.

PORTER, DAVID DIXON—As a Navy lieutenant in command of the storeship, *Supply*, David D. Porter (1813-1891) landed a shipment of 34 camels at Indianola, Texas on May 14, 1856. The shipment of animals from Smyrna, Turkey was the first of the species to be brought into the New World for commercial purposes. The Army would experiment with them as pack animals.

Porter, foster brother of another famous naval hero, David G. Farragut, distinguished himself in campaigns of the Mexican and Civil Wars. He was superintendent of the Naval Academy and was promoted to full admiral in 1870 following his tenure at Annapolis.

Founder of French Anarchism

PROUDHON, PIERRE JOSEPH—Called the "father of anarchy" in Europe, Frenchman Pierre Proudhon (1809-1865) was active in the socialist revolution of 1848 and was founder and editor of the *Le Peuple* series of radical newspapers from 1848 to 1850. Proudhon's many treatises and pamphlets on radicalism scorned all existing political organizations. His studies on poverty led him to the conclusion that "property is theft," an idea which led him to anarchism and syndicalism. One of his severest critics and ideological opponents was the German Communist, Karl Marx.

First U.S. Attorney General

RANDOLPH, EDMUND JENNINGS—At the outbreak of the American Revolution in 1776, Edmund Randolph (1753-1813) became an aide to General George Washington. Later, following the lessening of hostilities with Britain, he served as a delegate to the Continental Congress (1779-1782) and as Governor of Virginia (1786-1788). At the Constitutional Convention of 1787, Randolph proposed the idea of creating two congressional houses. In the act that established the Judicial Courts of the new country, Randolph was appointed the first Attorney General (1789-1794) by Washington and later State Secretary (1794-1795).

First U.S. Congresswoman

RANKIN, JEANNETTE—The first United States congresswoman, Jeannette Rankin (1880-1973), was elected to the House of Representatives as a Republican from Montana in 1916, and again in 1940. She cast a vote against American participation in World War I on April 7, 1917, and against participation in World War II on December 8, 1941. She remarked once that she hoped she would never see a third world war. But, if she was in a position to, "I'd surely vote against it."

Active in the fight for women's suffrage, Rankin was a member of the National Women's Trade Union League and, between congressional terms, served as a lobbyist and social worker in Montana and Washington, D.C.

Winner of Shortest War

RAWSON, SIR HARRY H.—From 9:02 to 9:40 a.m. on the morning of August 27, 1896, the shortest recorded war in history was fought. The battle between Great Britain and Zanzibar consisted of the British fleet's 38-minute bombardment of the palace of the Sultan Sa'id Khalid.

The sultan, who had taken control of the British owned African state, was ordered to surrender. Upon his refusal, Rear-admiral Harry Holdsworth Rawson, the British fleet commander, ordered his men to shell the palace; thirty-eight minutes later the sultan raised the white flag. Rawson received the Brilliant Star of Zanzibar for his efforts to restore the Sultanate to Hamud ibn Muhammad.

First Female in House of Lords

READING, STELLA—The House of Lords, the upper branch of the legislature of Great Britain, is made up of the nobility and high ranking clergy. The parliamentary body never had a female member until 1958, when the Marchioness of Reading took her seat for the first time. Stella Reading (1894-1971), a prominent British social worker, had founded and chaired the Women's Voluntary Services for Civil Defense in 1938. After the war, she sponsored the Women's Home Industries, Ltd.

First Nuclear Submarine

RICKOVER, HYMAN—The United States nuclear submarine, *Nautilus,* was launched at Groton, Connecticut on January 21, 1954. The first atom-powered vessel in history, capable of traveling at a speed of 20 knots, was designed by Admiral Hyman Rickover to carry 96 men.

The maiden voyage of the *Nautilus,* under the command of Captain E. P. Wilkinson, lasted two years and covered 69,138 miles before needing refueling. Submerged, the nuclear vessel displaced 3,747 tons of water. The *Nautilus* has since made extensive polar explorations as well as setting long distance records for submerged sailing.

Only Four-Term U.S. President

ROOSEVELT, FRANKLIN D.—The extensive traveling done by the thirty-second president of the United States, Franklin D. Roosevelt (1882-1945), was of landmark significance. As president, Roosevelt was the first to visit a foreign country (Brazil) during wartime. He was also the first president to broadcast in a foreign country and in a foreign language (French), the first to fly in an airplane, and the first president whose mother was able to vote for him (his was the first president's mother to be alive after suffrage was passed). Most importantly, FDR served as president for four terms, from 1933 until his death in 1945, and guided a stricken world through the Great Depression and World War II.

Handshaking Record

ROOSEVELT, THEODORE—On New Year's Day, 1907, President Teddy Roosevelt shook hands with a record-making 8,513 people during the New Year's presentation at the White House. (Although no previous handshaking record was in existence, this count has become an acknowledged standard.)

Roosevelt, who lived from 1858 to 1919, was renowned as a conservationist and naturalist before and after his two-term presidency. In 1906, he became the first American to win a Nobel Prize. The Peace prize was awarded to Roosevelt for negotiating a conclusion to the Russo-Japanese War of 1904-1906.

First U.S. Abolitionist

RUSH, BENJAMIN—American physician Benjamin Rush was born near Philadelphia, Pennsylvania in 1745. In the late 1700s, he founded the first anti-slavery society in America. In 1769, Rush delivered lectures on chemistry at the Philadelphia Medical School and, later, at the University of Pennsylvania.

Surgeon General of the Continental Army during the Revolution, Dr. Rush was a signer of the Declaration of Independence. He lived his entire life in Philadelphia and was treasurer of the United States Mint, located in his hometown, from its beginnings during Washington's administration until his death in 1813.

Record Pole-Sitter

SAINT DANIEL—Not to be confused with Daniel the prophet, this monk lived in the Middle East from 409 to 493 A.D. St. Daniel was known as Stylites, Greek for "man of the pillar."

In Syria, St. Daniel sat atop a pillar of stone for 33 years and three months, which is undoubtedly the all-time pole-sitting record. The modern record for pole-sitting was set by a woman in Yakima, Washington; she lingered for a mere 252 days. Although he sat for meditative and ascetic purposes only, St. Daniel's feat is considered to be the oldest recorded human *stunt*.

Longest Tenure of a Head of State

SALAZAR, ANTONIO—Antonio de Oliviera Salazar (1899-1970) served as the Portuguese Council of Ministers' president for more than 36 years, the longest tenure of any head of state not designated to rule for life. Salazar took office in politically unstable Portugal in 1932 and, by adopting policies of conciliation and appeasement with both the Fascists and the Allies, steered his country clear of direct involvement in the Spanish Civil War and World War II. The virtual dictator of what has been called Western Europe's most backward country, Salazar was succeeded by Marcello Caetano after he fell into a coma on September 16, 1968.

Man with the Most Medals

SELASSIE, HAILE—His Imperial Majesty Haile Selassie of Ethiopia, known as the Lion of Judah and descended from Solomon and the Queen of Sheba, wore over 50 medals among the 14 rows of ribbons on his chest. Selassie, who ruled Ethiopia during the period of Italian dictator Mussolini's invasion of his country, fought for international assistance in the League of Nations. Help was denied, thus making clear the League's impotence. The Ethiopian ruler, born Ras Tafari Makonnen in 1892, was deposed in a military coup in 1974 and died while under house arrest in 1975.

Many of the emperor's medals were bestowed upon him by foreign nations who had been moved by his impassioned defense of Ethiopia (then Abyssinia) against the Fascists and, later, during World War II.

First American-Born Saint

SETON, ELIZABETH—Elizabeth Seton, the daughter of a Protestan doctor, was born in New York City in 1774. Upon her conversion to Catholicism after a visit to Italy in 1804, she was forced to leave her home because of the existing hostility toward Papists. She resettled in Emmitsburg, Maryland, where she set up a convent and a school. Her subsequent devotion to teaching and humanitarian principles led to her founding and leading the first American sisterhood, the Sisters of Charity of St. Joseph in 1809. Forty-six-year-old Mother Seton died of tuberculosis in 1821 at St. Joseph's, which has since become a college for women.

On September 14, 1975, at 9:30 a.m., Pope Paul VI proclaimed sainthood upon Mother Elizabeth Seton as Saint Elizabeth Ann. The choir that sang at her canonization ceremony was directed by Sister Jane Marie Perrot, the first woman ever to direct a choir at a papal function.

First Emperor of China

SHIH HUANG TI—By the age of 12, Shih Huang Ti was the chief warlord of the State of Ch'in. By the age of 32, he consolidated all of the small warring states of China into one unified nation and appointed himself its first emperor. Living between 259 and 210 B.C., Shih began the construction of the Great Wall of China, but also destroyed many of China's libraries and educational institutions.

Only American to Marry Reigning King

SIMPSON, WALLIS WARFIELD—On June 3, 1937, Wallis Simpson of Baltimore, Maryland married Edward VIII, Edward Albert Christian George Andrew Patrick David, future Duke of Windsor. The marriage ceremony was performed in Monts, France by the Reverend Robert Anderson Jardine.

Edward, who had acceded to the British throne on January 20, 1936, abdicated on December 11, 1936, before officially receiving the crown. The abdication was brought on by the opposition of the British government to the marriage of their king to Wallis Simpson, a foreigner and twice-divorced woman. Upon his abdication, Edward was named Duke of Windsor, a position which demanded that he carry out specified royal functions. As part of his duties, he acted as governor of the Bahamas between 1940 and 1945. The Duke of Windsor died in 1972.

The Duchess performed supervisory work with the Red Cross during the war and has since become a patron of high fashion and art.

Founder of Mormon Church

SMITH, JOSEPH—The Church of Jesus Christ of the Latter-Day Saints was founded by Joseph Smith (1805-1844) in Fayette, New York, following the publication, in 1830, of *The Book of Mormon*. A visionary from the age of ten, Smith claimed that, in a vision, he had been brought golden tablets by an angel; the translation of these tablets formed the basis for his *Book*.

Claiming to be as valid as the scriptures of Christians and Jews, *The Book of Mormon's* most controversial tenet is polygamy, or the freedom of a man to take more than one wife. It was over this issue that Smith was lynched by a mob in Carthage, Illinois in 1844 while on a pilgrimage with his followers. The Mormons have (1976) an estimated 1.5 million followers in the United States.

"Mr. Europe"

SPAAK, PAUL-HENRI—Paul-Henri Spaak (1890-1972), a Belgian statesman, worked tirelessly for the recovery of Europe after World War II. One of the writers of the United Nations charter, he became the first president of the General Assembly in 1946.

In 1957, Spaak signed the Treaties of Rome, creating the Common Market. Spoken of as "Mr. Europe" for his humanitarian efforts, he helped form the North Atlantic Treaty Organization, and served as its secretary-general from 1957-1961.

First Colonial Military Leader

STANDISH, MILES—Captain Miles Standish (1584?-1656) was a soldier in England before undertaking to accompany the Pilgrims (the band of English Puritans who founded Plymouth Colony) to America in 1620. Neither a Puritan nor an Independent, Standish was looked upon as a protector of the settlers, and was elected unanimously as the captain of the colony's military force in 1621.

First American Suffrage Group

STANTON, ELIZABETH CADY—A preeminent American suffragette, Elizabeth Cady Stanton (1815-1902) organized the first women's convention supporting women's voting rights. The meeting was held in July, 1848 at Seneca Falls, New York. Stanton, along with Susan B. Anthony, formed the National Women's Suffrage Association in 1869. On January 20th of that year, when she addressed the Senate in support of voting rights for Washington, D.C. women, Elizabeth became the first female witness at a United States congressional hearing.

First Jewish U.S. Cabinet Member

STRAUS, OSCAR S.—A member of the family which owned a controlling interest in the Macy's department store chain, Oscar S. Straus (1850-1926), was a minister to Turkey (1887-1889, 1898-1900) and, later, a permanent member of the Hague Tribunal, a world court established in 1899 for the settling of international legal disputes. In 1906, when the Department of Commerce and Labor was established by President Theodore Roosevelt, Straus was chosen as its first secretary. The first Jewish member of a presidential cabinet was also one of the founders of the American Jewish Historical Society and the Young Men's Hebrew Association in New York (1874). When Turkey was recognized as a sovereign power by the United States in 1909, Oscar Straus became the first United States ambassador to that country (1909-1910).

World's Largest Religious Building

SURYAVARMAN II—Between 1113 and 1150 A.D., Angkor Wat ("City Temple") was built to honor the Hindu god, Vishnu. Covering 402 acres, the religious structure is the largest of its kind ever built. King of the Khymers, Suryavarman II, had the temple constructed in what is now Khymers, Cambodia. Its outermost wall, the curtain wall, measures 1,400 by 1,400 yards. Angkor Wat was abandoned by the Khymers in 1432 and, up until the later years of the Vietnam War, was a popular attraction for lovers of architecture. At its height, 80,000 people frequented Angkor Wat.

First Air Force Secretary

SYMINGTON, WILLIAM STUART—President Harry S. Truman created the Department of the Air Force and Stuart Symington was chosen as its first secretary. Sworn in on September 18, 1947 in Washington, D. C. by Chief Justice of the Supreme Court Frederick Moore Vinson, Symington served until April 24, 1950, his successor being Thomas Knight Finletter. Long distinguished in government, Symington is presently the senior senator from the state of Missouri, having first won election there in 1952, the first time he had ever run for office.

Only President to Become Chief Justice

TAFT, WILLIAM HOWARD—William Howard Taft (1857-1936), an eminent jurist, was appointed the first United States civil governor of the Philippines in 1901. Under Theodore Roosevelt, Taft was secretary of war and provisional governor of Cuba. He was elected President Roosevelt's successor in 1908, but ran unsuccessfully in 1912; Roosevelt opposed him, splitting the vote and giving the election to Woodrow Wilson. In 1910, Taft became the first president to throw out the first ball of the baseball season. On June 30, 1921, Taft was appointed Chief Justice of the Supreme Court, the only ex-president to have been so honored.

Inventor of the Submachine Gun

THOMPSON, JOHN T.—The Auto-Ordinance Company, organized by Brigadier General John Taliaferro Thompson (1860-1940) in 1915, attached the Thompson submachine gun (a light-weight semiautomatic rifle) to the recently invented automobile, producing a valuable military aid.

Thompson, chief of the U.S. Army Ordinance Corps Small Arms Division (1917-1919) produced his submachine gun between 1913 and 1915, refining its cooling and cartridge flow mechanism after the First World War.

The "Tommy gun," as it came to be called, was capable of firing up to 800 rounds of .45-calibre rifle bullets per minute, and had the advantage of being easy for an infantryman to carry. After being successfully used in the First World War, the Thompson submachine gun found its way into the hands of bootleggers and racketeers, who used it extensively in their bloody gang wars. Public sale was forbidden in the late 1920s.

First Senator Elected by Write-In Vote

THURMOND, STROM—In 1954, Democrat Strom Thurmond, running as an independent write-in candidate, garnered 139,106 votes and took the South Carolina senatorial election from the legitimate Democratic candidate, Edgar Brown. Brown, the state Democratic Executive Committee nominee, received 80,956 votes. Thurmond, elected on November 2, 1954, served until January 3, 1961. Thurmond was later re-elected as the Democratic candidate and has been a member of the Senate ever since.

Inventor of the Revolving Gun Turret

TIMBY, THEODORE RUGGLES—The rather unprepossessing name of Theodore Ruggles Timby (1822-1909) will forever be associated with a military device that revolutionized naval warfare. Timby invented the revolving gun turret, first used on the Union ironclad, *Monitor*. The turret enabled gunners to fire in a 360-degree arc, thereby eliminating all previous naval strategy involving ship positioning and "broadsides." Timby, who also suggested the use of ironclad protection for vessels, had explained his idea to the War Department as early as 1841. It was not implemented, however, until the historic battle with the Confederate ironclad, *Virginia*, on March 9, 1862, more than 20 years later.

First Grand Inquisitor of Spain

TORQUEMADA, TOMAS DE—Tomas de Torquemada (1420-1498), a Dominican monk, rose to be prior of Segovia. As his influence with Spain's rulers, Isabela and Ferdinand, increased, the cruel prelate arranged for the creation of the Holy Office of the Inquisition. Having received the approval of Pope Sixtus IV, Torquemada became the first inquisitor general of Spain. Beginning in 1480, the Inquisition was responsible for burning 2,000 people at the stake. A Spanish state tribunal, the Inquisition tried religious minorities (especially Jews) and political dissidents. Torture was employed regularly as a means of judicial inquiry. Torquemada jailed his fellow Dominican, the Archbishop of Toledo, for 17 years and twice jailed Ignatius of Loyola. The Inquisition was finally abolished 350 years later.

Most Self-Dedicated Statues

TRUJILLO, RAFAEL—The man who raised the most statues to himself was the president of the Dominican Republic, Generalissimo Dr. Rafael Leonidas Trujillo y Molina (1891-1961). When counted in 1960, there were more than 2,000 such self-tributes. In addition, Trujillo named the country's highest mountain, the capital city, and two provinces in his own honor.

Trujillo was assassinated on May 30, 1961, reportedly by agents of the American Central Intelligence Agency. Dominicans still celebrate the day as a public holiday.

First President Wed in Office

TYLER, JOHN—On June 25, 1844, President John Tyler (1790-1862) married Julia Gardiner in New York City. Never before had a president taken the marriage vows while in office. Tyler, the tenth president, took over the office upon the death of William Henry Harrison in 1841. When, in 1842, the House asked by what authority Tyler had created a New York Custom House investigation committee, he became the first president requested by Congress to justify the forming of a presidential committee.

After serving his presidential term, Tyler retired from public life. In 1861, however, he became the only president to be elected as an official of another nation (he was elected to the Provisional Congress of the Confederate States). Tyler died before the Congress convened for the first time.

First President Born a Citizen

VAN BUREN, MARTIN—The distinguished political figure from New York was born in Kinderhook on December 5, 1782, the first president to be born a citizen of the United States. Martin

Van Buren was a senator, governor of New York State, secretary of state under Andrew Jackson, and later his vice-president. He was elected to one presidential term in 1836, but the Panic of 1837 and its attendant depression cost him re-election in 1840. Van Buren's anti-slavery stand cost him the Democratic nomination in 1844. He died in 1862.

First U.S. Army Inspector General

VON STEUBEN, FRIEDRICH WILHELM—German Baron Friedrich Wilhelm von Steuben (1730-1794), a veteran of the Seven Years' War (1756-1763) and an aide to Frederick the Great of Prussia (1762), was persuaded to come to the Colonies to help the newly-organized Continental Army. In 1777, he was appointed Inspector General of the Colonial troops. In 1779, he published the first military drill manual printed in America. Von Steuben's excellent organization of the army was evident at the Battle of Monmouth (June 28, 1778) when he turned a retreat into a battle with his tactics and discipline. He was present at Valley Forge during the winter of 1778 and at Yorktown for the final United States victory. Von Steuben was rewarded with a pension and a tract of land by the new government, for his contribution to the American cause.

First Black on U.S. Coin

WASHINGTON, BOOKER T.—The founder of the Tuskegee Institute and the National Negro Business League, and the developer of the concept of "night school" was the distinguished American educator Booker T. Washington (1856-1915). His struggle to provide American black people with the educational facilities needed to advance their cause included extended lecture tours, fund-raising projects and registration drives. He authored many books on education as well as an autobiography, *Up From Slavery*, and was the recipient of honorary degrees from Harvard and Dartmouth Universities. In 1940, a ten-cent postage stamp bearing his likeness was issued. And, in 1946, a fifty-cent silver commemorative piece, the first U.S. currency to bear a black man's picture, was issued.

First U.S. President

WASHINGTON, GEORGE—George Washington (1732-1799) was the only president ever to run for the office unopposed. When he began his term in 1789, he coined the title "Mr. President" in response to citizen confusion about whether to call him "Your Majesty" or "Your Highness."

Washington was appointed the first General of the Continental Army by the Second Continental Congress on June 15, 1775. He was to be paid $500 a month, but served without recompense. He was also the recipient of the first mule on American soil: King Charles III of Spain sent him two jacks on October 26, 1785, the first animals of their kind in America.

Currency with a Woman's Picture

WASHINGTON, MARTHA—Excluding the female depiction of "Liberty," Martha Washington (1732-1802), our first First Lady (1789-1797), is the only woman to appear on United States currency. In 1886, the one-dollar silver certificate bore her portrait, the reverse being a field of green with lathe work ornamentation.

A commemorative quarter piece, bearing the face of Queen Isabella of Spain was struck for the World's Columbian Exposition in 1893, but these coins were few in number. They were snapped up as collector's items and never reached general circulation.

Most Expensive Watch

WELLESLEY, ARTHUR—The first Duke of Wellington, Arthur Wellesley (1769-1852), the heroic British general who defeated Napoleon at Waterloo in 1815, released a homing pigeon from a ship off the Ichabo Islands, West Africa on April 8, 1845. Fifty-five days later, it dropped dead a mile from its home loft in London, England, having flown an estimated 7,000 miles, the longest recorded flight for a homing pigeon.

A watch carried by Wellington brought $77,000 at an auction in 1964. Made in Paris in 1807, it is the highest auction price ever paid for a watch.

World's Wealthiest Woman

WILHELMINA, PRINCESS—Wilhelmina Helena Pauline Maria (1880-1962) of Orange-Nassau was probably the world's richest woman. Born in 1880, she became queen of the Netherlands at the age of 10. One of the best loved Dutch queens, she reigned until her abdication on September 4, 1948.

Wilhelmina's fortune was estimated at over $500,000,000. She fled her country when the Nazis assumed power in 1940, but returned after liberation and ruled until ill health forced her to yield the throne to her daughter, Juliana.

Founder of R. I. Baptist Church

WILLIAMS, ROGER—Having been forced to leave both England and the Massachusetts colony because of his religious beliefs, Roger Williams (1603?-1683) established Providence, Rhode Island in 1636. Known as the "Apostle of Religious Liberty," Williams established America's first Baptist Church in 1639 in Providence. Five years later, in Newport, Rhode Island, Dr. John Clarke set up a First Baptist Church, under the direction of Williams. About the same time, Williams himself rejected all formal creeds, and declared that people of all religions were welcome to live in his colony. He received a royal charter for Rhode Island in 1644 and served as its president from 1654 to 1657.

League of Nations Founder

WILSON, WOODROW—President and former professor of Princeton University, Woodrow Wilson (1856-1924) resigned to run for president of the United States. The twenty-eighth president was elected to two consecutive terms of office, serving from 1913 to 1921. He guided the country through prohibition and a world war, and created the Federal Reserve system and the Federal Trade Commission.

As head United States delegate to the World War I peace negotiations, Wilson pushed for the establishment of the League of Nations. This American patriot, who was awarded the Nobel Peace Prize in 1919, was honored posthumously in 1934 when his picture was placed on the highest denomination currency ever issued—the United States $100,000 bill.

First Apple Importer in America

WINTHROP, JOHN—As colonial governor of Massachusetts, John Winthrop (1588-1649) imported the first apples to America, from England, in 1629. The seeds he planted near Boston grew the first apple trees in the New World and, on October 10, 1639, their first fruit was harvested. Winthrop's successor as governor, John Endicott, planted the first apple nursery at Danvers, Massachusetts.

First Female U.S. Presidential Candidate

WOODHULL, VICTORIA CLAFLIN—The Equal Rights Party, which was organized at the convention of the National Women's Suffrage Association, nominated the first woman presidential candidate on May 10, 1872. Their nominee, Victoria Claflin

Woodhull (1838-1927), was also endorsed by the People's Party and the National Radical Reformers. Ulysses S. Grant was elected that year by a landslide.

A journalist by trade, Woodhull had founded the *Woodhull and Claflin's Weekly* with her sister, Tennessee Claflin, two years before her nomination. In it, she stated her platform—complete emancipation of women in all political and social areas—and drew many readers with her exposés of the sex scandals of the day.

SCIENCE

Father of Electromagnetism

AMPÈRE, ANDRÉ MARIE—A French mathematician and physicist, André Marie Ampère (1775-1836), did his important work while his native France was embroiled in revolution. He developed the Ampère law of electromagnetism, which postulated that magnetism is a form of electricity. He explained aspects of his theories of electrodynamics in two publications: *Ampère's Rule* (sometimes called *The Right-Hand Rule*) and *Ampère's Theorem* (which dealt with magnetic fields). Ampère's idea that electrical currents move in different directions depending on the magnetic field, is one of the important scientific discoveries of his age. The *ampère,* the standard unit for measuring the strength of an electric current is named for him.

Discoverer of the Positron

ANDERSON, CARL DAVID—In physics, an *electron* is a negatively-charged atomic particle; a *proton* is a positively-charged unit. In 1932, Carl D. Anderson (1905-) discovered the *positron,* which he described as an electron with a positive electrical charge. With his associate, Seth Neddermeyer, Anderson proved that positrons could be produced by bombarding aluminum and lead with gamma rays. In 1937, they discovered the *meson,* a particle with a mass between that of a proton and an electron. These discoveries were made while Anderson was conducting a study of cosmic rays, for which he shared the 1936 Nobel Physics Prize with the Austrian scientist, Victor Hess.

The Apgar Score System

APGAR, VIRGINIA—The Apgar Score System, devised and refined in the 1950s, is a reliable method of evaluating the health of newborn children. In the system, various physiological and heredity factors, and observed tendencies are combined to give an accurate portrait of the condition of an infant. The developer of the method, Dr. Virginia Apgar (1909-1974), worked for the National Foundation of the March of Dimes, first as division head for Congenital Malformations, later as director of Basic Research and, finally, as senior vice-president for Medical Affairs. In 1972, she co-authored *Is My Baby All Right?*, a best-selling handbook for young mothers.

The Lever Principle

ARCHIMEDES—The Greek scientist, Archimedes, born in Syracuse in 287 B.C., was the first man to understand how the lever works. In introducing the principle, Archimedes dramatically stated: "Give me a place to stand and I'll move the world," affirming his belief that a long flat object placed under a heavy object and on top of a pivotal object (fulcrum) could lift that heavy object when pressure was applied to its other end.

Archimedes was also the inventor of a method of raising water by simply turning a wooden screw, a method still used today for irrigation purposes. The *Archimedean Screw* is made up of a helix inside a water tight tube, the lower end of which is dipped in the water. When the helix is turned, the water circles up to the top of the tube, thus raising the water level. His law of hydrostatics was also an important scientific breakthrough.

The Lightest Metal

ARFWEDSON, JOHAN AUGUST—Chemist Johan Arfwedson, born in Sweden in 1792, is the discoverer of lithium, the lightest of all metals. In 1817, Arfwedson found that lithium, light golden brown in color, has a density of a mere 0.5333 grams per cubic centimeter. Its isotope, Li6, is even lighter: its density is 0.46.6 gram per cubic centimeter. Li6 is so chemically reactive that it must be stored under naptha. Other forms of lithium, particularly lithium salts, are used for medicinal purposes.

First to Band Birds

AUDUBON, JOHN JAMES—American ornithologist, painter and naturalist John J. Audubon (1785-1851) traveled extensively in

North America in the early nineteenth century. In 1803, he banded a group of phoebes with silver wire for purposes of identification at Mill Grove Farm, Pennsylvania, the first recorded banding of birds to take place. He later recovered two of the banded birds for use in his migration studies.

Audubon compiled *The Birds of America,* a collection of more than one thousand (435 were hand-colored plates) illustrations of 490 species, along with copious notes on their habits and migratory patterns. The work is still considered one of the greatest wildlife books ever produced. The first ten engravings appeared in 1827, but it was not until 11 years and several publishers later that the complete *Birds* was made available. The total number of copies in print is less than 200.

First Heart Transplant

BARNARD, CHRISTIAAN—On December 2, 1967, in Cape Town, South Africa, Louis Washansky, a sufferer of heart disease, received the heart of Denise Darvali, the 25-year-old victim of a traffic accident. The intricate operation performed by Dr. Christiaan Barnard lasted six hours and required the assistance of 30 doctors and nurses. Eighteen days later, heart transplant recipient Washansky died of pneumonia.

First New World Botanical Garden

BARTRAM, JOHN—Carl Linnaeus, the Swedish botanist, called John Bartram "the greatest natural botanist in the world." Former botanist to English King George III, Bartram moved to America in the 1720s. He settled in Philadelphia, where he set up a laboratory to conduct his studies. In 1728, Bartram laid out the first New World botanical garden. The visual wonder, which occupies six acres on the Banks of Philadelphia's Schuyler River, between Eastwick and 43rd Streets, still exists today.

The Wilson Cloud Chamber

BLACKETT, P. M. S.—P. M. S. Blackett (later Baron Blackett) (1897-1974), a distinguished British nuclear physicist, was one of the heroes of the Battle of Britain during World War II. His research in the field of radar was immeasurably helpful when Western Europe realized that German bombing attacks were imminent. Blackett's research on the nature of matter was used by the Allies to correctly identify objects appearing on the radar screen.

In 1948, Blackett was awarded the Nobel Physics Prize for his improvements of the Wilson Cloud Chamber, which allows the tracks of radio-active particles to be photographed as they pass through a vaporized enclosure. Cosmic ray showers and positive and negative electrons were among the phenomena discovered by Blackett utilizing the improved Cloud Chamber. His cosmic radiation studies led him to first develop the idea of operations research, which he taught for two decades at the University of London and Victoria University in Manchester.

First Woman Doctor

BLACKWELL, ELIZABETH—The male medical students at the Geneva Medical Institute were given the option by the institute's administration of admitting or rejecting the application of Elizabeth Blackwell. Much to the administration's surprise, the males accepted her application unanimously. On January 23, 1849 Elizabeth Blackwell received her M.D. degree, thus becoming the first professionally qualified woman doctor.

In 1876, in London, Dr. Blackwell published *Counsel to Parents on the Moral Education of Their Children*, the first sex education manual.

The Gasoline Pump

BOWSER, SYLVANUS F.—Sylvanus F. Bowser (1851-1915), with his brother, Augustus, of Fort Wayne, Indiana, produced the first gasoline pump in 1885. First sold to one Jake D. Gomper for the purpose of fueling his stove, the one-barrel tank was modified and adapted to the automobile later in the century. Patented in 1887, the device had valves made of Vermont marble and mechanical parts made of wood. The Bowsers embarked on a highly successful business in 1888.

First Presidential Photo

BRADY, MATHEW B.—In 1843, Samuel F. B. Morse, the inventor of the telegraph code, taught Matthew Brady (1823?-1896) how to develop photographs. Brady soon set up his own studio in New York City and, in 1849, made the first daguerrotype of President James Knox Polk.

Brady was granted Army permission to follow the troops during the Civil War. As a result, he produced the first news photographs—an extensive documentary (7,000 photographs) —of the conflict. Brady, who also experimented successfully with a new developing process called the *wet-plate process,* is perhaps best known for his photographs of President Lincoln, taken after 1860.

First Cathode Ray Tube

BRAUN, CARL FERDINAND—The first commercially successful cathode ray tube was produced by Carl Braun in 1897. The cathode ray tube is one of the devices used by Boris Rosing of Russia in the earliest "electric vision" machine, or television, in 1907.

Braun's experiments with electricity, while he was director of the Physical Institute in Strasbourg, Germany, led to the invention of the *Braun electrometer,* a device which measures voltage but doesn't draw current while doing so. He was also instrumental, with Marconi, in the development of the wireless telegraph and shared with him the 1909 Nobel Prize in Physics.

The Bunsen Burner

BUNSEN, ROBERT WILHELM—The German chemist, Robert Wilhelm Bunsen (1811-1899), evolved a method of gas analysis which led to his discovery of the elements *cesium* and *rubidium.* Perhaps as important is his invention of the *Bunsen burner,* a small gas burner that produces a hot, blue flame. The burner consists of a hollow metal tube with adjustable holes in the bottom for admitting air to be mixed with gas. It is one of the most important tools used by chemists the world over.

The Differential Analyzer

BUSH, VANNEVAR—The mathematical robot which later became the basis for the *analog* computer was invented by Vannevar Bush (1890-1974) in the 1930s. This *differential analyzer,* used for the quick solution of long mathematical problems, later led Bush to invent the *network analyzer,* a device used to test the strain on electric power systems by miniaturizing them electronically in the same way that the differential analyzer miniaturizes sets of data for compact evaluation. This computer was used during World War II to solve military problems involving acoustics, atomic physics and ballistics. Bush was one of the driving forces behind the mobilization of United States scientists in support of the Allied war effort. He also improved upon the vacuum tube design and the four-engine bomber and was the inventor of such devices as the justifying typewriter, the rapid selector and the cinema integraph.

Greek Fire

CALLIMACHUS—The continuous push to the West by the medieval Arabs, called Saracens, prompted the development of many ingenious weapons of war by the Greeks in the Balkan area. For the defense of the Greek-owned city of Constantinople in 670 A.D., a projectile was fashioned out of semisolid pitched tar mixed with sulphur and naptha; the projectile exploded into flame upon contact. When doused with water, the flame spread still further.` The inventor of this weapon, Callimachus (also called Callinicus, 620 A.D.- ?) of Constantinople, called it "Greek Fire." For 400 years, Greek Fire changed the tactics of war.

Discoverer of Hydrogen

CAVENDISH, HENRY—The son of British royalty, Henry Cavendish was a recluse for most of his adult life. Despite this, his scientific observation about the nature of heat was remarkably accurate.

In 1766, Cavendish discovered a gas which he called "inflammable air." (Lavoisier later termed it "hydrogen.") After much experimentation, Cavendish concluded that water was made up of oxygen and his "inflammable air." Later, based on measurements of hydrogen, he made astute analyses of the density of matter.

Discoverer of the Neutron

CHADWICK, JAMES—While working with the great British scientist Ernst, discoverer of the proton in 1922, James Chadwick (1891-1974) learned about the effect of alpha particle bombardment on a nucleus. This laid the groundwork for his 1932 discovery of the *neutron*, the projectile that makes uranium fission possible. The neutron is a particle in the nucleus of an atom which has no electrical (plus or minus) charge. A neutron is of slightly greater mass than a proton; the two particles are now considered the basic building blocks of all atomic nuclei. Chadwick won the 1935 Nobel Prize in Physics for his discovery.

In 1941, he began work with "Tube Alloys," the code name for British nuclear weapons. For his work with a British research team during World War II, Chadwick was knighted in January of 1945.

Decoder of Egyptian Hieroglyphics

CHAMPOLLION, JEAN-FRANCOIS—Until 1822, the secrets of the ancient Egyptians had been obscured by the mystery of their language. In that year, a young ancient history professor named Jean-Francois Champollion discovered the key to the mystery. By deciphering the Rosetta stone, a tablet of black basalt found at Rosetta (a town in Egypt at one of the mouths of the Nile), he discovered that hieroglyphics are comprised of figurative, ideographic and alphabetic elements. The stone had writings in three different languages and Champollion, translating the ancient Greek passages, was able to compare it to the Egyptian pictographs and break the code.

First Electric Telegraph

COOKE, W. F. & WHEATSTONE, CHARLES—W. F. Cooke, a retired Indian Army soldier, developed the first electric-powered telegraph in 1837. He found it an efficient means of communication along the rapidly expanding railway lines. Professor Wheatstone of King's College in England went into partnership with Cooke and, in 1838, the pair installed their first telegraph line along the Great Western Railway between London and West Drayton. The original telegraph had five needles that pointed to various letters. By 1838, a code had been developed which required only two needles.

Inventor of the Aqualung

COUSTEAU, JACQUES-YVES—Cousteau, the great French oceanographer and explorer, was a commandant in the French Navy in the summer of 1943 when he devised a means of supplying oxygen to deep sea divers. His invention, the *aqualung* or *scuba* (self-contained underwater breathing apparatus), utilizes a regulator that forced compressed air into the lungs of the swimmer.

After World War II, Cousteau set up his own floating laboratory, the *Calypso,* and, on July 29, 1956, anchored it in Romanche Trench in the Atlantic Ocean. The anchor, secured to a 5½-mile nylon cord, was lowered 24,600 feet in the water, the deepest an anchor has ever been dropped.

First to Use Machine Valve

CTESIBIUS—Though primitive valves have an ancient beginning, it was the Greek scientist Ctesibius who, in fashioning a force-pump, introduced the earliest documented valve for machine use. Described as "coins" at the tops of the pipes, which allowed water to enter but not leave the pipes, these flap-valves were circular in shape. Such "coins" were also used for the ventilation of roofs. Ctesibius used another kind of valve—the *slide valve*—in his hydraulic musical organ.

Ctesibius, who attended and later taught at a school of mechanics in Greece under the Ptolemaic pharaohs, probably lived between 300 and 230 B.C., under the reigns of Philadelphus and Euergetcs I (246-221 B.C.).

The Radio Amplifier

DeFOREST, LEE—The man who introduced the original radio girl in 1916 and who had, in 1910, first broadcast Enrico Caruso from the Metropolitan Opera House was Lee DeForest (1874-1961), one of radio's great pioneers. The revolutionary *audion tube,* which he perfected in 1906, made possible the electrical amplification of sound over radio transmitters and receivers. This radio amplifier was based on the triode, a three-electrode vacuum tube with the capability of boosting the transmission of sound in hearing aids, public address systems, television and phonographs. DeForest also worked on a process that would make it possible to add sound to motion picture film.

Founder of Analytical Geometry

DESCARTES, RENÉ—René Descartes' (1596-1650) principle of the thinking self ("I think, therefore I am") was the cornerstone of all his pioneer work in physiology, music theory and algebra. His philosophy, called *Cartesianism,* postulated the distinctness and clarity of ideas as a criterion for truth. He devised a system of plotting curves represented by equations—the so-called *Cartesian coordinates*—paving the way for Newton and Leibniz to produce the calculus. Descartes introduced the use of exponents and the square root sign. He set up the system of constants as the first letters of the alphabet and variables as the last ones still in use today. For combining algebra and geometry in a way which defines geometric figures using algebraic functions, Descartes can be said to be the founder of *analytical geometry.*

Discoverer of the Heaviest Gas

DORN, FRIEDRICH ERNST—Element number 86 is, in its gaseous state, the isotope Em 222, the heaviest of all gases. Although Baron Rutherford was working on its identification independently in England at about the same time, this element, *radon,* was discovered by German chemist Friedrich Dorn (1848-1916) in

1900. Radon is 111.5 times heavier than hydrogen gas. Also known as *niton*, it has a radioactive half-life of 3.825 days. Radon emanates radium salts and decays into an isotope of polonium.

The Iron Lung

DRINKER, PHILIP—An *iron lung* is a mechanical means of aiding the respiration of patients with lung disease or other respiratory problems. In 1929, American inventor Philip Drinker developed the first such device, which was also the first machine made to simulate human bodily functions.

Drinker's iron lung was a vacuum box into which a patient was placed; only the patient's head remained exposed. A rhythmic, controlled artificial air pressure was introduced into the box. The principles of gravity and atmospheric pressure were employed to aid the patient's respiration.

First Electronic Computer

ECKERT, J. P. AND MAUCHLY, J. W.—Since the invention of Pascal's early calculator in the seventeenth century, and Charles Babbage's "analytical engine" in 1823, scientists have sought to lessen the drudgery of solving long and complicated mathematical equations. In 1946, Eckert and Mauchly developed the ENIAC, the first electronic computer.

The ENIAC contained 18,000 radio valves; it was extremely bulky, temperamental and difficult to keep cool. But its biggest shortcoming was that the valves were not very reliable. Not until the invention of the transistor were computers of real value developed.

Syphilis Cure

EHRLICH, PAUL—Paul Ehrlich shared the 1908 Nobel Prize in Physiology and Medicine with Elie Metchnikoff for his work in immunology. He worked at his Institute for Serum Research, Steiglitz, Germany, and, in 1909, developed the first chemotherapeutic drug, *Salvarsan 606*, which was successful in fighting syphilis. Dr. Ehrlich later developed *neosalvarsan*, a less toxic form of the anti-syphilis drug.

Cure for Beriberi

EIJKMAN, CHRISTIAAN—While stationed in the Netherlands Indies in 1886, a Dutch Army surgeon, Christiaan Eijkman (1858-1930), investigated beriberi, a deficiency disease characterized by extreme weakness, paralysis, anemia and wasting away. As director of pathology in Batavia, Eijkman was the first to produce a dietary deficiency disease experimentally. The doctor caused a chicken to develop beriberi by feeding it only polished rice. From his observations, he deduced that it was the lack of an "essential food factor" in the diet (later identified as *antineuritic vitamins*) that was the cause of the disease. For his work in this field, Eijkman shared the 1929 Nobel Prize in Physiology and Medicine.

Theory of Relativity

EINSTEIN, ALBERT—The principle that the character of all motion, mass, velocity, etc. in the universe is relative rather than absolute is basic to Albert Einstein's (1879-1955) *Theory of Relativity*, which is perhaps the most important scientific discovery of the twentieth century. In 1905, the German-born physicist, who became an American citizen in 1940, made a thorough mathematical analysis of the Brownian movement in atoms. His research led him to couple the theory of Planck's Constant with ideas he'd been mulling over as a teacher in Switzerland; the result was his Theory of Relativity. For his work, Einstein was awarded the Nobel Prize in Physics in 1921. Einstein's famous equation was used in the 1940s to perfect the hydrogen bomb. Element 99, einsteinium, is named for him.

Electrocardiograph Inventor

EINTHOVEN, WILLEM—Born in the Dutch West Indies in 1860, Einthoven earned a medical degree in 1885. His major contribution to the profession was his development of the *electrocardiogram,* a tracing showing the changes in electric potential produced by the contractions of the heart. The *electrocardiograph,* the instrument for making an electrocardiogram, is made up of a *galvanometer* (also invented by Einthoven) placed near the patient's heart and a recording machine to trace the electrical changes. Einthoven won the 1924 Nobel Prize in Medicine for his achievement.

The Naval Screw Propeller

ERICSSON, JOHN—A Swedish-born, American naval engineer, John Ericsson (1803-1889), invented a device made of revolving blades which, attached to a steam engine, was able to propel a ship at a steady and significant rate of speed. Ericsson patented the naval *screw propeller* in London in 1839. He built the first screw propeller ship, the *Vandalia,* for the United States Navy in 1841.

In 1855, he built the first frigate equipped with a turret, called the *Roanoke*. In 1862, he built the first ironclad, turreted warship called the *Monitor*. And in 1894, he built the *Ericsson*, the first inland water warship. The *Monitor's* epic battle with the Confederate ironclad, *Virginia* (also known as the *Merrimac*), is said to have been the beginning of the end for wooden warships. Ericsson also contributed to naval knowledge about boilers and anti-recoil artillery mechanisms.

Earliest Study of Geometry

EUCLID—Around the year 300 B.C., while a teacher in Alexandria, Egypt, Euclid wrote *Elements*. Twenty-two centuries later, mathematics students are still being taught from this same book, the earliest to be written on the subject of geometry.

The *Elements* are contained in 15 volumes, 13 of which were written by Euclid himself and two by later writers. The book is, in itself, geometric in design. Many later thinkers—Hobbes, Descartes and Spinoza, for example—employed this geometric style in propounding their philosophical theories.

Pioneer in Electrodynamics

FARADAY, MICHAEL—Brilliant British chemist and physicist Michael Faraday (1791-1867) made many contributions to modern science. He discovered *electromagnetic induction* and formulated the laws of *electrolysis*. Faraday also developed the first *electric motor* and the first *transformer* (1831), and set forth ideas on the *vaporization* of mercury. The *faraday*, a unit of quantity of electricity, and the *farad*, an electromagnetic unit of capacitance, are named after him. Faraday is also the discoverer of *benzene*, a liquid used as a solvent for fats and in making lacquers, varnishes, dyes, and many organic compounds.

Nuclear Chain Reaction

FERMI, ENRICO—On December 2, 1942, Enrico Fermi and the staff of the Metallurgical Laboratory at the University of Chicago demonstrated the first self-sustaining nuclear chain reaction. Performed before 40 witnesses, the purpose of the experiment was to release the energy of an atom—and *control* it. The atoms of uranium (or uranium oxide), embedded in a pattern within a block of graphite, were permitted to collide with neighboring atoms, starting a chain reaction and causing the atoms to split. The Italian scientist won the Nobel Prize for Physics in 1938.

First Workable Spectroscope

FRAUNHOFER, JOSEPH VON—In 1666, Isaac Newton discovered that white light is composed of all known colors. This knowledge was not formally utilized until 1814 when Joseph von Fraunhofer assembled the first *spectroscope,* an optical instrument used for forming spectra for study. Employing a prism, a lens and a low-power observation telescope, Von Fraunhofer measured how light was dispersed. In the sunlight, he recorded about 700 dark bands, called *Fraunhofer lines.*

The Compound Lens

FRESNEL, AUGUSTIN JEAN—Augustin Jean Fresnel was employed by the French government as an engineer. He noticed that light waves travel transversely, unlike sound waves which are longitudinal, and in 1922, invented a compound lens that was used to produce parallel beams of light with its ribbed glass. The *Fresnel lens,* as it became known, was originally used in lighthouses; in a more sophisticated form it is still widely used in lighthouses and in theaters today. Fresnel died five years after inventing the compound lens, unaware of the significance of his discovery.

Father of Psychoanalysis

FREUD, SIGMUND—Born in Freiburg at Moravia in 1856, Sigmund Freud graduated from the University of Vienna in 1881 with a Doctor of Medicine degree. Uncertain of what branch of medicine to pursue, Freud did pioneer work with cocaine as a local anesthetic and, in 1886, entered private practice as a neurologist. He began to develop an interest in disorders of the mind, which led him into the study of hypnosis, a method of treatment popular among his colleagues. Unsatisfied with the effectiveness of hypnosis, he developed a method of treating neuroses and other disorders of the mind. The method was based on the assumption that such disorders are the result of the rejection by the conscious mind of factors which then persist in the unconscious mind, causing conflicts. The conflicts may be resolved by discovering and analyzing the repressions through use of such techniques as free association and dream analysis. Freud called his method *psychoanalysis,* which is often referred to simply as *analysis.* The father of the revolutionary, new way of treating disorders of the mind wrote many books explaining his theories and research findings. *The Interpretation of Dreams,* first published in 1900, is one of his most significant works. Freud died in London in 1939.

The Thermometer

GALILEO—Around the time of Christ, Philo of Byzantium had built a *thermoscope,* an instrument that indicated changes in temperature, without accurately measuring them. In 1592, Italian astronomer Galileo Galilei (1564-1642) developed an instrument consisting of a graduated glass tube with a sealed capillary bore in which mercury rose or fell according to change in temperature. This instrument was the first thermometer as we know it today. With his invention, Galileo was able to prove the difference between light and heat, an important advance for medicine. Galileo is credited with the development of the laws of motion. With the advent of the telescope, he was able to demonstrate the accuracy of the Copernican theory of the solar system, a belief for which he had previously been labelled a heretic.

The Geiger Counter

GEIGER, HANS—The *Geiger counter* is the instrument of radiation detection most used today. Hans Geiger (1882-1945), a physicist at Manchester University in England, began performing radiation experiments in association with Baron Rutherford. He invented an instrument, later named after him, for detecting and counting ionizing particles that pass through it. The instrument consists of a needlelike electrode inside a hollow metallic cylinder filled with gas which, when ionized by the radiation, sets up a current in an electric field.

First Air Pump

GUERNICKE, OTTO VON—The first *air pump* was devised in 1650 by Otto von Guernicke, Mayor of Magdeburg, Germany. Fashioned after an existing water pump, the air pump differed in that all parts were made airtight. It was based on the principle of vacuums, with which other scientists of the day were experimenting.

Von Guernicke demonstrated his air pump to Emperor Ferdinand III. The emperor was impressed by the feats of strength that could be performed by using the power of the vacuum.

Inventor of Electromagnet

HENRY, JOSEPH—Nineteenth-century American physicist Joseph Henry (1797-1878) invented the *electromagnet,* a current-carrying wire wrapped around a steel tube. Since the day he presented it to the Albany Institute in 1828, the invention has been used in its original form. In 1831, in his invention of the *electric bell,* Henry first introduced insulated iron ore. In 1840, utilizing his discovery of *self-induction,* the process whereby a field of objects, such as atoms, magnetizes itself electrically, he transmitted the first fireless radio impulse, a result of his earlier work on an electromagnetic telegraph. The *henry,* the unit of inductance used to represent the increase in magnetic flux as current is increased, is named for him. Henry was the first secretary of the Smithsonian Institute, from its inception in 1848 until his death.

Discoverer of Radio Waves

HERTZ, HEINRICH—Following the principles as described by James Clerk Maxwell, Heinrich Hertz (1857-1894) was the first to practically apply the theory of electromagnetic waves. In 1887, he produced such waves with a spark from a short-circuited condenser. After initial experimentation, he further utilized the theory to outline the principles of the radio. The radio waves he finally produced were called *Hertzian waves.* Marconi used the radio theories developed by Hertz to make the first transatlantic radio communication.

Discoverer of LSD

HOFFMAN, ALBERT—*LSD-25,* a d-Lysergic Acid Diethylamide tartrate, the most powerful synthetically-manufactured drug in existence, was originally produced in 1938 to aid in researching the common cold. The Swiss chemist, Dr. Albert Hoffmann, introduced LSD-25 as a hallucinogen in April 16, 1943, and its effects are still under the most careful scrutiny.

Chemically written as $C_2 H_{25} N_{0} O$, LSD was the subject of much controversy in the 1960s and early 1970s due to its ingestion by large numbers of young people in the United States and elsewhere. It has recently been used experimentally with victims of terminal cancer in an effort to ease their pain.

School for the Mentally Retarded

HOWE, SAMUEL GRIDLEY—A prominent Boston physician and philanthropist, Dr. Samuel Howe (1801-1876) was responsible for setting up the Massachusetts School for the Idiotic and Feeble Minded Youth in 1848—the first school of its kind in America. Still in existence, this institution for the retarded is now called the Walter E. Fernald State School. Dr. Howe was also associated with numerous schools for the blind and for needy children of school age. Howe was the husband of Julia Ward Howe, the authoress of "Battle Hymn of the Republic."

First Pendulum Clock

HUYGENS, CHRISTIAAN—Dutch physicist, astronomer, and mathematician Christiaan Huygens (1620-1695) is credited with an impressive list of scientific discoveries. The son of Dutch poet and statesman Constantijn Huygens, Christiaan was intrigued by Galileo's experimentation with pendulums and, in 1656, made the first pendulum clock. A member of Britain's Royal Society, Christiaan also did pioneering work with telescopic lenses, polarization and the solar system (he discovered Saturn's three concentric "rings").

First Safe Vaccination

JENNER, EDWARD—It took English physician Edward Jenner (1794-1823) 20 years to establish a connection between cowpox and smallpox. On May 14, 1796, he inoculated James Phipps with a compox serum with the hope of immunizing him to smallpox. Dr. Jenner's method was greeted by initial hostility but, by 1802, the vaccination was acclaimed both safe and workable. The perfection of the vaccination technique has greatly contributed to man's fight to overcome epidemic diseases.

Inventor of the Googol

KASNER, EDWARD—While a professor of mathematics at Columbia University, Dr. Edward Kasner contributed greatly to the understanding of relativity, horn angles, differential equations, polygonic functions and invariants. He coined the word *googol* for the number 10^{100}, or 10,000 sexdecillion. Ten raised to the power of a googol is called a *googolplex*, the value of which probably exceeds the number of atoms in the universe. The word googol is also sometimes used to refer to any very large number.

Youngest College Graduate

KELVIN, BARON—William Thomson (1824-1907) entered Glasgow University at the age of 10 and matriculated one month later. The British physicist became a professor at Glasgow and was made Baron Kelvin by Queen Victoria in 1892. A pioneer in the field of thermodynamics, Kelvin was instrumental in the laying of the transatlantic cable and in making improvements on navigational equipment for ships. He also devised the *Kelvin scale,* a scale of temperature measured in degrees centigrade from absolute zero. He was president of the Royal Society, a British scientific organization, from 1900 to 1904.

Earliest Kidney Machine

KOLFF, WILLEM—Willem Kolff was a patriotic Dutchman living in the Netherlands during the German occupation of World War II. He developed the first kidney machine in 1944 and used it initially to save the lives of several of his fellow Dutch partisans. The device, used to filter impurities out of the bloodstream when the kidneys have stopped functioning, led to the development of artificial kidneys in the early 1960s, and to sophisticated dialysis machines which can be used by patients without supervision for extended periods.

Inventor of the Stethoscope

LAENNEC, RENE HEOPHILE HYACINTHE—Watching children at play with long wooden sticks, putting one end of a stick to their ears to hear sounds while scratching the other, gave Rene Laënnec an idea. The day after his observation in 1816, he rolled up a sheet of paper, tied it with a string, and improved upon it by fashioning a cylinder of wood, which was sectioned in two parts for portability. He thus created the first *stethoscope*. Laënnec used the instrument to study heart disease, of which, ironically, he died in 1826.

Developer of the Cyclotron

LAWRENCE, ERNEST ORLANDO—The *cyclotron,* an apparatus sometimes referred to as a spiral "atom smasher," was developed in 1934 at Berkeley by Dr. Ernest O. Lawrence (1901-1958). Employing an 80-ton magnet and producing a 15-million volt ray, the cyclotron sends out high energy impulses from helium atoms. These impulses, called *alpha particles,* along with high-energy protons and deuterons, are used to bombard other atoms, thereby altering their structure and allowing for study of the atomic make-up of elements. Using the cyclotron, artificially radioactive elements and neutrons useful in chemical and nuclear research were produced. Lawrence received the 1939 Nobel Physics Prize for his invention.

Man's Earliest Ancestors

LEAKEY, RICHARD—Louis B. Leakey (1903-1972) was a renowned anthropologist who devoted his life to the search for the remains of man's ancestors in the Olduvai Gorge in Kenya. His son, Richard, discovered the earliest known remains of the genus *Homo*. East of Lake Rudolf in northern Kenya, Leakey and his associates announced on November 9, 1972 that they had found an almost complete skull and other bones estimated to be 2.8 million years old. Leakey is director of the Kenya National Museum's Centre for Pre-History and Palaeontology.

Bacteria and Protista

LEEUWENHOEK, ANTON VAN—A microscopist from Delft, Holland, Anton van Leeuwenhoek (1632-1723) manufactured more than 247 microscopes capable of magnifying objects up to 270 times. His pioneering descriptions of red blood cells and his discoveries of bacteria and protozoa were qualification enough to entitle him to membership in England's Royal Society. In 1676, he discovered *protista,* the name for all one-celled animals or plants.

Binary Arithmetic

LEIBNITZ, GOTTFRIED WILHELM VON—In 1679, Gottfried von Leibnitz (1646-1716) revealed his system of *binary arithmetic,* a system in which only two numbers, one and zero, are used. He related the system to his religious beliefs, *one* being God and *zero* meaning nothing. Leibnitz also developed a method of the calculus which resulted in a dispute with Isaac Newton over its discovery. In 1700, he became the first president of the Berlin Academy of Science.

First Operation Using Anesthesia

LONG, CRAWFORD W.—Having received his M.D. at the University of Pennsylvania in 1839, Dr. Crawford W. Long involved himself in careful experimentation in the field of anesthesiology for many months. Long knew he was pioneering in potentially dangerous territory. Using diethel ether, he removed a cyst from the neck of James Venable on March 30, 1842. He did not, however, make it public until four years later when the drug had been more thoroughly tested. That operation, performed in Jefferson, Georgia, was the first in which anesthesia was utilized.

Discoverer of the Laser

MAIMAN, THEO—Light Amplification by Stimulated Emission of Radiation (Laser) was theorized by Albert Einstein in 1917. He speculated that an excited atom could be stimulated into releasing its excess energy in light form, if bombarded by light of the proper frequency. In 1960, at the Hughes Laboratory in Malibu, California, Theo Maiman used a small, dilute ruby to synchronize light waves into an intense light beam. The art of using light in this way, called *holography*, is very helpful in surgery as a welding agent.

Developers of Chromatography

MARTIN, A. J. P. AND SYNGE, R. L. M.—Chromatography has made two major contributions to modern science: the first complete chemical analysis of a protein and the first complete explanation of the process of photosynthesis. Invented by two British chemists, A. J. P. Martin and R. L. M. Synge, *chromatography* is a process used to identify the components of a mixture by measuring the speeds with which the components are absorbed by paper. Martin and Synge received the 1952 Nobel Prize in Chemistry for their discovery.

Boston Philosophical Society

MATHER, INCREASE—One of a long line of American clergymen, Increase Mather (1639-1723) was pastor of Boston's North Church for nearly 60 years, serving as president of Harvard College between 1685 and 1701. In 1683, he set up the Boston Philosophical Society, recognized as the first American group dedicated to discussion and research in the fields of natural history and philosophy. Increase Mather's son (1663-1728) was known for helping create the atmosphere that led to the Salem Witch Trials of 1692, when many innocents were killed for allegedly having practiced witchcraft.

Electromagnetic Wave Theory

MAXWELL, JAMES CLERK—Nineteenth-century Scottish physicist James Maxwell (1831-1879) was successful in applying the principles of higher mathematics to the problems of physics. His *electromagnetic wave theory* stated that light consists of waves moving perpendicularly to the intersection of electric and magnetic waves. He propounded this theory between the years 1860 and 1870. Heinrich Hertz later employed the principles set forth by Maxwell in his work on radio waves.

The Science of Genetics

MENDEL, GREGOR—A nineteenth-century Roman Catholic monk and botanist, Gregor Johann Mendel (1822-1884), experimented in his Augustinian monastery at Brno, Moravia with the heredity characteristics of the garden pea. Based on his studies, Mendel formulated three principles of hereditary phenomena known as *Mendel's Laws*: 1) the law of independent unit characters; 2) the law of segregation; 3) the law of dominance. Mendel published his findings in 1865, but they received little scientific attention for another 35 years. Mendel's Laws form the basis of the modern science of *genetics*, the study of heredity.

Periodic Table of Elements

MENDELYEEV, DMITRI I.—A brilliant Russian chemist of the nineteenth century, Dmitri Ivanovich Mendelyeev (1834-1907) published his Periodic Arrangement of the Chemical Elements in 1869, and changed the science of chemistry forever. Using the table, not only could every known element be accounted for precisely, but the existence of unknown or as yet undiscovered elements could be postulated with accuracy. Element 101 (a radioactive chemical element), mendelevium, is named for him.

American Nobel Prize Winner

MICHELSON, ALBERT A.—As an instructor and researcher at the United States Naval Academy, Albert Abraham Michelson (1852-1931) discovered that light travels at exactly 186,508 miles per second, one of the foundations of Einstein's Theory of Relativity. It was in 1887 that Michelson first introduced the *interferometer,* a device of his invention which measures the interference of light waves. Used to calculate the smallest distances in space as well as the diameters of stars, the interferometer disproved the theory that light traveled on ether. In 1907, Michelson won the Nobel Prize for Physics, becoming the first American *and* the first Jew to receive a Nobel Prize.

Inventor of DDT

MULLER, PAUL—During World War II, most inventions and scientific advancements were in some way related to weaponry. Paul Muller's (1899-1965) development of the insecticide DDT in Switzerland in 1939 is an exception.

Crop-devouring insects have long been among man's most feared enemies. Möller's discovery of DDT (*dichlorodiphenyl trichloroethane*), which was tested successfully against the Colorado potato beetle and which earned him the 1948 Nobel Prize, for some time seemed to have solved the problem. Subsequent research showed, however, that while DDT is an effective pesticide, it is also a powerful environmental pollutant. Consequently, its use has been banned in many countries.

Formulator of Logarithms

NAPIER, JOHN—Scottish mathematician John Napier (1550-1617) was the eighth Laird (wealthy landowner) of Merchiston. *Marifici Logarithmorum Canonis Descriptio* was his introduction to his new discovery: logarithms. Published in 1614, the work described how to use the logarithm table he had perfected for 20 years. Logarithms (the exponent of the power to which a fixed number must be raised in order to produce a given number) proved to be of great importance in the fields of navigation, astronomy and surveying.

Napier was a versatile scientist. In addition to formulating logarithms, he built and devised a calculator called *Napier's rods,* and discovered that salt could be used as an agricultural fertilizer.

A Reflecting Telescope

NEWTON, ISAAC—Newton's (1642-1727) contributions to eighteenth-century science are many, particularly in the fields of mathematics (he devised a calculus), astronomy (he invented a reflecting telescope), physics (his laws of gravitation and motion are still in use), and the nature of light (he was a pioneer in the use of prisms and spectrums). Sir Isaac studied at Britain's Cambridge University, where he later became a professor. He was knighted by Queen Anne in 1705 during her visit to Cambridge. Newton represented Parliament and was president of the Royal Society from 1703 until his death in 1727. He is buried in Westminister Abbey.

Inventor of Dynamite

NOBEL, ALFRED—Alfred Nobel (1833-1896) came from a distinguished Swedish family of inventors. His father, Immanuel Nobel, the inventor of plywood, influenced him to experiment with gunpowder. Alfred carefully studied the experiments of Ascanio Sobrero, the discover of nitroglycerin, and, in 1865, Nobel made a powerful explosive combining nitroglycerin with mercuric fulminate. The result was: dynamite! Nobel developed a brisk business, despite a slow start due to heavy competition from gunpowder factories such as DuPont.

Nobel was also an industrialist and philanthropist. He established the Nobel prizes, which are awarded annually by the Nobel Foundation for distinction in physics, chemistry, medicine, literature, and for the promotion of peace.

Pure Aluminum

OERSTED, HANS CHRISTIAN—Aluminum, the most common element in the earth's crust, does not exist naturally in its pure form. The observations of Danish physicist and chemist Hans Christian Oersted (1777-1851) based on Sir Humphry Davy's (1778-1829) experiments in isolating aluminum oxide, led to the development of a process capable of producing pure aluminum. But the purifying process developed by the Dane was so expensive that, for years after he first produced it, aluminum was considered a semiprecious metal. In 1886, a cheaper method of obtaining aluminum was discovered, and today it is widely used in alloyed forms.

Unit of Resistance

OHM, GEORG—In 1827, Georg Simon Ohm (1787-1854) first published the equation $E = IR$, E being the electromotive force volts), I the electrical current (ampères), and R the electrical resistance (ohms). Ohm named the unit of resistance after himself. The unit of electrical conductance, called the mho (ohm spelled backwards), was named by Baron Kelvin in Ohm's honor. The Danish physicist's important equation states the basic relationship which governs the flow of electricity in any circuit.

First Atomic Bomb

OPPENHEIMER, J. ROBERT—In 1930, J. Robert Oppenheimer (1904-1967) disproved Englishman Paul Dirac's theory about anti-electrons, paving the way for the discovery of the positron two years later. In 1943, he was put in charge of the Los Alamos, New Mexico Atomic Research Laboratory, where the first atomic bomb was designed, constructed and tested. Oppenheimer provided information about atomic fission which he had gained from his work with charged particles. In 1935, he had experimented with splitting a heavy hydrogen atom with a positively-charged atomic nucleus, the theoretical basis of the hydrogen bomb. In 1974, he became chairman of the advisory council to the Atomic Energy Commission and, in 1963, received the Enrico Fermi Award for his nuclear research.

The Calculating Machine

PASCAL, BLAISE—Throughout his life, Blaise Pascal (1623-1662) was regarded as a philosopher and mathematician of genius. At the age of 16, he wrote a respected treatise on conic sections. In 1642, at the age of 19, the Frenchman invented a calculator to aid his father in his clerking duties. The primitive machine, which contained a clutch device to facilitate the turning of more than one digit at a time, was well received; a model was even presented to the king of France. In 1654, Pascal became a follower of the Jansenist religious sect, which profoundly influenced his work and life.

The Pasteur Treatment

PASTEUR, LOUIS—Louis Pasteur (1822-1895), the eminent French chemist and bacteriologist, is renowned for his germ theory of disease, a theory which resulted in the *Pasteur treatment*. The treatment was a method of preventing certain diseases, especially rabies, by successive inoculations with the specific virus in increasing strength.

Also a result of his germ theory was the development of the process called *pasteurization*, a method of destroying disease-producing bacteria in milk, beer, wine and other potables.

Nobel Prize Double Winner

PAULING, LINUS—Born on February 28, 1901, Linus Pauling has worked at the California Institute of Technology since 1931 as a professor of chemistry. He received the Nobel Chemistry Prize in 1954 and the Nobel Peace Prize in 1962, the only individual to have won two Nobel prizes. Madame Marie Curie and Professor John Bardeen have had a share in two prizes, and the International Red Cross has won three prizes, but Dr. Pauling remains the only individual to have been awarded the prize twice.

Inventor of Refrigeration

PERKINS, JACOB—Jacob Perkins (1776-1849) was an American who carried out most of his scientific work in England. His experiments with freezing and the properties of ice led him, in 1834, to create a machine whose degree of coldness could be regulated indefinitely. His vapor compression cycle, in which volatile liquids were evaporated to produce cooling, was the forerunner of the first marketed "fridge" in 1862.

Among Perkin's other inventions were: a method of silver-plating shoe buckles, several engraving and printing devices for currency, high pressure steam boilers and engines, ship pumps and ventilation devices. The latter two brought him Britain's Vulcan Gold Medal and other awards.

Deepest Ocean Descent

PICCARD, JACQUES—Piccard, a Swiss doctor, and his assistant, United States Navy Lieutenant Donald Walsh, dove into the waters of the Marinas Trench, off Guam, in the bathyscaphe (a deep-sea diving apparatus) *Trieste* on January 23, 1960. The duo dove 35,817 feet—the deepest ocean descent ever made by man—and remained under water for eight hours. Picard and his research teams made many important oceanographic discoveries relating to currents, pressure and mapping the huge underwater mountain ranges.

Inventor of Oral Contraceptive

PINCUS, GREGORY—Dr. Gregory Pincus of the Worcester Foundation in Shrewsbury, Massachusetts carefully studied fertility in animals. On the suggestion of Margaret Sanger, director of the first birth control advice center (1916), the doctor undertook the development of an oral contraceptive. In 1955, after many disappointing tries, Pincus discovered that the hormone norethisterone was an effective female contraceptive which could be ingested orally.

Upon the doctor's death at the age of 64 in 1957, an endowment in his name was established by Harvard University, where he had received his doctorate and had taught for some years.

The Quantum Theory

PLANCK, MAX—The German physicist Max Planck (1858-1947) theorized that energy, like matter, exists in particles and that it is not infinitely divisible. He called one of these energy particles a *quantum* (Latin for "how much?"). The ratio of the frequency of an electromagnetic radiation and the size of its particular quantum is called *Planck's Constant*, "h."

Planck's Theory, perhaps the single most revolutionary discovery in the history of physics, states that the size of the particle for any form of electromagnetic radiation is in direct proportion to its frequency. The theory was used by Einstein in 1905, and by Niels Bohr in 1913 to redefine many laws of atomic theory and physics. The Nobel Physics Prize was awarded to Planck in 1918.

The Wire Recorder

POULSEN, VALDEMAR—Danish scientist Valdemar Poulsen (1896-1942) made practicable the notion that a varying magnetic field can be used to reproduce sound waves. With this principle in mind, he invented the *wire recorder* (patented in 1898), a machine for recording sound electromagnetically on a thin wire running between two spools. Unable to get financial backing for his invention, Poulsen did not live to see the device perfected. With the advent of phonograph records, Poulsen's invention seemed superfluous. But in the 1940s, when the principles were carefully studied, the machine was refined and used widely.

The Raman Effect

RAMAN, VENKATA—The tendency of light to change its wave length and color when diffused is known as the *Raman effect*. Its discoverer, Venkata Raman (1895-1970), received the 1930 Nobel Physics Prize for the achievement and was knighted by the king of England. Raman also did pioneer work in acoustics and crystallography while teaching at the University of Calcutta. From 1947 until his death, he directed the Raman Research Institute in India.

Argon, Neon, Krypton and Xenon

RAMSAY, WILLIAM—A Scottish scientist whose specialty was the rare gases that make up the outer reaches of the earth's atmosphere, William Ramsay (1852-1916) discovered the existence of argon, neon, krypton, xenon and helium in 1895. He isolated the rare gaseous elements and his laboratory colleagues later found them to be radioactive by-products. For his discovery of these gases (also called the *noble,* or *inert,* gases because they do not form compounds), Ramsay was knighted. In 1904, he was awarded the Nobel Prize for Chemistry.

The Speed of Light

ROEMER, OLAUS—Olaus (or Ole) Roemer, born in Jutland, in the north of Denmark, in 1644, became a professor of astronomy at the University of Copenhagen. It had always been assumed that light was an instantaneous phenomenon, but Roemer proved that it travels at a finite speed. In watching the eclipses of the moons of Jupiter, whose speeds varied with the distances of the earth from that planet, Roemer was able to measure the speed of light. The Danish scientist also invented the first practical transit instrument, which aided navigators and astronomers in the measurement of distances between heavenly bodies.

Inventor of the X-ray

ROENTGEN, WILHELM KONRAD—In 1888, Wilhelm Roëntgen 1845-1923) was appointed professor of physics and director of the Wurzburg Physical Institute, Germany. He was studying the then-new vacuum tubes developed by Sir William Crookes when he noticed that a piece of paper painted with barium platino-cyanide would glow brightly when current was passing through one of the tubes. Roëntgen discovered that invisible rays, not able to penetrate dense materials, could successfully pass through paper or wood. Further work by the German physicist led to the development of *Roëntgen rays*, or *X-rays*. For his contribution to science, Roëntgen was awarded the Nobel Prize for Physics in 1901.

The Anti-Polio Vaccine

SALK, JONAS—Dr. Jonas Salk, born in 1914, had been a teacher and research professor in various American colleges while search-ing for a cure for poliomyelitis (infantile paralysis). In 1953, and 1954, he tested an anti-polio vaccine on his family—with successful results. Unfortunately, unknown to Salk, another vaccine, which had not been thoroughly tested, was distributed in 1955. It resulted in 200 cases of polio and 11 deaths. Salk's improved and tested vaccine, distributed the following year, proved effective. Salk has since devoted his time to cancer research.

Nitrogen, Manganese, Barium and Chlorine

SCHEELE, KARL WILHELM—An eighteenth-century Swedish chemist, Karl Wilhelm Scheele (1742-1786) made many im-portant contributions to man's understanding of the world's chemical make-up. In 1774, his experiments with nitrogen proved that yellow-green gas has both the highest melting and boiling points of the normal temperature gases. Scheele published his treatise on manganese in 1774, which later helped him isolate barium. The Swede also discovered chlorine and experimented with glycerin and other acids.

Highest-Priced Orchid

SCHROEDER, BARON—Sanders of St. Alban's received $6,000 from Baron Schroeder of Germany for an *Odontoglossum cris-*

pum, the highest price ever paid for an orchid. The flower, of the variety *pittianum,* was sold at auction at Protheroe & Morris in London on March 22, 1906. What the Baron received was one rare species of 100 in the *Odontoglossum* genus which are epiphytical in nature; that is, these nonparisitic plants grow on other plants but get their nourishment from the air. They are found throughout Central America and the high West Range of the Andes Mountains which run through South America.

Discoverer of Eight Elements

SEABORG, GLENN T.—For his work which led to the discovery of americium, plutonium, berkelium, californium and curium while a professor of chemistry at the University of California at Berkeley, Glenn T. Seaborg (with E. M. McMillan) was awarded the Nobel Prize for Chemistry in 1951. Working with physicists such as Albert Ghiorso, S. G. Thompson, Ralph James and Kenneth Street, Seaborg (1912-) produced evidence of the existence of lawrencium, mendelevium and einsteinium. He also did significant work in artificial radioactivity, and was appointed head of the Atomic Energy Commission in 1961.

Alternating Current and Induction

TESLA, NIKOLA—Nikola Tesla (1856-1943) was a Croatian immigrant who began his inventing career with Thomas Edison. He left Edison's shop after an argument with his boss on the relative merits of alternating and direct current. This began a life-long feud between the two that indirectly caused the Nobel Prize committee to change their minds about awarding them a joint prize and, instead, honored neither of them. In 1892, Tesla developed a transformer system for the efficient transfer of alternating current electricity. Alternating current became the form of power most used in the United States (rather than Edison's direct current method). The unit of magnetic flux density is called the *tesla* in his honor.

Vaccine for Yellow Fever

THEILER, MAX—Physician and bacteriologist Max Theiler (1899-1972) born in South Africa and schooled in London, spent many years investigating yellow fever, an acute infectious tropical disease caused by a virus transmitted by the bite of certain mosquitoes and characterized by fever, jaundice and vomiting. Theiler's research, conducted mostly at New York's Rockefeller Institute in the 1920s and 1930s, led to his discovery of a preventive vaccine against the disease in 1937. Theiler won the 1951 Nobel Prize for Medicine and Physiology for his contribution to medical science. He taught at Yale until his retirement in 1967.

Inventor of the Barometer

TORRICELLI, EVANGELISTA—Evangelista Torricelli (1608-1647), a pupil of Galileo, listened to his master expound on nature's abhorrence of a vacuum. The Italian physicist experimented with the nature of mercury in a vacuum, and the six inches of airless space at the top of his first mercury-filled tube became known as the *Torricellian vacuum.* He had discovered the principle of the *barometer,* the instrument used for measuring atmospheric pressure. The French scientist, Blaise Pascal, confirmed Torricelli's theory of watching the mercury fall as he scaled a mountain.

Discoverer of Heavy Water

UREY, HAROLD C.—In 1931, it was announced at the annual meeting of the American Association for the Advancement of Science that American chemist Harold Clayton Urey had discovered an isotope of hydrogen that had double the atomic weight of regular hydrogen. The isotope, named deuterium, is a basic element of "heavy water," which is used in the creation of atomic energy. Urey also discovered U-235, the uranium isotope used in atomic reactions. He won the 1934 Nobel Chemistry Prize for his monumental discoveries. Although they have resulted in the creation of atomic bombs, Urey has consistently denounced the use of his discoveries for destructive purposes. The peaceful production of atomic energy, he maintained, is a far more valuable tool. In 1976, he was Professor Emeritus at the University of California at Berkeley.

Discoverer of Borax

VEATCH, JOHN A.—On January 8, 1856, Dr. John A. Veatch (1804-1871) discovered an impure form of *borax* in the mineral water of Tuscan Springs, California. Eight years later, a crystallization process was found to successfully extract the impurities from borax, thus making the mineral available to industry. Veatch's discovery is used in the manufacture of glass and enamel, as a fertilizer, as a flux in soldering, and as a food preservative. It is most popularly used as a cleanser.

Earliest Human Remains

VERTES, LASZLO—Between 300,000 and 450,000 years ago, the first man, or *Homo sapiens*, walked the earth. On August 24, 1965, Dr. Laszlo Vertes, a Hungarian anthropologist, discovered the earliest-known remains of the species. In a limestone quarry approximately 30 miles west of Budapest, he unearthed part of a skull with a cranial capacity of nearly 85 cubic inches, a size comparable to that of modern man. The occipital bone found by Vertes belonged to a class of man known as *Homo sapiens palaeohungaricus*.

The Electric Battery

VOLTA, ALESSANDRO—A count in Bologna, Alessandro Volta (1745-1827) worked with his fellow countryman, Luigi Galvani (after whom *galvanization* is named). Through their experiments, Volta achieved the first continuous source of electric current by stacking alternating discs of copper and zinc and binding them together with moistened cloth. These stacks of metal discs became known as *voltaic piles*. Napoleon commanded Alessandro Volta to demonstrate his remarkable invention before the court of France in 1801.

The unit of electromotive force, the *volt*, is named after Volta.

Father of Modern Dermatology

VON HEBRA, FERDINAND—Ferdinand von Hebra (1816-1880) was a physician in Austria when he demonstrated that skin diseases are caused more by local irritation than by a condition of the body fluids. The latter theory was put forth by believers in humoral pathology and Von Hebra did much to discount it. His further experiments in skin disease paved the way for the founding of the modern science of dermatology.

First to Use "Antibiotic"

WAKSMAN, SELMAN A.—Microbiologist Selman A. Waksman (1888-1973), born in Russia, was a member of the faculty of Rutgers University for 40 years, founding the Rutgers Institute of Microbiology and acting as its chairman for 19 years. In 1943, he discovered *streptomycin*, one of the more than 500 antibiotics now used to treat disease. Waksman first used the term "antibiotics" in 1942 to describe the wonder drugs that were produced in the 1930s and early 1940s. The winner of the 1952 Nobel Prize for Medicine authored *My Life with the Microbes* in 1954.

Successful Radar Demonstration

WATSON-WATT, ROBERT—The names of the scientists involved in the development of radar reads like a roll call of the great electromagnetic pioneers. Heinrich Hertz, Clerk Maxwell, Nikola Tesla, Edward V. Appleton and Gregory Breit—all made significant contributions to the theory and application of detecting objects by using radio waves (radar). But it was Robert Watson-Watt who conducted the first successful demonstration.

Watson-Watt was a member of the British Air Ministry. In 1934, while working on a "death ray" at the Government Radio Research Station, he developed a practical way of demonstrating radio-location. Watson-Watt tested it—and successfully—on moving aircraft.

Psychology Laboratory

WUNDT, WILHELM MAX—In Leipzig in 1878, Dr. Wilhelm Wundt (1832-1920) founded the first experimental laboratory for the fledgling science of psychology. Wundt, a prominent German physiologist, took up the study of psychology and became intrigued by its potential contribution to the understanding of man. To further the science, which had been the subject of ridicule in some conservative scientific circles, Wundt set up his Leipzig lab, where many of the great names in German psychology received early training.

Electron Microscope and Iconoscope

ZWORYKIN, VLADIMIR C.—Born and educated in Russia, Dr. Vladimir Zworykin (1889-) continued his studies in France and in the United States. He came to work for the Radio Corporation of America in 1929. As an outgrowth of his research, Zworykin developed the *iconoscope*, the "electric eye" of television which transmits the electrical output to a cathode-ray tube receiver. The receiver changes the impulses into light energy. He also perfected the *kinescope*, a form of cathode-ray receiving tube used for live television transmissions. In 1939, Zworykin's research group produced the *electron microscope*, which was able to magnify an object up to 100,000 times its size. The 1,000-pound instrument stood more than 10 feet tall. In the 1950s, Zworykin formulated a plan for an electronic highway system which would reduce accident rates by electronically notifying cars of impending collisions.

AVIATION AND OUTER SPACE

First on the Moon

ARMSTRONG, NEIL ALDEN—Neil Alden Armstrong and Edwin
E. Aldrin, Jr. landed their lunar module, *Eagle,* on the moon on
July 21, 1969. Armstrong, command pilot of the Apollo XI mission, stepped onto the moon's surface at 02:56.26 a.m. GMT;
Aldrin followed shortly after. The first men on the moon performed numerous scientific experiments, and gathered soil and
rock samples.

Armstrong, the first nonmilitary man to become an astronaut, was born in Wapakoneta, Ohio on August 5, 1930. He is
presently (1976) teaching at the University of Cincinnati College of Engineering. Aldrin is a colonel in the Air Force and
currently teaches at the Aerospace Research Pilots School at
Edwards Air Force Base, California.

Group Flight to U.S.

BALBO, ITALO—As air minister of Italy, General Italo Balbo
(1896-1940) brought the first group of foreign aircraft across
the Atlantic to America on July 15, 1933. He led 24 seaplanes on
the 6,100-mile, 48-hour flight from Ortobello, Italy to Chicago,
Illinois, making several stopovers along the way. Balbo was
promoted to air marshall by Benito Mussolini upon his return.
He was accidentally shot down by Italian anti-aircraft guns
while, as governor-general of Libya, he was making an inspection
flight over Tobruk.

First WWI Downed Pilot

BALSLEY, CLYDE—Even before the United States formally entered World War I in 1917, many Americans served with the French Foreign Legion in the Lafayette Escadrille. Many of those American pilots were poorly trained. Thus, when the Escadrille, a squadron of the French Air-Service, first saw frontline action in June of 1916, casualties were suffered almost immediately. Clyde Balsley was shot down above Verdun on June 18, 1916 while flying his Nieuport-17 fighter at 10,000 feet. He escaped death, however, and was awarded the War Cross and the Military Medal. Balsley went on to become an ace pilot for the Allies.

Glider License #1

BARNABY, RALPH AND HATTIE—On February 5, 1931, Navy Commander Ralph Stanton Barnaby received license #1 for Class C glider piloting from the National Aeronautic Association. To qualify for the license, Barnaby was required to make a five-minute flight, maintaining altitude throughout. On August 12, 1931, his wife, Hattie Meyer Barnaby, satisfied the requirements near Washington, D.C., and became the first woman to receive a glider license. She was awarded license #37.

Flight Across English Channel

BLÉRIOT, LOUIS—French aviator Louis Blériot (1872-1936) flew an aircraft of his own design from Les Baraques, France to Dover Castle, England on July 25, 1909. His monoplane, the *Blériot XI*, was powered by a 23-horsepower Anzani engine. Blériot took off at 4:41 a.m.; thirty-seven minutes later he had set his aerial record.

Blériot-designed aircraft were officially adopted for use by the French and Belgian air services at the outbreak of World War I.

Furthest Known Object

BURBIDGE, ELEANOR MARGARET—The object designated as QSO OQ172 is 91,700,000,000,000,000,000,000 miles from the earth. It is the most remote object yet detected in our universe, so remote, in fact, that its physical properties are only vaguely known. It is believed to be a dense gas formation, possibly a star or a star system. Dr. Eleanor Burbidge, director of the Greenwich Royal Observatory in Sussex, England, announced the discovery on June 7, 1973. She was working with a 120-inch telescope near San Jose, California.

Flight Over Both Poles

BYRD, RICHARD E.—On May 9, 1926, United States Navy Lieutenant Commander Richard Evelyn Byrd (1888-1957), accompanied by Floyd Bennett, flew the Fokker trimotor monoplane *Josephine Ford* over the North Pole on a flight from King's Bay, Spitzbergen. The 1,545-mile, nonstop flight took the duo 15½ hours to complete. On November 28, 1929, Byrd and a crew of three flew from the base at Little America. They reached the southern polar cap at nine o'clock the following morning, where they dropped an American flag. Among Byrd's discoveries at the Little America base was the southernmost plant life ever seen.

Longest Space Flight

CARR, GERALD P.; POGUE, WILLIAM R.; GIBSON, EDWARD G.—Lieutenant Colonel Gerald Carr of the Marines, Lieutenant Colonel William Pogue of the Air Force, and Dr. Edward Gibson constituted the crew of the United States space program's *Skylab 4*. On November 16, 1973, *Skylab 4*, an orbiting laboratory, was launched. The crew spent 84 days, one hour and 16 minutes in space, returning to earth on February 8, 1974.

The three astronauts traveled a record distance in space of 34.5 million miles; they circled the earth 1,214 times. This longest of space flights was chiefly devoted to study of the sun, the planets, Kohoutek's Comet, and the earth's atmosphere.

Inventor of the Glider

CAYLEY, GEORGE—In 1804, the founder of the science of aerodynamics, Sir George Cayley (1773-1857), used a kite as the main wing of the first glider ever built. Cayley had studied the properties of the wings of birds, noting how the curve of the wing catches the wind and uplifts the bird's body. Cayley's glider was the source of much of the knowledge employed by the Wright brothers in developing the first airplane.

Inventor of the Gas Balloon

CHARLES, J. A. C.—Physicist J. A. C. Charles was commissioned by the French government to build a hot air balloon based on the model of a successful one produced by the Montgolfier brothers in 1783. Charles believed that the only way to lift a balloon was by using a hot *gas*. When he saw a demonstration of the hot *air* balloon, he realized that he had invented something quite different.

The first flight of Charles' hydrogen balloon carried him and a friend 27 miles on December 1, 1783. His gas balloon, more practical than the hot air balloon, was used militarily throughout Europe.

Fastest Woman on Earth

COCHRANE, JACQUELINE—Piloting a North American F-86 Sabre Jet aircraft on May 18, 1953, Jacqueline Cochrane became the first woman to fly faster than the speed of sound. On May 11, 1964, she flew an aircraft faster than any woman in history. Her F104G1 *Starfighter* jet aircraft, flying above Edwards Air Force Base, California, was timed at 1492.2 miles per hour to set the world's record.

Now married, Mrs. Floyd Bostwick Odlum can be called the fastest woman on earth; the Russian cosmonaut, Valentina Tereschova, is the fastest space woman.

Ship-to-Ship Hydroplane Flight

CURTISS, GLENN H.—Glenn Hammond Curtiss (1878-1936), inventor of the Curtiss flying machine, set several records with his pioneering invention:

On May 29, 1910, he won a prize of $10,000 for racing his airplane against a train—and winning.

On August 31, 1910, in the first American overwater flight, he flew across Lake Erie for 78 minutes.

He flew the hydroplane version of his aircraft to and from the *U.S.S. Pennsylvania,* making the first ship-to-ship hydroplane flight, in 1911.

Curtiss was issued the first pilot's license by the Aero Club of America on June 8, 1911.

"Blind" Airplane Flight

DOOLITTLE, JIMMY—James Harold Doolittle was a successful racing flier. On September 24, 1929, newly-commissioned as a lieutenant in the United States Flying Corps, he made the first completely "blind" airplane flight, using only a radio beacon for guidance. Doolittle received the Congressional Medal of Honor for leading 16 carrier-based medium bombers on a raid over Tokyo, a flight that strengthened American morale after Japan's devastating early World War II victories. At the age of 47, Doolittle was made a lieutenant general, the youngest American to hold the rank.

First Woman to Fly Solo

EARHART, AMELIA—In 1928, Amelia Earhart (1898-1937) became the first female passenger to cross the Atlantic. In 1932, she bettered that record by becoming the first woman to fly solo both across the Atlantic and across the United States nonstop.

At 10:15 p.m., on Friday, January 11, 1935, Amelia took off from Wheeler Field in Honolulu, Hawaii. At 4:31 p.m. the following day, after traveling a distance of 2,408 miles in 18 hours and 16 minutes (at 133 miles per hour), she landed at the Oakland Airport, Oakland, California. She thus became the first woman to fly solo across the Pacific.

In 1937, Amelia Earhart Putnam was reported lost while flying over a remote part of the Pacific, near New Guinea. No trace of her was ever found.

First Man in Space

GAGARIN, YURI ALEKSEYEVICH—Born on a collective farm in the central Russian town of Gzhatsk on March 9, 1934, Yuri Gagarin was a test pilot before becoming a cosmonaut trainee. On April 12, 1961, at 9:07 a.m. Moscow time, he was propelled into space by a five-ton Sputnik satellite from Barkonin, U.S.S.R. His spaceship, *Vostok* (East), made one revolution around the earth, traveling at a speed of 17,000 miles per hour, in 89.1 minutes. He spent one hour and 48 minutes aloft before safely landing on snow-covered Russian soil. Gagarin—the first man in space—was named a Hero of the Soviet Union for his accomplishment. Ironically, he was killed on March 27, 1968 in a test plane flight.

First Human Drop

GARNERIN, JACQUES—Standing in a small bucket-shaped gondola attached to an observation balloon, Jacques Garnerin was raised into the air on October 22, 1797. At 3,000 feet, wearing the first parachute ever tested, he jumped. The canopy of the parachute, ribbed and semistiff, opened. Based on the design of a parasol made by Leonardo da Vinci in 1485, the chute had no hole in the top. Garnerin swayed violently from side to side, became ill, and had a very unsatisfactory ride. He returned to the drawing board to redesign the parachute.

First Powered Dirigible

GIFFARD, HENRI—The balloon was invented in 1783 by the Montgolfier brothers. Like the bicycle, many men worked on the development of a *powered* balloon. French engineer Henri Giffard is credited with the first successful flight of a heavier-than-air vehicle capable of moving under its own power. On September 24, 1852, he took off from the Paris Hippodrome and landed successfully 17 miles away, having traveled at a speed of six miles per hour. Others improved upon Giffard's invention, particularly in the area of engine strength; Giffard's machine was useless and even dangerous in anything more than a light breeze.

First American to Orbit Earth

GLENN, JOHN—Lieutenant Colonel John Herschel Glenn, Jr. orbited the earth three times aboard his Mercury capsule, *Friendship 7*, on February 20, 1962. He landed safely in the Atlantic after traveling 17,400 miles in space. The reception accorded the first American to orbit the earth was fantastic: he received the largest ticker-tape parade in the history of New York City, home of ticker-tape parades. The New York City Sanitation Department estimated that it cleaned up 3,474 tons of paper following the parade, topping the welcomes accorded General Douglas MacArthur in 1951 and Colonel Charles Lindbergh in 1927.

Liquid Fuel Rocket Flight

GODDARD, ROBERT H.—In Auburn, Massachusetts, on March 16, 1926, Professor Robert Hutchins Goddard tested the first liquid fuel rocket, for which he had been granted a patent on July 14, 1914. At the launch, energy was produced by an outside pressure tank and, while in flight, by an alcohol heater inside the rocket. The rocket traveled 184 feet in 2.5 seconds, attaining a speed of 60 miles per hour.

Goddard was working under a grant from Clark University of Worcester, Massachusetts. He had previously demonstrated the possibility of lifting a projectile by using liquid fuel in the forms of liquid oxygen or ether.

Two-Man American Space Flight

GRISSOM, GUS AND YOUNG, JOHN—The *Gemini III* satellite, *Molly Brown*, carried Major Virgil I. Grissom and Lieutenant Commander John Young into orbit on March 23, 1965. The four-hour, 53-minute expedition was the first American two-man space flight. The duo, launched into orbit by the 89-foot *Titan II* rocket, made three revolutions around the earth before landing in the Atlantic and being brought aboard the aircraft carrier *USS Intrepid*.

Born in San Francisco in 1930, Young later flew in *Apollo 10* (1969) and *Apollo 14* (1972) and still works for the National Aeronautics and Space Administration in Houston.

Grissom (1926-1967), one of the original seven astronauts, was the second American in space (1961). He died on January 27, 1967 when the first Project Apollo flight caught fire during a simulation.

The Diving Bell

HALLEY, EDMUND—Distinguished English astronomer Edmund Halley (1656-1742), who mapped and catalogued the stars of the Southern Hemisphere, made significant use of the magnetic compass in his lunar observations. While tracking the paths of comets in 1683, he noted that what had previously been described as several comets was actually one comet. Halley correctly predicted that this comet—later named *Halley's Comet*—would reappear every 75½ years. It was last seen in 1910.

Halley also invented the *diving bell*. Made of wood, the bell was fitted with a plate glass window, and was weighted with lead. The occupants of the 60-cubic-foot object could remain under water for long periods; fresh air was "sent down" in lead-encased barrels.

Discoverer of the Ionosphere

HEAVISIDE, OLIVER—In 1892, English physicist Oliver Heaviside (1850-1925) published an important work, entitled *Electrical Papers*. The publication, which established Heaviside as a leading electrical scientist, influenced the evolution of long-distance telephones. Heaviside studied the layers of the earth's atmosphere and conjectured that the upper atmosphere contains an ionized belt that reflects radio waves so that they travel parallel to the earth's surface. The *Heaviside layer*, which later became known as the *ionosphere*, is estimated as being from 30 to 200 miles above the earth's surface. Composed of oxygen and nitrogen, it serves to protect the earth's atmosphere from the high-frequency radiation constantly coming in from outer space.

Largest Airplane

HUGHES, HOWARD R.—Howard R. Hughes, a record-breaking flyer, constructed the aircraft with the largest wingspan, the H.2 *Hercules* flying boat. The first eight-engined airplane ever built, its wingspan was 320 feet. In its only flight, on November 2, 1947, the *Hercules* rose 70 feet above the ground and flew for a thousand yards off Long Beach, California with Hughes at the stick. The $40-million plane was designed to carry military troops or complete mobile hospital units. Hughes, who was reportedly one of the world's wealthiest men, stored the plane for many years at public expense, but later offered sections of it to several museums, the Smithsonian Institution in Washington, D.C. receiving the largest part. Hughes died in 1976.

The Radio Telescope

JANSKY, KARL—The invention of the radio telescope added a new dimension to astronomy. Man was no longer at the mercy of the earth's thick, light-warping atmosphere for "views" of the heavens. Working for the Bell Telephone Company in 1931, Karl Jansky (1905-1950), an American physicist, discovered that the earth was continually being bombarded by radio waves. His idea led to the development of the first radio "dish," which was built by amateur astronomer Grote Reber in 1937.

The unit of strength of radio-wave emission is called the *jansky* in his honor.

'Round the World Race

KILGALLEN, DOROTHY—Taking off from Lakehurst, New Jersey on September 30, 1936, *New York Evening Journal* (later the *Journal American*) reporter Dorothy Kilgallen (1913-1965) raced two of her male colleagues around the world in airplanes flown by commercial airlines pilots. The purpose of the race was to test commercial flying routes. The winner—Herbert R. Ekins of the *World Telegram*—finished in approximately 18 days 11 hours (six days and one hour ahead of Dorothy). He covered 25,654 miles.

Kilgallen, who wrote a book about the race, later became a regular on the television quiz show, *I've Got a Secret*. She also wrote a regular column for several New York newspapers, and co-hosted a radio program, *Breakfast with Dorothy and Dick*, with her husband, Dick Kollmar.

Artificial Satellite Designer

KOROLYOV, SERGEY PAVLOVICH—Launched from Tyuratam, U.S.S.R. on October 4, 1957, *Sputnik I* (meaning "fellow traveler") was placed into orbit around the earth at an altitude of between 142 and 588 miles. The spacecraft traveled through its orbit at a speed of more than 17,750 miles per hour. Spherical in shape, and with a diameter of 22.8 inches, the 184.3-pound *Sputnik* had a lifetime of 92 days, ending on January 4, 1958.

Sergey Korolyov, the Soviet designer of the craft, died in 1966, but he saw more than 50 of his designs successfully orbited and is often credited with being the man who kept the Soviets ahead in the "space race" until the 1969 American moon landing by Armstrong and Aldrin.

First Black Astronaut

LAWRENCE, ROBERT H., JR.—In 1963, black Air Force Captain Edward J. Dwight was appointed to the astronaut program. He failed, however, to qualify for training. On June 30, 1967, Air Force Major Robert Henry Lawrence, Jr. became the first black man to both be appointed and to qualify for the American astronaut training program. Lawrence met an untimely death six months later while accumulating flight time at Edwards Air Force Base in California. On December 8, 1967, the F-104 fighter jet being piloted by the major crashed on the base's runway, killing him instantly.

First Man to Walk in Space

LEONOV, ALEKSEY A.—Lieutenant Colonel Aleksey Arkhipovich Leonov left the Russian spacecraft, *Voshkod II,* on March 18, 1965, and, attached to a 16-foot nylon cord, spent 12 minutes and nine seconds floating in space. From 8:30 to 8:42, Leonov floated a distance of over 3,000 miles at a speed of 17,500 miles per hour. He then safely returned to the craft.

First Rocket Air Mail

LEY, WILLY—With the assistance of Louis Goodman and H. F. Pierce, Willy Ley (1906-1969) invented the first rocket to carry mail. Called the *Gloria,* the 11-foot-long rocket had a wingspan of 15 feet. On its first flight on February 23, 1936 from Greenwood Lake, New York, it carried 4,323 letters and 1,826 postcards to New York City in eight minutes.

Willy Ley, a pioneer in the field of rocket propulsion, was the author of several books on astronomy and missile travel. Among them are *Rockets, Missiles and Space, Beyond the Solar System* and *The Exploration of Mars.*

First Transatlantic Solo Flight

LINDBERGH, CHARLES A.—At 12:52 p.m. on May 20, 1927, American aviator Charles Lindbergh (1902-1974) took off from Roosevelt Field, Long Island, in a 220-horsepower Ryan monoplane, called *The Spirit of St. Louis.* Thirty-three hours, 29½ minutes and 3,610 miles later, he landed at Le Bourget airfield near Paris, France. As the first man to travel solo across the Atlantic, Lindbergh won $25,000 and world-wide acclaim. He was also honored by being appointed a colonel in the Air Force.

In 1935, Lindbergh assisted Dr. Alexis Carrel with the invention of the first artificial heart, which was a spirally coiled glass tube and pump.

The Refracting Telescope

LIPPERSHEY, JOHANNES—Eyeglasses had been in use for 300 years before man got the idea to combine two eyeglass lenses for purposes of magnification. Johannes (or Hans) Lippershey (1587-1619) noticed that when he viewed a weathervane atop his church's steeple through two such lenses he could see it more clearly. He mounted his discovery onto wooden tubes and, on October 2, 1608, sold them to the Dutch government as a secret war weapon. The device was soon brought to the attention of Galileo who, in constructing his own telescope, made the lenses more powerful and used them for astronomical rather than military observations.

First U.S. Aeronautical Degree

LOENING, GROVER C.—Grover C. Loening (1888-1976), the Wright Brothers' invaluable assistant and manager of their Dayton, Ohio aircraft factory, was a member of their original aircraft design team. He was taught to fly by Orville himself. In 1910, Columbia University honored Loening with the first aeronautical degree ever awarded in the United States. In 1912, while working for Blériot in France, he built one of the world's first amphibious airplanes, the *Aeroboat*. He later improved on this model and invented many important aviation devices. During World War II, Loening pioneered the use of helicopters and helped found Pan American Airways and Grumman Aircraft Corporation.

Greatest Altitude Attained by Man

LOVELL, JAMES A.; SWIGERT, JOHN L.; HAISE, FREDERICK W.—On April 11, 1970, the crew of *Apollo XIII* reached an altitude of 248,665 miles above the surface of the earth, and went into orbit around the moon. Lovell, Swigert and Haise were forced to abort their moonbound mission due to an oxygen explosion resulting in complete power loss in *Apollo XIII's* service module. The crew began the return home, using the Lunar Module as a "life boat," and splashed down safely on April 17.

First "Jet-Setter"

LOWESTEIN-WERTHEIM, PRINCESS VON—On the 21st day of May, 1914, Princess von Lowestein-Wertheim chartered a Handley-Page H.P.7 to take her from Britain to Paris for an urgent social function. Fog and inclement weather forced her to be late for the function, but the princess was so impressed with the idea of flying to parties that she commissioned the chairman of Handley-Page Aircraft to build a plane to fly her across the Atlantic for her transoceanic engagements. World War I broke out, however, and the idea was scrapped.

First Pilot Awarded Medal of Honor

LUKE, FRANK—Known as "the Arizona Balloon Buster" and "the American Wonder," Frank Luke (1897-1918) was the first pilot to receive the Congressional Medal of Honor, America's highest military decoration. Luke received his award posthumously for his feat of shooting down eight German observation balloons in four days (September 12-15, 1918) in Murvaux, France. Attached to the United States 27th Flying Squadron, Second Lieutenant Luke, who flew a Spad XIII pursuit ship, was especially adept at firing at the gas balloons used by the Germans for artillery observation. Although he was only in combat for two months, the Phoenix-born Luke destroyed 14 such balloons and four German aircraft. Shot down behind enemy lines on September 29, 1918, Luke fought with a handgun until he was outwitted by enemy infantrymen.

Greatest Jet Ace

McCONNELL, JOSEPH C.—Captain Joseph C. McConnell of the United States Air Force shot down 16 jet aircraft during his tours in the Korean War (1950-1953). This represents the greatest number of "kills" made by a pilot in jet-to-jet combat. McConnell almost always piloted the F-86 Sabre Jet; his targets were usually Russian-made MIG-15s.

Pilots of the Israeli and Egyptian air forces may have downed greater numbers of aircraft in the Six-Day War of 1967 and the Yom Kippur War of 1973, but the identities of any such pilots is still classified.

First Battleship Sunk by Plane

MITCHELL, WILLIAM—On July 21, 1921, General William Mitchell (1879-1936), an early advocate of a strong air force, attempted to convince the United States government to allot greater appropriations for the funding of the fledgling United States Air Corps. To demonstrate the potential effectiveness of a strong air force, he used the captured German battleship, *Ostfriesland*, hitting it directly with three 1,000-pound bombs dropped from Martin bombers. An additional seven bombs scored near misses, but shook open the seams of the vessel, causing it to run on its port side and sink. The government was unconvinced; it took two decades and a devastating Japanese attack on American warships at Pearl Harbor for the United States to realize the importance of air superiority.

First Hot Air Balloon

MONTGOLFIER, JOSEPH M. AND JACQUES E.—On June 5, 1783, Joseph Michel Montgolfier and his younger brother, Jacques Etienne, launched a hot air balloon of their invention. The passengers on the ten-minute flight, near Annonay, France, were a sheep, a duck and a rooster.

The Montgolfier brothers, papermakers by trade, had observed that debris rose from fire. Their experimentation with paper bags led them to the construction of a cloth balloon, 110 feet in circumference. They fastened paper to the cloth using buttons. After their successful flight on June 5, they prepared for the first manned flight, which was completed successfully later in 1783 with Pilatre de Rozier aboard.

Inventor of the Wind Tunnel

MUNK, MAX MICHAEL—Working with the National Aeronautics Advisory Committee at Langley Field, Virginia, Max Munk (1881-1947) developed the idea of the *wind tunnel* for testing new aircraft designs. In April, 1923, Dr. Munk prepared a tunnel which tested models traveling at an air speed of 80 miles per hour. The simulated conditions were achieved through use of compressed air and a propeller.

Inventor of the Jet Engine

OHAIN, HANS VON—The Heinkel Hel 78, a turbo-jet-engined aircraft, invented by Dr. Hans von Ohain, was first flown in 1939. The centrifugal-flow jet engine was designed for the rapidly developing Nazi Luftwaffe. Von Ohain's engine was originally used in heavy, bomber-type aircraft, but later was successfully used against the Allies as a fighter engine, most significantly the Messerschmitt Me262. The Germans also produced the first successful rocket-engined warplane, the Me163 Komet, first flown in 1944 against the Allies.

Discoverer of Great Comet

OLBERS, HEINRICH WILHELM—A physician by trade and an amateur stargazer throughout his life, Heinrich Wilhelm Olbers made many important astronomical discoveries. Most of his research was concentrated in the field of comets, and the great comet which he discovered in 1815 was named in his honor.

In 1807, Dr. Olbers discovered the only asteroid (or *planetoid,* as he called them)—Vesta, with a diameter of 206 miles—visible to the naked eye. He also discovered the asteroid Pallas in 1802, which he was led to believe consisted of remnants of a planet which had exploded.

Stratosphere Explorer

PICCARD, AUGUSTE—The stratosphere, with a fairly constant temperature of 67° F., begins at an altitude of about seven miles above the earth's surface and continues to the ionosphere. In the late 1920s, Swiss physicist Auguste Piccard (1884-1962) invented a high-altitude balloon which, in 1931 with Piccard aboard, penetrated the *stratosphere.* The physicist thus became the first man to pass through the lowest layer of the earth's atmosphere. Piccard's twin brother, Jean Felix, also explored the stratosphere in a balloon, setting further altitude records.

Auguste also invented the *bathyscaphe,* a submersible vehicle capable of traveling into the ocean depths. In 1954, he descended 12,285 feet in his craft. The marine work was continued by his son, Jacques, who set many depth records.

World Solo Airplane Flight

POST, WILEY—Wiley Post, born in Texas oil field country in 1898, had an adventurous nature. He began his career as a parachute jumper, playing country fairs. In 1933, Post flew his Lockheed "Vega"-type monoplane around the world in seven days, 18 hours and 49 minutes, stopping ten times for fuel. His plane, *Winnie Mae,* had made a successful flight around the world two years previously, carrying Post and another man. So, when on July 22, 1933 Post returned safely to Floyd Bennett Field in New York City, he became the first man to fly around the world *twice.*

On his solo flight, Post spent a total of 115 hours, 36 minutes, 30 seconds in the air—flying first to Berlin, across Russia and down through Alaska and Canada. He lost his life in 1935 while flying the satirist Will Rogers to a speaking engagement.

World War I Ace

RICHTHOFEN, MANFRED VON—Manfred von Richthofen (1892-1918) is credited with having shot down 80 Allied airplanes during his World War I service in the German air force. The leader of Jagstaffel 11, which saw extensive service on the French-Belgian border, he flew several types of aircraft, including the Albatros D5, the Fokker D7 and the Fokker DR1 triplane.

Von Richthofen was killed in an aerial duel with Captain Roy Brown of the British air force, over Amiens, France on April 21, 1918.

Most Distinguished Service Crosses

RICKENBACKER, EDWARD V.—America's top World War I ace, Captain Edward Vernon Rickenbacker (1890-1973) shot down 26 enemy aircraft during his brief tour on the Western Front. While in service during the Second World War, his plane was shot down over the Pacific. He survived many days on the ocean before being rescued.

For his impressive war record, Eddie Rickenbacker was awarded the Distinguished Service Cross ten times, winning the nation's second highest decoration more than any other serviceman. He later served as president of Eastern Airlines until his death in 1973.

American in Space

SHEPARD, ALAN B.—On May 5, 1961, a 2,000-pound *Mercury* capsule manned by Alan B. Shepard was launched on a 15-minute suborbital flight from Cape Canaveral, Florida. The launch was powered by a Redstone booster rocket delivering 75,000 pounds of thrust, and enabling the craft to travel at a ground speed of 4,500 miles per hour. Shepard reached an altitude of 115 miles and remained weightless for five minutes. Three days after the mission, he was awarded the first N.A.S.A. Distinguished Service Medal by President John F. Kennedy.

Helicopter Pioneer

SIKORSKY, IGOR—Igor Ivan Sikorsky (1885-1972) made a fortune building bombers for the Russian Air Force during World War I, but was forced to flee his native land following the revolution of 1917. He settled in the United States in 1919. On April 17, 1941, Sikorsky made the first helicopter flight from water. The helicopter, a Vought-Sikorsky of his own design, was mounted with rubber bags to keep it afloat. Two days earlier, on April 15, 1941, the craft had made the first helicopter flight of more than one hour's duration. On May 13, 1942, another helicopter of Sikorsky's design made the first cross-country helicopter flight, with test pilot C. S. Morris at the stick.

Fastest Humans

STAFFORD, THOMAS P.; CERNAN, EUGENE A.; YOUNG, JOHN W.—On May 26, 1969, traveling at 24,791 miles per hour upon re-entry into the earth's atmosphere in *Apollo X's* Command Service Module, Stafford, Cernan and Young set a new record for human speed. The trio was at an altitude of 400,000 feet when they reached maximum speed.

The crew also set an absolute altitude record for humans during their orbit of the moon, a record which was later to be broken by *Apollo XIII*.

The mission of *Apollo X* was to fly close to the moon to scout possible landing sites for *Apollo XI* and to test separation and docking procedures for landing.

Woman in Space

TERESHKOVA, VALENTINA V.—Junior Lieutenant (now Lieutenant Colonel) Tereshkova (born on March 6, 1937) orbited the earth 48 times after being launched aboard *Vostok VI* on June 16, 1963. She traveled more than 1,225,000 miles in a flight which lasted two days, 22 hours and 46 minutes. During the flight, she came within three miles of *Vostok V*. In so doing, the Russian became the woman to have reached the greatest altitude above the earth (143.5 miles) and to have traveled the fastest (17,470 mph).

Transporter of Atomic Bombs

TIBBETS, PAUL W., JR.—Paul Tibbets was commander of the B-29 Superfortress bomber, *Enola Gay*, when it dropped atomic bombs on the Japanese industrial towns of Hiroshima and Nagasaki in August of 1945. The aircraft had been stripped and specially prepared to carry and discharge the bulky bombs, which released a force equivalent to 20,000 tons of TNT. The bombardier, Major Thomas W. Forebee, entered a mental institution after learning of the bombs' destructive results. *Enola Gay* is now in the Smithsonian Institute.

Discoverer of Pluto

TOMBAUGH, CLYDE W.—Long predicted by Dr. Percival Lowell in *Memoirs on a Trans-Neptunian Planet* (1915), Pluto, the outermost planet of our solar system, was discovered and verified photographically on February 18, 1930 by Clyde W. Tombaugh. An astronomer working in Lowell's observatory in Flagstaff, Arizona, Tombaugh, following mathematical directions given by Lowell, found the planet in almost precisely the spot estimated by the eminent scientist. Pluto, which is more than 3.6 billion miles away from the sun, takes nearly 248 years to circle that body. Surface temperature on Pluto is approximately — 400° F.

Rocket Pierces Outer Space

VON BRAUN, WERNHER—At the age of 20, Wernher von Braun (1912-), head of a German Army rocket research center, helped develop the V-1 and V-2 rocket bombs that destroyed much of London during World War II. Captured by the Allies, Von Braun was brought to the United States to teach rocketry. On February 24, 1949, he fired a V-2 with an American Wac Corporal warhead into outer space for the first time.

Earliest Astronomer in America

WINTHROP, JOHN—John Winthrop (1714-1779), great-grandson of the colonial governor of the same name, observed sun-spots in April of 1739, making the first significant contribution to astronomy in America. In 1761, the Commonwealth of Massachusetts outfitted the first scientific expedition in the New World and Winthrop, a physicist, was selected to lead the Newfoundland-bound group. On the expedition, Winthrop made the second series of his observations of the planet Mercury.

First Sustained Flight

WRIGHT, ORVILLE—Orville Wright (1871-1948) was piloting the airplane he and his brother, Wilbur, had built when, on December 17, 1903, at 10:35 a.m., it remained aloft for 12 seconds on Kill Devil Hill, Kitty Hawk, North Carolina. The craft, the *Flyer I*, a 12-horsepower, chaindriven bi-plane, attained an airspeed on that day of 35 miles per hour. Five witnesses looked on.

In 1909, Orville and Wilbur Wright sold the United States government its first airplane for a sum of $30,000. The Dayton, Ohio-built aircraft was called *Miss Columbia;* it attained a speed of 42 miles per hour to qualify for the government contract.

Orville was awarded the Civil Aeronautics Administration's first honorary license on August 19, 1940.

Underwater Jet Engine

ZWICKY, FRITZ—Originally interested in astronomy, Fritz Zwicky (1898-1974) was the first to explain the phenomena of flashing *supernovae*, huge stars, visible from earth, which exploded millions of years ago. While Zwicky served as director of the Aerojet Engineering Corporation (1943-1949), the jet engine was developed and rocket propellants were tested. In 1949, Zwicky patented the underwater jet engine and was awarded the Presidential Freedom Medal.

ADVENTURERS AND DAREDEVILS

First to Reach South Pole

AMUNDSEN, ROALD—Between 1903 and 1906, Norwegian explorer Roald Amundsen (1872-1928) navigated the Northwest Passage, accomplishing what Columbus and others had attempted but failed to do.

In October of 1911, Amundsen and a party of four landed their exploration vessel, *Fram,* in the Bay of Whales. Fifty-three days later, on December 1, 1911, after a long and arduous trip by dog sled, they became the first men to reach the southern tip of the world—the South Pole.

Lion and Tiger Tamer

BEATTY, CLYDE—Although there is differing opinion as to whether it is more dangerous to tame lions by themselves or with tigers, Clyde (Raymond) Beatty (1904-1965) thought a mixed lot was more challenging. He tamed 40 of the beasts simultaneously, a record. Beatty was a featured attraction at Ringling Brothers circus during the 1940s and 1950s.

First Electrically-Lit Steamboat

BENNETT, JAMES GORDON—When James Bennett (1841-1918), son of the founder and editor of the *New York Herald,* took over the management of the newspaper in 1867, he did not abandon the journal's sensational style. The younger Bennett was a man who always sought excitement. He loved steamships, and his *Jeannette,* the first steamship to use electric lights, was designed for an exploration of the Bering Strait between Siberia and Alaska. The vessel met an unfortunate fate: 'it sank during its main voyage in 1879. Bennett had better luck with another of his nautical acquisitions. The *Henrietta* won the first transatlantic yacht race in 1866, which included a $90,000 prize.

In 1876, Bennett introduced polo to the United States, a game he enjoyed so much during a visit to England that, upon his return to the United States, he purchased stables of horses and formed a league. He is also credited with having sent Stanley to find Livingston in darkest Africa.

Niagara Falls Tightrope Walker

BLONDIN, CHARLES—Charles Blondin was the stage name of Jean Francois Gravelet, the greatest wire walker of the nineteenth century. On July 30, 1855, Blondin made the first crossing of Niagara Falls on a three-inch, 1,100-foot-long wire suspended 160 feet above the cataract. By the time Blondin reached the other side, he was soaking wet from the spray.

Five years later, on September 30, 1860, Blondin repeated the feat—only this time he carried a man on his back. The brave man was Harry Colcord, the wirewalker's agent.

Woman Globe-Trotter

BLY, NELLIE—Reporter Elizabeth Cochrane (1865?-1922), under the pseudonym Nellie Bly, toured the globe in 72 days, six hours, 11 minutes and 14 seconds under the sponsorship of the *New York World*. She began her voyage aboard the *Augusta Victoria* from New York City on November 14, 1889 and returned to New York aboard the Chicago Express train on January 25, 1890. Total traveling time was 56½ days, but Cochrane spent some of that time in Russia and Japan. She later wrote extensively for the *World* about her experiences.

Most Remote Island Discoverer

BOUVET DE LOZIER, J.B.C.—On New Year's Day, 1739, the French Antarctic explorer, J. B. C. Bouvet de Lozier, sighted Liverpool Island. The island, now called Bouvet Oya in his honor, is a possession of Norway located in the South Atlantic 1,050 miles from the nearest land, Queen Maud Land, which, like Bouvet Oya, is uninhabited. Man first set foot on Bouvet Oya (located at 5426'S by 324'E) 86 years later in the person of Captain George Norris.

Inventor of the Bowie Knife

BOWIE, JAMES—Although it is only legendary that Jim Bowie invented the first Bowie knife, the fact that he used one as early as 1835 is not disputed. His alleged invention, with single-edged blade and curved point, was not as long as the Roman short sword but longer than the average hunting knife. Bowie possibly got the idea for the new kind of weapon when his regular sword was broken off 20 inches from the hilt. He found that it was still useful for close range combat and proceeded to fashion another one from a file. Bowie became a colonel in the Texas army during its revolt against the Mexicans and was leader of the Alamo defenders when the outpost was overrun by Santa Ana's army in 1836.

First Woman Parachutist

BROADWICK, TINY—Having jumped from balloons many times as part of her traveling parachute show, on June 21, 1913, Tiny Broadwick became the first woman to parachute from an airplane. She free-fell for 100 feet and then, buoyed by an 11-pound silk chute, floated an additional 900 feet to the ground, landing in a barley field near Griffith Field, Los Angeles, California. Appearing on the Groucho Marx quiz show, *You Bet Your Life,* in 1957, Broadwick claimed that she had more parachute jumps to her credit than any woman in history.

First New-World Pirate

BULL, DIXIE—The story goes that Dixie Bull (?-1638) had just moved in to clear a piece of land he had purchased near York, Maine in 1631 when a pinnace (a small sailing ship) of the French government landed on his Penobscot Bay property. His boat was seized with the large supply of provisions he had brought from England to make his way in the New World. Dejected, Bull turned to a life of piracy which began with the looting of Bristol, Maine in November of 1632. Hoards of his plunder are said to be buried on remote islands off Nova Scotia; the first pirate in America was killed before he was able to claim his loot.

Fastest Transatlantic Solo Sail

CHICHESTER, FRANCIS—In 1970, Francis Chichester (1901-   ) of Great Britain sailed his 57-foot vessel, *Gypsy Moth V,* from Portuguese Guinea on the West Coast of Africa to Nicaragua. The 22.4-day trip was the fastest East-West solo transatlantic crossing ever made by boat. Chichester followed the less treacherous southern route; the record for the northern route, set in 1934 by Captain R. D. Graham, had taken two days longer. The adventurer traveled an average 179.1 miles per day during his three-week voyage.

Chichester was knighted by Queen Elizabeth II for his feat of sailing around the world alone in a boat similar to the *Gypsy Moth,* completing his nine-month 28,500-mile voyage on May 18, 1967.

Earliest Wild West Show

CODY, BUFFALO BILL—William Frederick Cody (1846-1917) produced the first Wild West show as part of the Fourth of July celebration in North Platte, Nebraska in 1883. The next year, he followed that success with a commercialized and expanded touring version of the show. Cody featured trick shooters, such as Annie Oakley, and famous Indian chiefs and mountain men. The first stop of the tour was Omaha, Nebraska.

First to Cross Antarctic Circle

COOK, JAMES—Aboard the *Resolution,* English navigator James Cook (1728-1779) crossed latitude 66°30′ South on January 17, 1773. During that exploratory voyage, during which he set out to map the South Pacific, Captain Cook discovered New Caledonia, New Hebrides, Norfolk Island and the Cook Islands.

In all, the captain made three voyages around the Horn. The first one, in *Endeavour,* took him to Australia and New Zealand. His third and last voyage took him to the Sandwich Islands, later the Hawaiian Islands, where he was killed by natives.

First American-Born of English Parents

DARE, VIRGINIA—Born in Roanoke Island, North Carolina on August 18, 1587, Virginia Dare was the daughter of Ananias and Eleanor (White) Dare. Her grandfather, John White, was the governor of the colony that had been set up by Sir Walter Raleigh earlier that year. The vessel that had brought the Dare family to the New World returned to England for more supplies nine days after her birth. When they returned four years later, the colony that had been established was in ruins and no trace of the colonists, including Virginia Dare, was in evidence.

First White Man to See Old Miss

DE SOTO, HERNANDO—The largest river on the North American continent, now known as the Mississippi, was first seen by white men when a Spanish explorer, Hernando De Soto (1500?-1542), and his men landed at the village of Chisca in May, 1541. The following year, after having succumbed to exhaustion and fever, De Soto was buried at the bottom of this same river which they called the "Rio de Espiritu Santu," in what is now Louisiana.

A conquistador with Pizarro in Peru and a governor of Cuba around 1536, De Soto explored what are now Florida, Georgia, Tennessee, Alabama, Mississippi and Oklahoma in search of the seven cities of gold. He never found them.

First Christian Service on West Coast

DRAKE, FRANCIS—During his circumnavigation of the world in 1577, English admiral Francis Drake (1543?-1596) held the first Christian religious service on the American West Coast. The Holy Communion was read on June 24, 1579 near San Francisco, California. The chaplain who performed that first service, Francis Fletcher, wrote an account of Drake's 'round-the-world voyage aboard the *Golden Hind*. From this account, we learn that Drake and his crew realized 500,000 English pounds on the venture, which included plundering all the Spanish gold and trading settlements they passed.

Sir Francis Drake, knighted for his three-year voyage by Queen Elizabeth, was later instrumental in defeating the Spanish Armada in 1588. His brilliant maritime record is cause for him to be regarded as the founder of British naval tradition.

First White Man in North America

ERICSON, LEIF—Around the year 1000 A.D., a small band of Vikings, led by Leif Ericson, son of Eric the Red, the ruler of Greenland, landed on the North American continent somewhere between Labrador and Virginia. Ericson called the land Vinland because of the abundance of grapes thereabouts. Leif and his men were the first whites to reach the New World, antedating Columbus by 500 years. Ericson's nephew, Snorro, was the first white child to be born in North America.

First Route through Rockies

FREMONT, JOHN CHARLES—The Oregon Trail, the first overland route to the American West Coast, stretched from Independence Landing, Missouri to the mouth of the Columbia River in Washington. The trail was blazed in 1842 by John Fremont (1813-1890), who was on a surveying and mapping expedition for the United States government.

Fremont soon became an important West Coast political figure, first as civil governor of California and, in 1850, as a United States senator. He ran for president in 1856 on the Free Soil Party ticket, but was defeated by James Buchanan. During the Civil War, the defeated presidential candidate became a general officer and, from 1878 to 1883, was governor of the Arizona Territory.

First to Climb Mount Everest

HILLARY, EDMUND PERCIVAL—Edmund Hillary, born in Auckland, New Zealand in 1919, yearned for excitement even during his early days as a beekeeper. After World War II, he took up mountain climbing in the Himalayas, the world's largest mountain range. On May 29, 1953, he and Tenzig Norgay, a Sherpa tribesman, reached the top of the 29,028-foot Mount Everest, the highest mountain peak in the world. Hillary was knighted by Queen Elizabeth for the accomplishment.

In 1957, Sir Edmund blazed the trail for the first transantarctic expedition. In 1960, in search of the Abominable Snowman, he climbed the 27,780-foot Mount Makalu.

First to Wear Tights

HOWER, NELSON—Nelson Hower was a bareback horse rider with the traveling Buckley & Wicks Show of Chicago. The conventional costume for the show's performers was a tight-fitting jacket and waistcoat, knee breeches and long stockings. One night during the company's tour in 1828, the costume wagon failed to arrive in time for the show. The undaunted Hower followed the old adage that "the show must go on" and out he went standing on the bareback of a horse—in his woolen long underwear. He found maneuverability far greater in his longjohns than in the constrictive show uniform he was accustomed to wearing. From then on he appeared in a specially-made costume of knit fabric closely resembling his underwear.

First to Seek Northwest Passage

HUDSON, HENRY—When it became known that Columbus had not discovered a route to the Indies, European explorers and geographers reasoned that there must be a northern route around America. Beginning in 1607, English navigator Henry Hudson (?-1611) searched for this imagined Northwest Passage. He never found it, of course, but, during his four voyages, he did find Chesapeake Bay, Delaware Bay and the Hudson River. On his last trip, in 1611, he travelled to the far north, where he discovered Hudson's Bay. But, Hudson was unable to obtain enough food to sustain his men. They mutinied, casting Hudson, his son and eight others into a boat. The explorer and his family were never heard from again.

Workmen's Compensation Agreement

KIDD, WILLIAM—A Scottish-born sailor who later settled in New York, Captain William Kidd (1645?-1701) commanded the 787-ton privateer, *Adventure Galley*. Sailing in service for the British, he was rewarded, in 1691, for his successful resistance of French privateers which had been attacking British ships. On January 26, 1695, he announced to his crew that 600 pieces of eight or six dismembered slaves would be awarded to any man who lost an arm or leg in battle; one hundred pieces would be awarded for a joint lost. Kidd was hanged as a pirate in 1701, but not before he had established the first workman's compensation benefits plan.

Stunt Driver Injuries

KNIEVEL, EVEL—Montana-born stunt driver Robert Craig "Evel" Knievel (1938-) has successfully jumped over the fountains at Caesar's Palace, 19 automobiles (129 feet), 14 Mack trucks (once in a soccer stadium in England and, on another occasion, in Canada), and has made a variety of long ramp-to-ramp leaps on a motorcycle. In 1972, Knievel broke 431 bones, including his neck, skull, back, both arms, both legs, shoulderblade, ribs, pelvis, hands and a foot. He claims that his greatest stunt was the traversing of the Snake River Canyon in Montana on September 7, 1974 on a rocket-powered BSA motorcycle, called a Skycycle. Due to a faulty parachute mechanism, he did not make it to the other side of the canyon. But, he suffered only a bloody nose and collected over one million dollars for his effort.

First Army Balloon Pilot

LAHM, FRANK P.—A West Point graduate, Frank Lahm won the Bennett Cup International Balloon Race in Paris in 1906. In 1912, during his Army career, he organized the aviation service of the Philippines and commanded the Second Army Air Service during World War I. Between 1926 and 1930, he organized the Air Corps training centers in the United States. The first United States Army pilot rose to the rank of brigadier general and assistant to the chief of the Air Corps. He died in 1976.

Most Unusual Swim

LaLANNE, JACK—Jack LaLanne has made a fortune from his network of 1,000 health spas, physical fitness aids and a regular television program on which, for the past 20 years, he has demonstrated proper exercise methods. For the more than 40 years that he has been in the business, LaLanne has tried to demonstrate that advancing age need not be a liability to keeping oneself fit. To prove his point, in October of 1975, 61-year-old LaLanne swam a distance of two miles across San Francisco Bay. Wearing a diver's wetsuit, and with his hands and feet bound in chains, LaLanne towed a 2,000-pound boat across the bay. He swam underwater using a compressed air breathing apparatus. Commenting on the two-hour swim, LaLanne later said: "Anything is possible with proper food and exercise." His wife maintained that it was not a publicity stunt.

Expedition Across North America

LEWIS AND CLARK—Captain Meriwether Lewis (1774-1809) and Captain William Clark (1770-1838) undertook an expedition from St. Louis, Missouri to the Pacific Coast on May 14, 1804. The party reached the mouth of the Columbia River on November 8, 1805 and returned to St. Louis on September 23, 1806.

Accompanying Lewis and Clark were 14 United States Army soldiers, nine Kentucky volunteers, two French explorer/adventurers, and a Negro servant. They employed the services of the Indian woman, Sacajaweya, as a guide through the mountainous and wooded terrain of the Northwest.

Circumnavigation of Earth

MAGELLAN, FERDINAND—After long service to King Manuel I of Portugal, including explorations to India and the Spice Islands, Ferdinand Magellan (1480?-1521) set out to find the "bottom" of the earth. He discovered what became the Strait of Magellan and crossed the Pacific to the Philippine Islands. In the Philippines, the Portuguese navigator became involved in a native war, in which he was killed. When the battling had ended, only one of the seven ships with which Magellan and crew had begun their mission from Spain remained intact. The lone vessel, the *Vittoria*, continued its voyage, circling Africa and returning to Spain two years and 30,700 miles later.

Mile-a-Minute Bicyclist

MURPHY, CHARLES MINTHORN—On June 30, 1899, Charles Minthorn Murphy rode a bicycle over a distance of one mile in 57.8 seconds, the first cyclist to travel a mile a minute. "Mile-a-Minute" Murphy, as he came to be called, paced himself behind a Long Island Railroad train going from Farmingdale to Maywood, Long Island on a three-mile measured course. The train was equipped with a special wind-breaking device so Mile-a-Minute wouldn't have to battle the breezes.

Biggest TV Quiz Winner

NADLER, TEDDY—By September, 1958, Teddy Nadler had won a total of $264,000 on American television quiz programs. He appeared on the most popular, including the *$64,000 Question*. Nadler, now unemployed, reportedly paid more than $150,000 in income taxes on his winnings.

Following a series of scandals involving cheating and fraud in quiz shows, regulations were tightened. Today, a contestant can win no more than $25,000 on a quiz or game show.

First to Ski Across Greenland

NANSEN, FRIDTJOF—The 1922 Nobel Peace Prize winner, Fridtjof Nansen (1861-1930), a man of varied talents, was knowledgeable in the fields of oceanography, zoology and diplomacy. In attempting to prove that the polar ice packs flow in a manner that draws the ice steadily towards the northern or southernmost point, he fastened his exploration vessel, the *Fram,* into a pack of ice in 1893 and floated to within 85° 14′ North. Subsequently, in 1895, he walked further north, to 86° 14′, thus establishing a record for northern exploration.

Nansen skied across the ice packs of Greenland in 1888, becoming the first to accomplish that feat. Between 1906 and 1908, he acted as Norway's first minister to England, following his successful peace negotiations between Norway and Sweden. His later work with World War I refugees won him the Nobel Peace Prize.

First Black to See New World

NIÑO, PEDRO ALONZO—When Christopher Columbus crossed the Atlantic to the New World in 1492 in three ships, the navigator of one of those ships—the *Niña*—was Pedro Alonzo Niño (1470?-1524?). Niño, a black man, had "signed on" with Columbus in the summer of 1492. He was chosen by the ship's captain, Vicente Pinzón, to act as the navigator of the *Niña.*

Fastest Swim Around Manhattan Island

NYAD, DIANA—On October 1, 1975, Diana Nyad, a swimming coach at Columbia University, set a mark of seven hours 57 minutes for a 28-mile swim around Manhattan Island, New York, breaking the old record by almost an hour. Acknowledged as the greatest living female long-distance swimmer, Nyad made the swim clockwise to avoid the dangerous Hell's Gate currents. The 65-degree Fahrenheit water (despite the fact that she had covered herself in pure lanolin) was icy cold. She lost 10 pounds during the swim.

Nyad's future plans include a swim across Lake Ontario and a swim around the perimeter of the Bermuda Triangle.

Greatest Trick Shooter

OAKLEY, ANNIE—For 35 years, between the ages of 27 and 62, Annie Oakley, the semilegendary frontier woman, toured in Buffalo Bill's Wild West Show, demonstrating a unique shooting prowess. She could shoot 100 out of 100 clay pigeons, could split a playing card head-on at 25 yards, hit a dime in mid-air and shoot a cigarette from the lips of Frank Butler, her husband.

Born Anne Mozee in 1860, she toured the American West and Midwest with such Wild West luminaries as Chief Sitting Bull of the Dakota tribe which defeated General G. A. Custer at the Battle of the Little Bighorn in 1876. Annie died in 1926.

First to Sight Antarctica

PALMER, NATHANIEL B.—With his 44-ton sloop, *Hero,* and a crew of six, Captain Nathaniel Brown Palmer (1799-1877) sailed south from Stonington, Connecticut on July 25, 1820. He passed through the Drake Passage and the South Shetland Islands and, on November 18, 1820, he sighted the tip of Antarctica, the largest uninhabited body of land on earth. The tip of land, located at approximately 64° South latitude by 60° West longitude, south of Argentina, was named the Palmer Peninsula in his honor. Palmer returned to his point of departure in July of 1821.

Largest Meteorite Found

PEARY, ROBERT E.—A 68,085-pound meteorite, known to the Eskimos of Greenland as the "Abnighito," was found near Cape York, Greenland by Commander Robert Edwin Peary during his polar explorations of 1897. The "Tent" meteorite, as it is known, is the largest one to be exhibited in any museum and is now on exhibit at the Hayden Planetarium in New York City.

Peary (1856-1920) is credited with the discovery of the North Pole in 1908, although proof of the discovery is hard to find. By a special act of Congress the American rear admiral's many contributions to arctic exploration were recognized in 1911. Peary Land, in North Greenland, is named after him.

Highest Tightrope Walker

PETIT, PHILIPPE—Philippe Petit (1948-   ), of Nemours, France, sneaked past maintenance men in the early hours of August 7, 1974, and using a crossbow, shot a tightrope from one of the twin World Trade Center towers to the other. He then proceeded to walk the rope, 1,350 feet above the streets of downtown New York City, a feat no man had ever before dared. After successfully completing his walk, Petit was arrested and "sentenced" to perform his act in Central Park for a group of underprivileged children. He is currently employed by Ringling Brothers, Barnum and Bailey Circus.

First New World Beer

RALEIGH, WALTER—Walter Raleigh, the English explorer, statesman, courtier, historian and poet, was born around the year 1552. A favorite of Queen Elizabeth, he was the first to bring potatoes and tobacco to England from the New World. He had established an early colony on Roanoke Island, Virginia in 1585 and, in 1587, at that English encampment, the first beer in the New World was brewed. To manufacture the beverage, the available malt, hops and maize showed to them by the Indians was used.

Raleigh's expeditions in North and Central America, in search of the fabled El Dorado, led to his discovery of Guinea, Trinidad and the Orinoco River. During his travels, the adventurer wreaked havoc in Spanish settlements. He was beheaded in 1618 after the Spanish ambassador to England convinced James I that Raleigh was a pirate.

First Moving Train Robbery

RENO BROTHERS AND SPARKS, FRANK—As the 9:02 was pulling out of Seymour, Indiana on October 6, 1866, three men leaped aboard the baggage and express car and put guns to the heads of the surprised guards. The bandits, John and Simeon Reno, with their accomplice, Frank Sparks, threw two safes off the train and then themselves jumped to safety. This was the first robbery of a moving train in history. The $45,000 that had been taken was recovered when the gang was caught soon after. The trio was never tried for the Seymour, Indiana crime, but the Ohio & Mississippi Railroad finally brought them to justice for later crimes against the line.

First Tobacco Crop by White Man

ROLFE, JOHN—On May 13, 1607, the first English settlers arrived in the New World and set up a settlement in Jamestown, Virginia. John Rolfe was one of the original 108 who tried to make a life with the Indians. Rolfe learned about tobacco from the Indian princess, Pocahontas, and, in 1612, planted his first crop. He married Pocahontas in 1613 after her conversion to Christianity.

Gas Turbine Auto Test

ROSE, MAURI—The General Motors Corporation introduced the first gasoline-fueled turbine car in 1954 in New York City. The vehicle, which was never commercially-produced because of its rapid fuel consumption, had been tested the previous year in Milford, Michigan by three-time Indianapolis 500 winner Mauri Rose, who had at one time been rated as one of the top three drivers in the world. Rose is said to have tested the vehicle, the XP-21 Firebird, at speeds in excess of 235 miles per hour (although its listed speed was a mere 150), a *very* fast car for its time. The Firebird, which was powered by a 370-horsepower Whirlfire Turbojet, could only seat one person.

Southernmost Active Volcano

ROSS, JAMES CLARK—British rear-admiral and polar explorer Sir James Clark Ross (1800-1862) discovered Ross Sea, Ross Shelf Ice and Ross Island. On Ross Island, he found an active volcano, Mount Erebus, on January 26, 1841; it is the southernmost active volcano known. The 12,450-foot volcano was not climbed until 67 years later, by Tannatt W. E. David and a party of five. Ross, who located the North Magnetic Pole in 1831, made several extensive voyages to the northern polar cap and to Antarctica. In 1818, in the company of his uncle, Sir John Ross, he made his first expedition in search of the Northwest Passage.

First Solo Globe Circumnavigation

SLOCUM, JOSHUA—A retired mariner, Captain Joshua Slocum (1844-1909) was jokingly given the ruined remains of a boat by another captain who dared him to rebuild it. Slocum not only rebuilt it, but sailed it around the world *alone*. Starting from Newport, Rhode Island, on April 24, 1895, he completed his 46,000-mile journey on July 3, 1898, taking the westerly route through the Strait of Magellan.

After making his record voyage, Slocum lectured on seamanship. Longing to return to the water, the captain readied his old boat, a 37-foot gaff yawl called the *Spray*, and cruised the Atlantic and Caribbean for several years before disappearing. After an extensive search in the Bermuda Triangle, Slocum was officially reported "lost at sea."

First New World Kidnapping

VERRAZANO, GIOVANNI DE—Giovanni de Verrazano (1485?-1528?) was an Italian navigator in the service of France. On July 8, 1524, he wrote a letter to France's King Francis I, telling of his experiences on his voyage to the New World. He described how his men had unsuccessfully tried to kidnap an old woman and a young woman in the New World. The women had cried and struggled, successfully fending off their attackers. Verrazano's men abandoned the idea of abducting the two women and, instead, captured an Indian child. Whether or not the child was actually brought to France is unknown. What is known is that Verrazano and his men were responsible for the first known kidnapping in the New World.

First Human Cannonball

ZACCHINI, HUGO—While an artilleryman in the Italian Army during World War I, Hugo Zacchini conceived a circus act in which a human would be shot from a cannon. At the end of the war, he broached the idea to his father's troupe, The Zacchini Brothers, by whom it was received enthusiastically, and Hugo set about building his equipment.

On the island of Malta, in 1922, his act was unveiled for the first time: he safely fired himself 200 feet through the air and into a net. Zacchini toured Europe with his family for the next seven years before being contracted by John Ringling of the Ringling Brothers/Barnum & Bailey Circus, with whom he appeared for 40 years. Zacchini performed at the Rose Bowl, in New York's Madison Square Garden and at the 1939 New York World's Fair before retiring in 1961.

INDEX

Kolff, Willem, 188
Konig, Friederich, 107
Korolyov, Sergey Pavlovich, 209
Koufax, Sandy, 25
Kramer, Stanley, 60
Kreisler, Fritz, 61

Laennec, Rene H. H., 188
Lafayette, Marquis de, 146
La Follette, Philip, 146
Lahm, Frank P., 225
LaLanne, Jack, 226
Land, Edwin, 107
Landau, Martin, 61
Larsen, Don, 25
Lasker, Emanuel, 25
Laurens, Henry, 146
Laver, Rod, 26
Lawrence, E. O., 188
Lawrence, Mary Wells, 107
Lawrence, Robert H., Jr., 210
Leakey, Richard, 188
Led Zeppelin, 61
Leeuwenhoek, Anton van, 189
Leibnitz, Gottfried Wilhelm von, 189
Lenin, 147
Lennon, John, 62
Lenoir, Étienne, 108
Leo XIII, Pope, 147
Leonov, Aleksey A., 210
Lesseps, Ferdinand de, 108
Lewis and Clark, 226
Lewis, Fulton, Jr., 62
Ley, Willy, 210
Lie, Trygve, 147
Lincoln, Abraham, 147
Lincoln, Robert Todd, 148
Lind, Jenny, 62
Lindbergh, Charles A., 210
Lippershey, Johannes, 211
Loening, Grover C., 211
Long, Crawford W., 189
Long, Russell B., 148
Loubet, Emile F., 148
Louis XIII, King, 149
Louis XV, King, 149
Louis, Joe, 26
Lovell, James A., 211
Lowestein-Wertheim, Princess von, 212
Luke, Frank, 212

Macadam, John, 108
MacArthur, Douglas, 149
MacDonald, John Alexander, 150

MacIntosh, Charles, 108
MacMillan, Ernest, 63
MacMillan, Kirkpatrick, 109
Madison, James, 150
Magee, Carl C., 109
Magellan, Ferdinand, 226
Mahan, Larry, 26
Mahler, Gustav, 63
Maiman, Theo, 189
Mallon, Mary, 109
Mantle, Mickey, 26
Manutius, Aldus, 63
Marconi, Guglielmo, 109
Maris, Roger, 27
Marshall, George C., 150
Marshall, Thurgood, 151
Martin, A. J. P., 190
Martin, Dean, 63
Mather, Cotton, 151
Mather, Increase, 190
Matisse, Henri, 64
Mauchly, J. W., 181
Maxwell, James Clerk, 190
McCarthy, Charlie, 64
McCarthy, Joe, 27
McCartney, Paul, 62
McCay, Winsor, 64
McClellan, George Brinton, 152
McConnell, Joseph C., 212
McCormick, Cyrus H., 110
McWhirter, Ross, 65
Medici, Lorenzo de, 152
Meegeren, Hans van, 65
Mendel, Gregor, 190
Mendelyeev, Dmitri, 191
Menendez, Pedro de Aviles, 152
Merckx, Eddie, 27
Merzario, Arturo, 28
Mezzofanti, Giuseppe Caspar, 153
Michelson, Albert A., 191
Mill, Henry, 110
Miller, Glenn, 65
Mitchell, Billy, 212
Moog, Robert, 66
Montessori, Maria, 66
Montgolfier, Joseph M. and Jacques E., 213
Monti, Eugenio, 28
Moon, Sun Myung, 153
Moore, Garry, 66
Moore, Henry, 67
Morphy, Paul C., 28
Morrill, Justin, 153
Morse, Samuel F. B., 110
Morton, Levi P., 153

www.ingramcontent.com/pod-product-compliance
Lightning Source LLC
Chambersburg PA
CBHW021542260326
41914CB00001B/124